Advanced Deep Learning with R

Become an expert at designing, building, and improving
advanced neural network models using R

Bharatendra Rai

Packt>

BIRMINGHAM - MUMBAI

Advanced Deep Learning with R

Commissioning Editor: Sunith Shetty
Acquisition Editor: Reshma Raman
Content Development Editor: Nazia Shaikh
Senior Editor: Ayaan Hoda
Technical Editor: Utkarsha S. Kadam
Copy Editor: Safis Editing
Project Coordinator: Aishwarya Mohan
Proofreader: Safis Editing
Indexer: Tejal Daruwale Soni
Production Designer: Joshua Misquitta

First published: December 2019

Production reference: 1161219

Published by Packt Publishing Ltd.
Livery Place
35 Livery Street
Birmingham
B3 2PB, UK.

ISBN 978-1-78953-877-9

www.packt.com

Packt>

Subscribe to our online digital library for full access to over 7,000 books and videos, as well as industry leading tools to help you plan your personal development and advance your career. For more information, please visit our website.

Why subscribe?

- Spend less time learning and more time coding with practical eBooks and Videos from over 4,000 industry professionals

- Improve your learning with Skill Plans built especially for you

- Get a free eBook or video every month

- Fully searchable for easy access to vital information

- Copy and paste, print, and bookmark content

Did you know that Packt offers eBook versions of every book published, with PDF and ePub files available? You can upgrade to the eBook version at www.packt.com and as a print book customer, you are entitled to a discount on the eBook copy. Get in touch with us at customercare@packtpub.com for more details.

At www.packt.com, you can also read a collection of free technical articles, sign up for a range of free newsletters, and receive exclusive discounts and offers on Packt books and eBooks.

Contributors

About the author

Bharatendra Rai is a chairperson and professor of business analytics, and the director of the Master of Science in Technology Management program at the Charlton College of Business at UMass Dartmouth. He received a Ph.D. in industrial engineering from Wayne State University, Detroit. He received a master's in quality, reliability, and OR from Indian Statistical Institute, India. His current research interests include machine learning and deep learning applications. His deep learning lecture videos on YouTube are watched in over 198 countries. He has over 20 years of consulting and training experience in industries such as software, automotive, electronics, food, chemicals, and so on, in the areas of data science, machine learning, and supply chain management.

About the reviewer

Herbert Ssegane is an IT data scientist at Oshkosh Corporation, USA with extensive experience in machine learning, deep learning, statistical analysis, and environmental modeling. He has worked on multiple projects for The Climate Corporation, Monsanto (now Bayer), Argonne National Laboratory, and the U.S. Forest Services. He holds a Ph.D in biological and agricultural engineering from the University of Georgia, Athens USA.

Packt is searching for authors like you

If you're interested in becoming an author for Packt, please visit authors.packtpub.com and apply today. We have worked with thousands of developers and tech professionals, just like you, to help them share their insight with the global tech community. You can make a general application, apply for a specific hot topic that we are recruiting an author for, or submit your own idea.

Table of Contents

Section 4: Deep Learning for Natural Language Processing

Preface

Deep learning is a branch of machine learning based on a set of algorithms that attempt to model high-level abstractions in data. *Advanced Deep Learning with R* will help you understand popular deep learning architectures and their variants in R and provide real-life examples.

This book will help you apply deep learning algorithms in R using advanced examples. It covers variants of neural network models such as ANN, CNN, RNN, LSTM, and others using expert techniques. In the course of reading this book, you will make use of popular deep learning libraries such as Keras-R, TensorFlow-R, and others to implement AI models.

Who this book is for

This book is for data scientists, machine learning practitioners, deep learning researchers, and AI enthusiasts who want to develop their skills and knowledge to implement deep learning techniques and algorithms using the power of R. A solid understanding of machine learning and a working knowledge of the R programming language are required.

What this book covers

Chapter 1, *Revisiting Deep Learning Architecture and Techniques*, provides an overview of the deep learning techniques that are covered in this book.

Chapter 2, *Deep Neural Networks for Multiclass Classification*, covers the necessary steps to apply deep learning neural networks to binary and multiclass classification problems. The steps are illustrated using a churn dataset and include data preparation, one-hot encoding, model fitting, model evaluation, and prediction.

Chapter 3, *Deep Neural Networks for Regression*, illustrates how to develop a prediction model for numeric response. Using the Boston Housing example, this chapter introduces the steps for data preparation, model creation, model fitting, model evaluation, and prediction.

Chapter 4, *Image Classification and Recognition*, illustrates the use of deep learning neural networks for image classification and recognition using the Keras package with the help of an easy-to-follow example. The steps involved include exploring image data, resizing and reshaping images, one-hot encoding, developing a sequential model, compiling the model, fitting the model, evaluating the model, prediction, and model performance assessment using a confusion matrix.

Chapter 5, *Image Classification Using Convolutional Neural Networks*, introduces the steps for applying image classification and recognition using convolutional neural networks (CNNs) with an easy-to-follow practical example. CNN is a popular deep neural network and is considered the 'gold standard' for large-scale image classification.

Chapter 6, *Applying Autoencoder Neural Networks Using Keras*, goes over the steps for applying autoencoder neural networks using Keras. The practical example used illustrates the steps for taking images as input, training them with an autoencoder, and finally, reconstructing images.

Chapter 7, *Image Classification for Small Data Using Transfer Learning*, illustrates the application of transfer learning to NLP. The steps involved include data preparation, defining a deep neural network model in Keras, training the model, and model assessment.

Chapter 8, *Creating New Images Using Generative Adversarial Networks*, illustrates the application of generative adversarial networks (GANs) to generate new images using a practical example. The steps for image classification include image data preprocessing, feature extraction, developing an RBM model, and model performance assessment.

Chapter 9, *Deep Network for Text Classification*, provides the steps for applying text classification using deep neural networks and illustrates the process with an easy-to-follow example. Text data, such as customer comments, product reviews, and movie reviews, play an important role in business, and text classification is an important deep learning problem.

Chapter 10, *Text Classification Using Recurrent Neural Networks*, provides the steps for applying recurrent neural networks to an image classification problem with the help of a practical example. The steps covered include data preparation, defining the recurrent neural network model, training, and finally, the evaluation of the model performance.

Chapter 11 , *Text Classification Using a Long Short-Term Memory Network*, illustrates the steps for using a long short-term memory (LSTM) neural network for sentiment classification. The steps involved include text data preparation, creating an LSTM model, training the model, and assessing the model.

Chapter 12, *Text Classification Using Convolutional Recurrent Networks*, illustrates the application of recurrent convolutional networks for news classification. The steps involved include text data preparation, defining a recurrent convolutional network model in Keras, training the model, and model assessment.

Chapter 13, *Tips, Tricks, and the Road Ahead*, discusses the road ahead in terms of putting deep learning into action and best practices.

To get the most out of this book

The following are a few ideas for how you can get the most out of this book:

All examples in this book use R codes. So before getting started with it, you should have a good foundation in the R language. As per Confucius, "I hear and I forget. I see and I remember. I do and I understand." This is true for this book, too. A hands-on approach of working with the codes while going through the chapters will be very useful in understanding the deep learning models.

All the codes in this book were successfully run on a Mac computer that had 8 GB of RAM. However, if you are working with a much larger dataset compared to what has been used in this book for illustration purposes, more powerful computing resources may be required in order to develop deep learning models. It will also be helpful to have a good foundation in statistical methods.

Download the example code files

You can download the example code files for this book from your account at www.packt.com. If you purchased this book elsewhere, you can visit www.packtpub.com/support and register to have the files emailed directly to you.

You can download the code files by following these steps:

1. Log in or register at www.packt.com.
2. Select the **Support** tab.
3. Click on **Code Downloads**.
4. Enter the name of the book in the **Search** box and follow the onscreen instructions.

Once the file is downloaded, please make sure that you unzip or extract the folder using the latest version of:

- WinRAR/7-Zip for Windows
- Zipeg/iZip/UnRarX for Mac
- 7-Zip/PeaZip for Linux

The code bundle for the book is also hosted on GitHub at `https://github.com/PacktPublishing/Advanced-Deep-Learning-with-R`. In case there's an update to the code, it will be updated on the existing GitHub repository.

We also have other code bundles from our rich catalog of books and videos available at `https://github.com/PacktPublishing/`. Check them out!

Download the color images

We also provide a PDF file that has color images of the screenshots/diagrams used in this book. You can download it here: `https://static.packt-cdn.com/downloads/9781789538779_ColorImages.pdf`.

Conventions used

There are a number of text conventions used throughout this book.

`CodeInText`: Indicates code words in text, database table names, folder names, filenames, file extensions, pathnames, dummy URLs, user input, and Twitter handles. Here is an example: "We store the accuracy and loss values while fitting the model in `model_three`."

A block of code is set as follows:

```
model %>%
    compile(loss = 'binary_crossentropy',
    optimizer = 'adam',
    metrics = 'accuracy')
```

Bold: Indicates a new term, an important word, or words that you see onscreen. For example, words in menus or dialog boxes appear in the text like this. Here is an example: "**Recurrent neural networks (RNNs)** are well suited to working with data involving such sequences."

Warnings or important notes appear like this.

Tips and tricks appear like this.

Get in touch

Feedback from our readers is always welcome.

General feedback: If you have questions about any aspect of this book, mention the book title in the subject of your message and email us at customercare@packtpub.com.

Errata: Although we have taken every care to ensure the accuracy of our content, mistakes do happen. If you have found a mistake in this book, we would be grateful if you would report this to us. Please visit www.packtpub.com/support/errata, selecting your book, clicking on the Errata Submission Form link, and entering the details.

Piracy: If you come across any illegal copies of our works in any form on the Internet, we would be grateful if you would provide us with the location address or website name. Please contact us at copyright@packt.com with a link to the material.

If you are interested in becoming an author: If there is a topic that you have expertise in and you are interested in either writing or contributing to a book, please visit authors.packtpub.com.

Reviews

Please leave a review. Once you have read and used this book, why not leave a review on the site that you purchased it from? Potential readers can then see and use your unbiased opinion to make purchase decisions, we at Packt can understand what you think about our products, and our authors can see your feedback on their book. Thank you!

For more information about Packt, please visit packt.com.

Section 1: Revisiting Deep Learning Basics

This section contains a chapter that serves as an introduction to deep learning with R. It provides an overview of the process for developing deep networks and reviews popular deep learning techniques.

This section contains the following chapter:

- Chapter 1, *Revisiting Deep Learning Architecture and Techniques*

1
Revisiting Deep Learning Architecture and Techniques

Deep learning is part of a broader machine learning and artificial intelligence field that uses artificial neural networks. One of the main advantages of deep learning methods is that they help to capture complex relationships and patterns contained in data. When the relationships and patterns are not very complex, traditional machine learning methods may work well. However, with the availability of technologies that help to generate and process more and more unstructured data, such as images, text, and videos, deep learning methods have become increasingly popular as they are almost a default choice to deal with such data. Computer vision and **natural language processing** (NLP) are two areas that are seeing interesting applications in a wide variety of fields, such as driverless cars, language translation, computer games, and even creating new artwork.

Within the deep learning toolkit, we now have an increasing array of neural network techniques that can be applied to a specific type of task. For example, when developing image classification models, a special type of deep network called a **convolutional neural network** (CNN) has proved to be effective in capturing unique patterns that exist in image-related data. Similarly, another popular deep learning network called **recurrent neural networks** (RNNs) and its variants have been found useful in dealing with data involving sequences of words or integers. Another popular and interesting deep learning network called a **generative adversarial network** (GAN) has the capability to generate new images, speech, music, or artwork.

In this book, we will use these and other popular deep learning networks using R software. Each chapter presents a complete example that has been specifically developed to run on a regular laptop or computer. The main idea is to avoid getting bogged down by a huge amount of data needing advanced computing resources at the first stage of applying deep learning methods. You will be able to go over all the steps using the illustrated examples in this book. The examples used also include the best practices for each topic, and you will find them useful. You will also find a hands-on and applied approach helpful in quickly seeing the big picture when trying to replicate these deep learning methods when faced with a new problem.

This chapter provides an overview of the deep learning methods with R that are covered in this book. We will go over the following topics in this chapter:

- Deep learning with R
- The process of developing a deep network model
- Popular deep learning techniques with R and RStudio

Deep learning with R

We will start by looking at the popularity of deep learning networks and also take a look at a version of some of the important R packages used in this book.

Deep learning trend

Deep learning techniques make use of neural network-based models and have seen increasing interest in the last few years. A Google trends website for the search term **deep learning** provides the following plot:

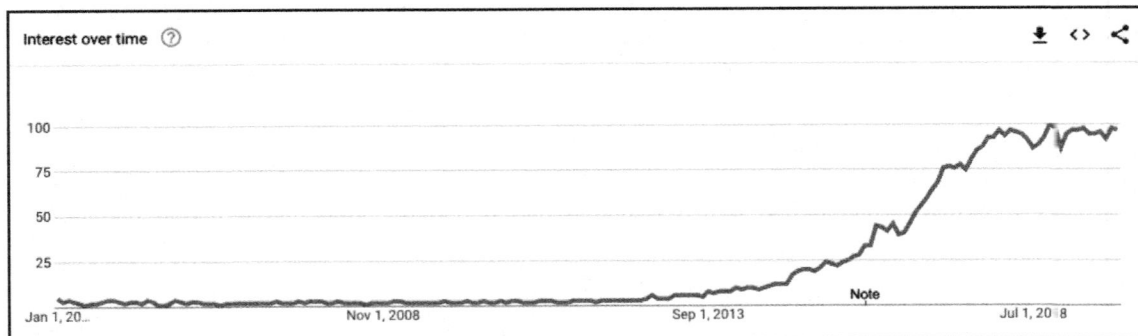

The preceding plot has 100 as the peak popularity of a search term, and other numbers are relative to this highest point. It can be observed that the interest in the term **deep learning** has gradually increased in popularity since around 2014. For the last two years, it has enjoyed peak popularity. One of the reasons for the popularity of deep learning networks is the availability of the free and open source libraries, TensorFlow and Keras.

Versions of key R packages used

In this book, we will use the Keras R package that uses TensorFlow as a backend for building deep learning networks. An output from a typical R session, used for the examples illustrated in this book, providing various version-related information, is provided in the following code:

```
# Information from a Keras R session
sessionInfo()

R version 3.6.0 (2019-04-26)
Platform: x86_64-apple-darwin15.6.0 (64-bit)
Running under: macOS 10.15

Matrix products: default
BLAS:
/System/Library/Frameworks/Accelerate.framework/Versions/A/Frameworks/vecLi
b.framework/Versions/A/libBLAS.dylib
LAPACK:
/Library/Frameworks/R.framework/Versions/3.6/Resources/lib/libRlapack.dylib

Random number generation:
 RNG: Mersenne-Twister
 Normal: Inversion
 Sample: Rounding

locale:
[1] en_US.UTF-8/en_US.UTF-8/en_US.UTF-8/C/en_US.UTF-8/en_US.UTF-8

attached base packages:
[1] stats graphics grDevices utils datasets methods base

other attached packages:
[1] keras_2.2.4.1

loaded via a namespace (and not attached):
 [1] Rcpp_1.0.2 lattice_0.20-38 lubridate_1.7.4 zeallot_0.1.0
 [5] grid_3.6.0 R6_2.4.0 jsonlite_1.6 magrittr_1.5
 [9] tfruns_1.4 stringi_1.4.3 whisker_0.4 Matrix_1.2-17
```

```
[13] reticulate_1.13 generics_0.0.2 tools_3.6.0 stringr_1.4.0
[17] compiler_3.6.0 base64enc_0.1-3 tensorflow_1.14.0
```

As seen previously, for this book we have used the 3.6 version of R that was released in April 2019. The nickname for this R version is Planting of a Tree. The version used for the Keras package is 2.2.4.1. In addition, all the application examples illustrated in the book have been run on a Mac computer with 8 GB of RAM. The main reason for using this specification is that it will allow a reader to go through all the examples without needing advanced computing resources to get started with any deep learning network covered in the book.

In the next section, we will go over the process of developing a deep network model that is broken down into five general steps.

Process of developing a deep network model

Developing a deep learning network model can be broken down into five key steps shown in the following flowchart:

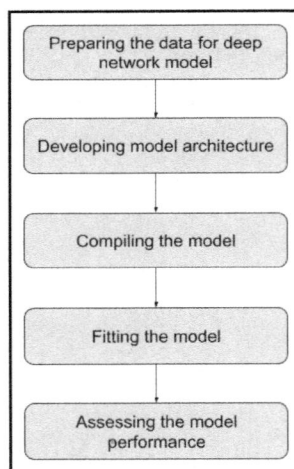

```
┌─────────────────────────────────────┐
│  ┌───────────────────────────────┐  │
│  │   Preparing the data for deep │  │
│  │        network model          │  │
│  └───────────────────────────────┘  │
│                 │                    │
│  ┌───────────────────────────────┐  │
│  │  Developing model architecture │ │
│  └───────────────────────────────┘  │
│                 │                    │
│  ┌───────────────────────────────┐  │
│  │       Compiling the model      │ │
│  └───────────────────────────────┘  │
│                 │                    │
│  ┌───────────────────────────────┐  │
│  │        Fitting the model       │ │
│  └───────────────────────────────┘  │
│                 │                    │
│  ┌───────────────────────────────┐  │
│  │     Assessing the model        │  │
│  │        performance             │  │
│  └───────────────────────────────┘  │
└─────────────────────────────────────┘
```

Each step mentioned in the preceding flowchart can have varying requirements based on the type of data used, the type of deep learning network being developed, and also the main objective of developing a model. We will go over each step to develop a general idea about what is involved.

Preparing the data for a deep network model

Developing deep learning neural network models requires the variables to have a certain format. Independent variables may come with a varying scale, with some variable values in decimals and some other variables in thousands. Using such varying scales of variables is not very efficient when training a network. Before developing deep learning networks, we make changes such that the variables have similar scales. The process used for achieving this is called **normalization**.

Two commonly used methods for normalization are z-score normalization and min-max normalization. In z-score normalization, we subtract the mean from each value and divide it by the standard deviation. This transformation results in values that lie between -3 and +3 with a mean of 0 and a standard deviation of 1. For a min-max normalization, we subtract the minimum value from each data point, and then divide it by the range. This transformation converts data to having values between zero and one.

As an example, see the following plots, where we have obtained 10,000 data points randomly from a normal distribution with a mean of 35 and a standard deviation of 5:

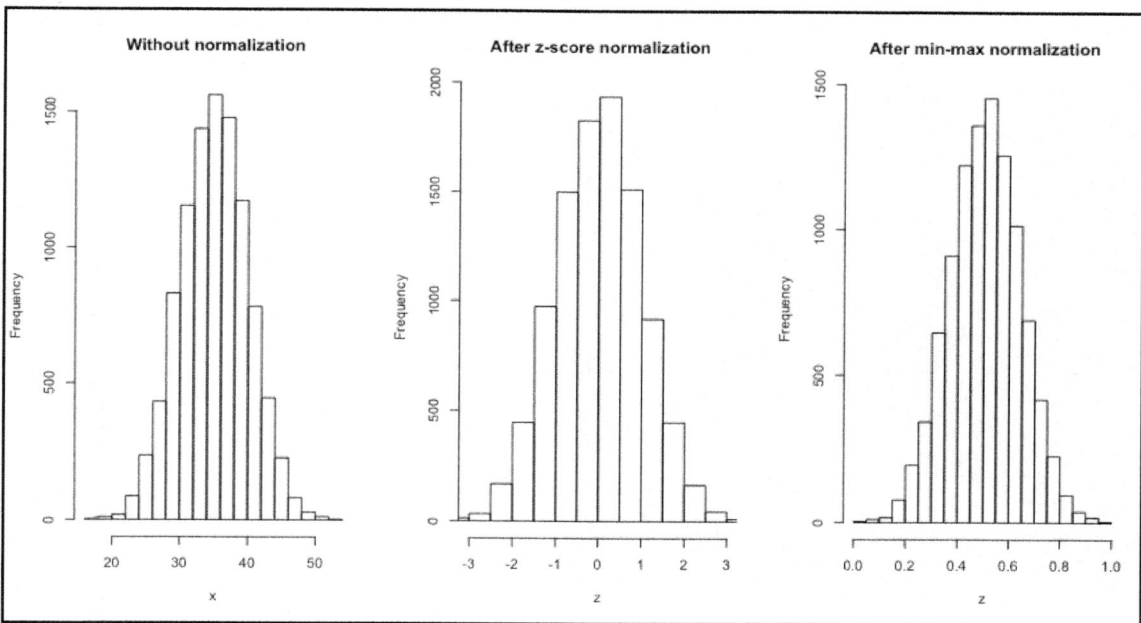

From the preceding plots, we can observe that after z-score normalization, the data points mostly lie between -3 and +3. Similarly, after min-max normalization, the range of values changes to data points between 0 and 1. However, the overall pattern seen in the original data is retained after both types of normalization.

Another important step in preparing data when using a categorical response variable is to carry out one-hot encoding. One-hot encoding converts a categorical variable to a new binary format that has values containing either 0 or 1. This is achieved very easily by using the `to_categorical()` function available in Keras.

Typically data processing steps for unstructured data, such as image or text, are more involved compared with a situation where we are dealing with structured data. In addition, the nature of data preparation steps can vary from one type of data to another. For example, the way we prepare image data for developing a deep learning classification model is likely to be very different from the way we prepare text data for developing a movie review sentiment classification model. However, one important thing to note is that before we can develop deep learning models from unstructured data, they need to be first converted into a structured format. An example of converting unstructured image data into a structured format is shown in the following screenshot, using a picture of the handwritten digit *five*:

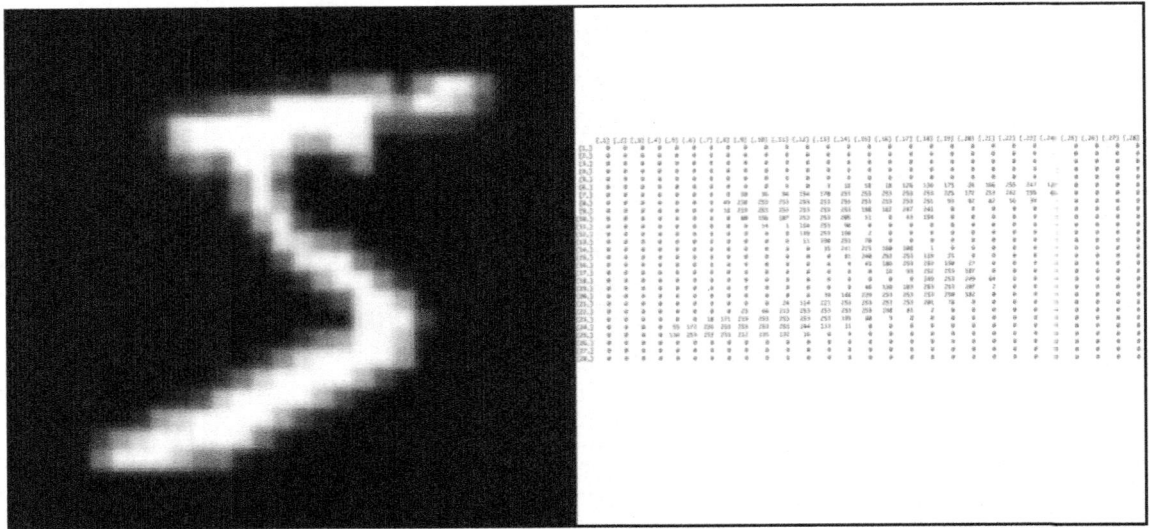

As can be observed from the preceding screenshot, when we read an image file containing a black and white handwritten digit *five* with 28 x 28 dimensions in R, it gets converted to numbers in rows and columns, giving it a structured format. The right-hand side of the screenshot shows data with 28 rows and 28 columns. The numbers in the body of the table are pixel values that range from 0 to 255, where a value of zero represents the black color and 255 represents the white color in the picture. When developing deep learning models, we make use of some forms of such structured data that are derived from image data.

Once the data for developing the model is prepared in the required format, we can then develop the model architecture.

Developing a deep learning model architecture

Developing the architecture of a model involves defining various items, such as the type and number of layers for the network, the type of activation function, the number of units or neurons to use in the network, and also providing the data-related input/output values. An example of specifying a simple sequential model architecture using Keras in R is shown in the following code:

```
# Model architecture
model <- keras_model_sequential()
 model %>%
 layer_dense(units = 8, activation = 'relu', input_shape = c(21)) %>%
 layer_dense(units = 3, activation = 'softmax')
```

Note that a sequential model allows us to develop models layer by layer. As seen from the preceding code, two layers of densely connected networks have been added as a part of the sequential model. Two important decisions while choosing a model architecture involve the number and type of layers and the type of activation function for a layer. The number and type of layers to use is guided by the nature and complexity of the data. For a fully connected network (also known as a multilayer perceptron), we can use a dense layer with the help of the layer_dense function available in Keras.

On the other hand, when working with image data, we are likely to use convolutional layers in the network, using the layer_conv_2d function. We will discuss more details about specific model architectures with examples in each chapter.

There are different types of activation functions that are used in deep learning networks. A rectified linear unit, or `relu`, is a popular activation function used in hidden layers, and it uses a very simple calculation. If the input is negative, it returns a value of zero and, for everything else, there is no change to the original value. As an example, let's look at the following code:

```
# RELU function and related plot
x <- rnorm(10000, 2, 10)
y <- ifelse(x<0, 0, x)
par(mfrow = c(1,2))
hist(x)
plot(x,y)
```

The preceding code generates 10,000 random numbers from a normal distribution with a mean of two and a standard deviation of 10, and stores the results in x. And then negative values are changed to zero and stored in y. A histogram of x and a scatter plot for x and y are given in the following graphs:

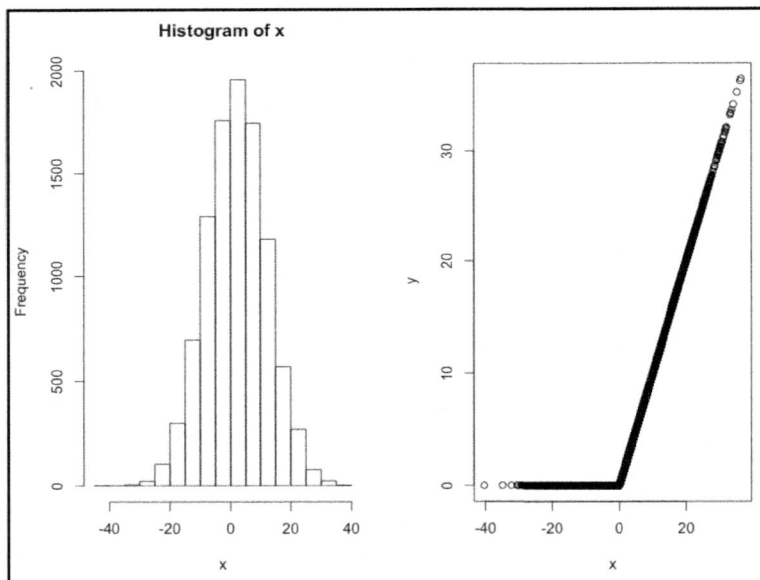

It can be observed from the preceding histogram that x has values that are both positive and negative. The scatter plot, based on the original x values and the modified y value that is obtained after converting negative values to zero, visualizes the impact of the `relu` activation function. In the scatter plot, the data points to the left of x = 0 are flat and have a zero slope. The data points to the right of x = 0 have a perfect linear pattern with a slope of 1.

One of the main advantages of using the `relu` activation function is its simple calculation. For developing deep learning network models, this becomes an important factor as it helps to reduce computational cost. For many deep learning networks, a rectified linear unit is used as the default activation function.

Another popular activation function used for developing deep networks is `softmax`, which is usually used in the outer layer of the network. Let's look at the following code to understand it better:

```
# Softmax function and related plot
x <- runif(1000, 1, 5)
y <- exp(x)/sum(exp(x))
par(mfrow=c(1,2))
hist(x)
plot(x,y)
```

In the preceding code, we have taken a random sample of 1,000 values from a uniform distribution that lies between 1 and 5. To use the `softmax` function, we can divide the exponential of each input value x by the sum of the exponential values of x. The resulting histogram, based on the x values, and the scatter plot of x and y values are shown in the following graphs:

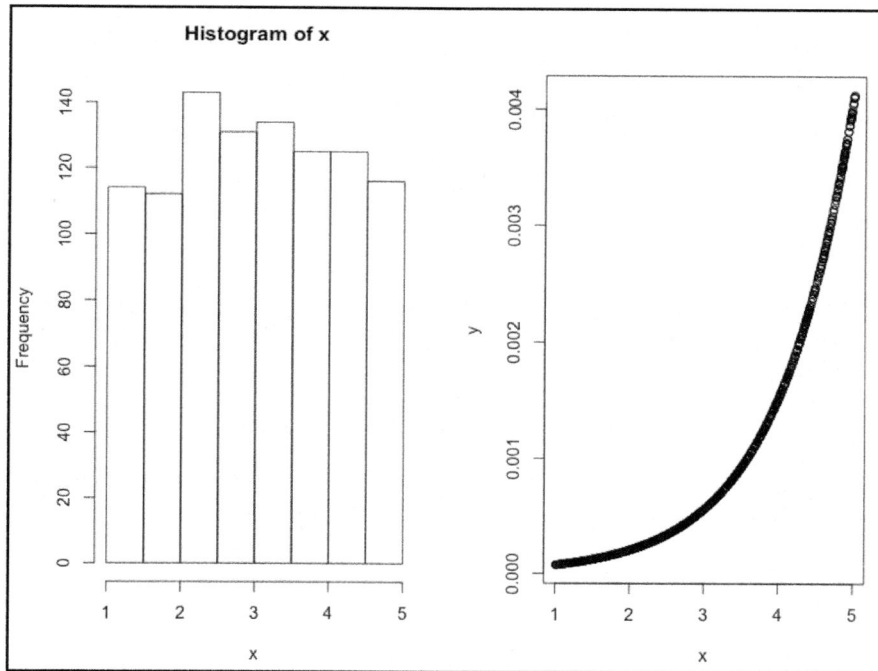

We can observe that the preceding histogram provides an approximate uniform pattern for the x values. The impact of the `softmax` function can be seen from the scatter plot where the output values now lie between 0 and 1. This conversion is very useful for interpreting the results in terms of probabilities as the values now are as follows:

- Lie between 0 and 1
- The total of these probabilities is 1

This aspect of the `softmax` activation function, where results can be interpreted in terms of probabilities, makes it a popular choice when developing deep learning classification models. It works well whether we use it for image classification or text classification problems.

Apart from these two activation functions, we also make use of others that may be more suitable for a specific deep leaning model.

Once a model architecture to be used is specified, the next step is to compile the model.

Compiling the model

Compiling a model typically involves specifying the loss function, choosing an optimizer, and specifying the metrics to be used. These choices, however, depend on the type of problem that is being addressed. The following code is an example of R for compiling a deep learning binary classification model:

```
model %>%
    compile(loss = 'binary_crossentropy',
    optimizer = 'adam',
    metrics = 'accuracy')
```

The preceding loss function specified is `binary_crossentropy`, which is used when the response variable has two classes. Binary cross-entropy can be calculated using the following formula:

$$-y \times log(yhat) - (1 - y) \times log(1 - yhat)$$

In the preceding formula, y represents the actual class and `yhat` represents the prediction probability. Let's consider two examples using the following code:

```
# Example-1
y <- c(0, 0, 0, 1, 1, 1)
yhat <- c(0.2, 0.3, 0.1, 0.8, 0.9, 0.7)
(loss <- - y*log(yhat) - (1-y)*log(1-yhat))
```

```
[1] 0.2231436 0.3566749 0.1053605 0.2231436 0.1053605 0.3566749
```

```
mean(loss)
```

```
[1] 0.228393
```

```
# Example-2
yhat <- c(0.2, 0.9, 0.1, 0.8, 0.9, 0.2)
(loss <- - y*log(yhat) - (1-y)*log(1-yhat))
```

```
[1] 0.2231436 2.3025851 0.1053605 0.2231436 0.1053605 1.6094379
```

```
mean(loss)
```

```
[1] 0.761505
```

As seen in `Example-1`, there are a total of six cases represented by y where the first three cases indicate the actual class to be 0, and the next three cases have the actual class as 1. The prediction probabilities captured by `yhat` is the probability that a case belongs to category 1. In `Example-1`, the `yhat` values correctly classify all six cases, and the average of all loss values is about 0.228. In `Example-2`, the `yhat` values correctly classify only four cases, and the average of all loss values now increases to about 0.762. The binary cross-entropy loss function in this way helps to assess the classification performance of a model. The lower the loss value is, the better the classification performance, and the higher the loss value is, the worse the classification performance of the model.

There are various other loss functions that are used based on the type of problem for which the deep learning network is being developed. For classification models where the response variables have more than two classes, we make use of the `categorical_crossentropy` loss function. For regression problems with numeric response variables, the mean square error (mse) may be an appropriate loss function.

When specifying an optimizer to be used by the model, `adam` is a popular choice for deep learning networks, giving good results in a wide variety of situations. Other commonly used optimizers include `rmsprop` and `adagrad`. When a deep learning network is being trained, the parameters of the network are modified based on feedback obtained from the loss function. How this modification of parameters takes place is based on which optimizer is used. The choice of a suitable optimizer is therefore important in arriving at a suitable model.

When compiling the model, we also specify a suitable metric that will be used for monitoring the training process. For classification problems, `accuracy` is a one of the most commonly used metrics. For regression problems, the mean absolute error is a commonly specified metric.

Once we compile a model, we are ready to fit it.

Fitting the model

Fitting or training of the model is carried out with the help of data. An example of a code used for fitting a classification model is provided as follows:

```
model %>%
  fit(training,
    trainLabels,
    epochs = 200,
    batch_size = 32,
    validation_split = 0.2)
```

In the preceding code, fitting a model includes `training`, which is the data on independent variables, and `trainLabels`, which contain labels for the response variable. The number of epochs is specified to indicate the number of iterations of all samples in the training data that will be used during the training process. Batch size refers to the number of samples from the training data to be used, after which the model parameters will be updated. In addition, we also specify any validation split, where a 0.2 or 20% split means that the last 20% of samples from the training data will be kept separate from the training process to assess the model performance.

When fitting a model, different layers in the network have a random initialization of weights. Due to this random initialization of network weights, if we fit a model again with the same data, same architecture, and same settings, we will get slightly different results. This will occur not only in a different session of R, but also in the same session when a model is trained again.

There are many situations where getting repeatable results is important. As an example, while publishing a deep learning-related article in a peer-reviewed international journal, you may need to generate more plots from the same model based on reviewer feedback. Another situation could be where a team working on the same project may like to share a model and also results with other members of the team. The easiest way to obtain the same results from the model is to save and then reload the model using the following code:

```
# Save/reload model
save_model_hdf5(model,
  filepath,
  overwrite = TRUE,
  include_optimizer = TRUE)
model_x <- load_model_hdf5(filepath,
  custom_objects = NULL,
  compile = TRUE)
```

We can save the model by specifying `filepath` and then reload when required. Saving a model allows us to obtain repeatable results when we use the model again. It also allows us to have a way to share the same model with others who can obtain exactly the same results, as well as helping in situations where each run takes a lot of time. Saving and reloading the model allows you to resume the training process when you train the model again.

Once a model is fit, its performance can be assessed using both training and testing data.

Assessing the model performance

Assessing the performance of a deep learning classification model requires developing a confusion matrix that summarizes predictions for actual and predicted classes. Consider an example where a classification model is developed to classify graduate school applicants in one of two categories where class 0 refers to applications that have not been accepted, and class 1 refers to accepted applications. An example of a confusion matrix for this situation explaining the key concepts is provided as follows:

		Actual Class	
		0	1
Predicted Class	0	208	73
	1	15	29

In the preceding confusion matrix, there are 208 applicants who were actually not accepted and the model also correctly predicts that they should not be accepted. This cell in the confusion matrix is also called the **true negative**. Similarly, there are 29 applicants who were actually accepted and the model also correctly predicts that they should be accepted. This cell in the confusion matrix is called the **true positive**. We also have cells with numbers indicating the incorrect classification of applicants by the model. There are 15 applicants who were actually not accepted, but the model incorrectly predicts that they should be accepted and this cell is called a **false negative**.

Another name for making an error when incorrectly classifying category 0 as belonging to category 1 is a type-1 error. Finally, there are 73 applicants that were actually accepted but the model incorrectly predicts them to belong to the not-accepted category, and this cell is called a **false positive**. Aanother name for such an incorrect classification is a type-2 error.

From the confusion matrix, we can calculate the accuracy of the classification performance by adding numbers to the diagonal and dividing the numbers by the total. So, the accuracy based on the preceding matrix is (208+29)/(208+29+73+15), or 72.92%. Apart from the accuracy, we can also find out the model performance in correctly classifying each category. We can calculate the accuracy of correctly classifying category 1, also called sensitivity, as 29/(29+73), or 28.4%. Similarly, we can calculate the accuracy of correctly classifying category 0, also called specificity, as 208/(208+15), or 93.3%.

Note, that the confusion matrix can be used when developing a classification model. However, other situations may call for other suitable ways of assessing the deep learning network.

We can now briefly go over the deep learning techniques covered in this book.

Deep learning techniques with R and RStudio

The term **deep** in deep learning refers to a neural network model having several layers, and the learning takes place with the help of data. And based on the type of data used, deep learning may be categorized into two major categories, as shown in the following screenshot:

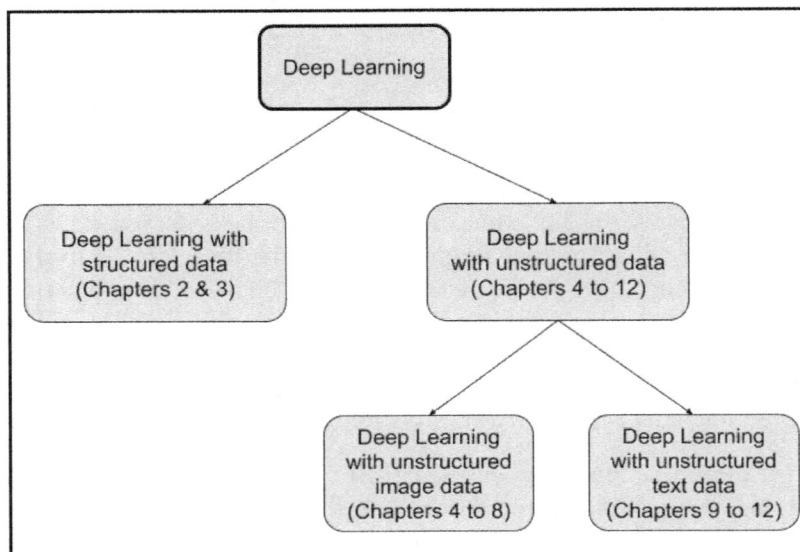

As shown in the preceding diagram, the type of data used for developing a deep neural network model can be of a structured or unstructured type. In Chapter 2, *Deep Neural Networks for Multi-Class Classification,* we illustrate the use of a deep learning network for classification problems using structured data where the response variable is of the categorical type. In Chapter 3, *Deep Neural Networks for Regression,* we illustrate the use of a deep learning network for regression problems using structured data where the response is a continuous type of variable. Chapters 4 to 12 illustrate the use of deep learning networks for mainly two types of unstructured data that involve images and text. In chapters 4 to 8, we provide application examples of some popular deep learning networks using image data, which is regarded as an unstructured type of data. Finally, in chapters 9 to 12, we cover some popular deep learning networks that are useful with text data, which is another major category within unstructured data.

Now, let's briefly go over the examples and techniques covered in chapters 2 to 12.

Multi-class classification

There are many problems where the main objective is to develop a classification model that uses data to classify observations into two or more categories. For example, a patient may be classified as normal, suspect, or pathological based on the data on several variables. The deep learning network in this case will use data on several patients where the outcome is already available, and it will learn to classify a patient into one of the three categories.

Another example of a classification problem could be where students send applications to a graduate school. An application from a student may be accepted or rejected based on variables such as GPA, GRE, and ranking of the school during their undergraduate degree. Another interesting example could be where student-related data is used for developing a model that helps to classify first-year students into those that are likely to stay with the current school and those who are likely to transfer to another school. A similar model can be developed to classify customers who are likely to stay with a business or switch to a competitor.

One of the challenges involved while developing a classification model is that of class imbalance. For example, when dealing with medical data, the number of patients classified as normal may be much larger than the number of patients who are classified as pathological. Similarly, when applying to a graduate program at one of the top universities, it is very likely that the data contains a significantly higher number of cases where an applicant is not accepted. Deep network models are useful in addressing such concerns easily. The Keras library used in this book provides a user-friendly interface not only to address such issues easily, but also to help in obtaining suitable classification models with the help of fast experimentation.

In Chapter 2, *Deep Neural Networks for Multi-Class Classification*, we provide an illustration of a multi-class deep learning classification model using R.

Regression problems

Structured data involving numeric response variables is classified as a regression problem. For example, the price of a house in a city may depend on variables such as the age of the house, the crime rate in the city, the number of rooms, and the property tax rate. Although statistical methods, such as multiple linear regression and elastic net regression, can also be useful for these situations, deep learning networks offer certain advantages. One of the main advantages of using neural networks in general is that they can capture non-linearity. Unlike statistical methods that require certain assumptions to be met before we can use them, neural network-based models are more flexible to use and do not require many assumptions to be fulfilled.

Many applications involving regression problems also call for identifying variables or features that have a significant impact on the response variable. However with deep learning networks, such feature engineering is inbuilt, and it doesn't call for any extra effort in extracting important features. One thing to note regarding deep learning networks is that the larger the dataset being used, the more effective the resulting prediction model will be. In Chapter 3, *Deep Neural Networks for Regression*, we provide an illustration of a deep learning regression model using R.

Image classification

Image data is classified as an unstructured type of data. One of the popular applications of deep learning networks involves developing image classification and recognition models. Image classification has various applications, such as face recognition on smartphones or on social media networks, classification of medical image data, classification of handwritten digits, and self-driving cars. Note that it is not possible to develop a classification model directly from unstructured data. The unstructured data needs to be first converted into a structured form before deep learning networks can be developed. For example, a black and white image may have dimensions of 21 x 21 and thus contain data on 441 (21 x 21) pixels. Once we convert an image into numbers representing all the pixels, it becomes feasible to develop image classification models. Although humans can classify a type of dress, a person, or certain object very easily, even when the images may have different sizes or orientation, training a computer to do so is a challenging task.

The Keras library provides several easy-to-use features for processing image data that helps in developing deep learning image classification networks. The effectiveness of having deep networks or neural networks with many layers especially comes to the fore when it comes to image recognition and classification problems. In `Chapter 4`, *Image Classification and Recognition*, we provide an illustration of applying a deep learning image classification model using R.

Convolutional neural networks

Image classification tasks become challenging when the number of categories increases and images within a category show significant variability. Such situations also require a larger number of samples so that features inherent in each category can be captured more accurately by the classification model. For example, a fashion retailer may have a large variety of fashion items and may be interested in developing a classification model from the image data of such fashion items. A special type of deep network, called a **convolutional neural network (CNN)**, has proven to be highly effective in situations that call for large scale image classification and recognition tasks. CNNs are the most popular networks for such applications and are regarded as the gold standard for large-scale image classification problems. These networks are capable of capturing various minute details in an image with the help of different types of layers in the network. In `Chapter 5`, *Image Classification Using Convolutional Neural Networks*, we provide an illustration of applying a CNN to image classification using R.

Autoencoders

Deep learning methods that involve classification and prediction models using data that has a response or a dependent variable are part of supervised deep learning methods. When working with structured or unstructured data, there are situations where the response variable is either not available or not used. Applications of deep learning networks that do not use a response variable are classified as unsupervised deep learning methods. For example, an application of deep learning may involve image data from which we want to extract important features in order to achieve dimension reduction. Another example involves handwritten images that contain unwanted noise and a deep network is used for denoising the images. In such situations, autoencoder networks have been found to be very useful for performing unsupervised deep learning tasks.

Autoencoder neural networks make use of an encoder and decoder network. When the image data is passed through an encoder and the resulting dimension is lower than that of the original image, the network is forced to extract only the most important features from the input data. And then the decoder part of the network reconstructs the original data from whatever is available from the output of the encoder. In Chapter 6, *Applying Autoencoder Neural Networks Using Keras*, we provide an illustration of applying an autoencoder neural network for dimension reduction, de-noising, and image correction when working with image data using R.

Transfer learning

Developing deep learning classification models when the image data has several categories is a challenging task. It becomes even more challenging when the number of images available is limited. In such situations, it may be possible to take advantage of an existing model that has been developed with the help of a much larger dataset and reuse the patterns it has learned by customizing it for another classification task. This reuse of a pretrained deep network model for a new classification task is known as transfer learning.

The Keras library provides various pretrained models for image classification tasks that are trained using over a million images, and that capture reusable features that can be applied to similar but new data. Transferring what a pretrained model has learned from a large number of samples to a model that is being built with a much smaller sample size helps to save computational resources. In addition, use of the transfer learning approach can help to outperform a model that is built from scratch using a smaller dataset. In Chapter 7, *Image Classification for Small Data Using Transfer Learning*, we cover transfer learning and illustrate the utilization of a pre trained deep learning image classification model using R.

Generative adversarial networks

An article in The Verge (Reference: https://www.theverge.com/2018/10/25/18023266/ai-art-portrait-christies-obvious-sold) reported that an artwork named *Portrait of Edmond Belamy* created using an artificial intelligence algorithm was sold for $432,500. This artwork was estimated to sell for about $7,000 to $10,000. The deep learning algorithm that was used to create this artwork is called a **generative adversarial network (GAN)**. The unique attribute of generative adversarial networks is that two deep networks are made to compete against each other to generate something meaningful. The two networks that compete against each other and try to outsmart one another are called generator and discriminator networks.

Consider a situation where we want to generate new handwritten images of the digit *five*. A generative adversarial network in this case would involve a generator network that creates fake images of the handwritten digit *five* from simply random noise and sends it to a discriminator network. The fake images are mixed with genuine images and the discriminator network, which is trained to differentiate between real and fake images of the handwritten digit *five*, will try its best to successfully differentiate between real and fake images. These two networks are made to compete against each other until the generator network starts making realistic-looking fake images that the discriminator network finds increasingly difficult to differentiate between. In addition to image data, application of generative adversarial networks can be extended to generate new text or even new music. We will illustrate an application of a generative adversarial network to generate new images in `Chapter 8`, *Creating New Images Using Generative Adversarial Networks*.

Deep network for text classification

Text data has certain unique characteristics that makes it a very different type of unstructured data compared to image data. As mentioned earlier, unstructured data requires extra processing steps to arrive at a structured format that can be used for developing a deep learning classification network. One of the applications of deep learning with text data involves developing a deep neural network sentiment classification model.

To develop a sentiment classification model, labels capturing sentiment related to the text data are needed. For example, we may use text data on movie reviews and a related sentiment label (positive review or negative review) to develop a model that can be used to automate the process. Another example could be the development of a sentiment classification model using text data on tweets. Such a model can be useful in comparing sentiments contained in thousands of tweets or and after an important event. Examples of such events where sentiment classification models can be useful include sentiments contained in tweets before and after the release of a new smartphone by a company, and sentiments contained in tweets before and after the performance of a presidential candidate in a live debate. A deep network for a sentiment classification model using text data is illustrated in `Chapter 9`, *Deep Networks for Text Classification*.

Recurrent neural networks

A unique characteristic of text data is the fact that the placement of words in a text sequence has some meaning. **Recurrent neural networks (RNNs)** are well suited to work with data involving such sequences. Recurrent networks allow output from the previous step to be passed as input to the following step. This process of feeding prior information at a step allows recurrent networks to have memory, which is very useful for dealing with data involving sequences. The name **recurrent** in RNN also comes from the fact that the output at a step depends on information from the previous step.

RNNs can be used to develop a sentiment classification model where the text data could be movie reviews, tweets, product reviews, and so on. Developing such a sentiment classification model will also need the labels that will be used for training the network. We go over steps for developing a recurrent neural network model for sentiment classification using R in `Chapter 10`, *Text Classification Using Recurrent Neural Networks*.

Long short-term memory network

Long short-term memory (LSTM) networks are a special type of recurrent neural network. LSTM networks are useful when data regarding the sequence of words or integers has long-term dependencies. For example, two words that are important for correctly classifying sentiment contained in a movie review may be separated by many words in a long sentence. A sentiment classification model using a regular RNN will have difficulty capturing such long-term dependency between words. A regular RNN is useful when dependency between words or integers in a sequence is immediate or when two important words are next to each other.

Apart from sentiment classification, the application of LSTM networks can also be useful for speech recognition, language translation, anomaly detection, time series forecasting, answering questions, and so on. An application of an LSTM network for movie review sentiment classification is illustrated in `Chapter 11`, *Text Classification Using Long Short-Term Memory Network*.

Convolutional recurrent networks

Convolutional neural networks (CNNs) are useful for capturing high-level local features from the image or text data, and LSTM networks can capture long-term dependencies in the data involving sequences. When we use both CNNs and a recurrent network in the same model architecture, it is called a **convolutional recurrent neural network (CRNN)**. As an example, if we consider data on articles and their authors, we may be interested in developing an author classification model where we can train a network to take text data containing an article as input and then help to make a prediction in terms of probability regarding the author. For this, we can first use a one-dimensional convolutional layer to extract important features from the data. These extracted features can then be passed to the LSTM recurrent layer to obtain the hidden long-term dependencies, which, in turn, are passed to a fully connected dense layer. This dense layer can then obtain the probability of correct authorship. CRNNs can also be applied to problems related to natural language processing, speech, and video. In `Chapter 12`, *Text Classification Using Convolutional Recurrent Networks*, we illustrate the use of CRNNs for developing a model that can classify an author, based on articles written by them.

Tips, tricks, and best practices

In this book, we provide an illustration of applying several popular deep learning methods using R. When working on more complex problems requiring the application of deep learning networks, the use of certain supporting tools may sometimes be very helpful. TensorFlow provides such a tool; it is called **TensorBoard** and is useful for visualizing deep network training performance, especially in situations that call for experimentation. Similarly, there is a package called **Local Interpretable Model-Agnostic Explanations (LIME)** that can help with visualization and interpretation of specific predictions. We also get many outputs, such as summaries and plots, when developing a deep network model. There is a package called **tfruns** that can help to keep everything in one place for easy reference. There is a callback feature in the Keras package that helps with stopping a network training at a suitable time. We will discuss all these tips, tricks, and best practices in `Chapter 13`, *Tips, Tricks, and the Road Ahead*.

Summary

Deep learning methods that make use of artificial neural networks have been increasing in popularity in recent years. A number of areas of application involving deep learning methods include driverless cars, image classification, natural language processing, and new image generation. We started this first chapter by looking at the popularity of the deep learning term as reported from a Google trend website. We described a general five-step process for applying deep learning methods and developed some broad ideas about details within each step. We then briefly looked at deep learning techniques covered in each chapter and situations in which they are applied, along with some best practices.

In the next chapter, we get started with an application example and illustrate steps for developing a deep network model for multi-class classification problems.

Section 2: Deep Learning for Prediction and Classification

This section contains two chapters that explain how to develop deep learning classification and regression models. The process of developing a deep network model is illustrated for multi-class classification and regression situations.

This section contains the following chapters:

- Chapter 2, *Deep Neural Networks for Multi-Class Classification*
- Chapter 3, *Deep Neural Networks for Regression*

2
Deep Neural Networks for Multi-Class Classification

When developing prediction and classification models, depending on the type of response or target variable, we come across two potential type of problems: the target variable is of categorical type (this is a classification type of problem) or the target variable is of a numeric type (this is a regression type of problem). It has been observed that about 70% of the data belongs to problems arising from classification categories and the remaining 30% are regression problems (here is the reference: `https://www.topcoder.com/role-of-statistics-in-data-science/`). In this chapter, we will provide steps for applying deep learning neural networks for classification problems. The steps are illustrated using the fetal cardiotocograms, or CTGs.

In this chapter, we will cover the following topics:

- A brief understanding of the fetal cardiotocogram (or CTG) dataset
- Steps for data preparation, including normalization, data partitioning, and one-hot encoding
- Creating and fitting a deep neural network model for classification problems
- Evaluating classification model performance and making predictions using the model
- Fine-tuning the model for performance optimization and best practices

Cardiotocogram dataset

In this section, we will provide information about the data used for developing a multiclass classification model. We will use only one library, which is Keras.

Dataset (medical)

The dataset used in this chapter is publicly available at the UCI Machine Learning Repository maintained by the School of Information and Computer Science at the University of California. You can access this at https://archive.ics.uci.edu/ml/datasets/cardiotocography.

It is to be noted that this URL enables you to download an Excel data file. This file can be easily converted to a .csv format by saving the file as a .csv file.

For data we should use the formatting which is used for .csv, as shown in the following code:

```
# Read data
library(keras)
data <- read.csv('~/Desktop/data/CTG.csv', header=T)
str(data)

OUTPUT
## 'data.frame': 2126 obs. of 22 variables:
## $ LB : int 120 132 133 134 132 134 134 122 122 122 ...
## $ AC : num 0 0.00638 0.00332 0.00256 0.00651 ...
## $ FM : num 0 0 0 0 0 0 0 0 0 ...
## $ UC       : num  0 0.00638 0.00831 0.00768 0.00814 ...
## $ DL       : num  0 0.00319 0.00332 0.00256 0 ...
## $ DS       : num  0 0 0 0 0 0 0 0 0 ...
## $ DP       : num  0 0 0 0 ...
## $ ASTV     : int  73 17 16 16 16 26 29 83 84 86 ...
## $ MSTV     : num  0.5 2.1 2.1 2.4 2.4 5.9 6.3 0.5 0.5 0.3 ...
## $ ALTV     : int  43 0 0 0 0 0 0 6 5 6 ...
## $ MLTV     : num  2.4 10.4 13.4 23 19.9 0 0 15.6 13.6 10.6 ...
## $ Width    : int  64 130 130 117 117 150 150 68 68 68 ...
## $ Min      : int  62 68 68 53 53 50 50 62 62 62 ...
## $ Max      : int  126 198 198 170 170 200 200 130 130 130 ...
## $ Nmax     : int  2 6 5 11 9 5 6 0 0 1 ...
## $ Nzeros   : int  0 1 1 0 0 3 3 0 0 0 ...
## $ Mode     : int  120 141 141 137 137 76 71 122 122 122 ...
## $ Mean     : int  137 136 135 134 136 107 107 122 122 122 ...
## $ Median   : int  121 140 138 137 138 107 106 123 123 123 ...
## $ Variance: int  73 12 13 13 11 170 215 3 3 1 ...
## $ Tendency: int  1 0 0 1 1 0 0 1 1 1 ...
## $ NSP      : int  2 1 1 1 1 3 3 3 3 3 ...
```

This data consists of fetal CTGs, and the target variable classifies a patient into one of three categories: normal, suspect, and pathological. There are 2,126 rows in this dataset. The CTGs are classified by three expert obstetricians, and a consensus classification label is assigned to each of them as normal (N) (represented by 1), suspect (S) (represented by 2), and pathological (P) (represented by 3). There are 21 independent variables, and the main objective is to develop a classification model to correctly classify each patient into one of the three categories represented by N, S, and P.

Preparing the data for model building

In this section, we will prepare the data for building the classification model. Data preparation will involve normalizing the data, partitioning the data into training and test data, and carrying out one-hot encoding of the response variable.

Normalizing numeric variables

For developing deep network models, we carry out the normalization of numeric variables to bring them to a common scale. When dealing with several variables, it is likely that different variables have different scales—for example, there could be a variable that shows revenues earned by a company and the values could be in millions of dollars. In another example, there could be a variable that shows the dimension of a product in centimeters. Such extreme differences in scale create difficulties when training a network, and normalization helps to address this issue. For normalization, we will use the following code:

```
# Normalize data
data <- as.matrix(data)
 dimnames(data) <- NULL
 data[,1:21] <- normalize(data[,1:21])
 data[,22] <- as.numeric(data[,22]) -1
```

As you can see from the preceding code, we first change the data to matrix format, and then we remove the default names by assigning NULL to the dimension names. In this step, the names of 22 variables will be changed to V1, V2, V3,..., V22. If you run str(data) at this stage, you will notice the change in format of the original data. We normalize the 21 independent variables using the normalize function, which is a part of the Keras package. When you run this line of code, you will notice that it uses TensorFlow as a backend. We also change the target variable, NSP, to numeric from the default integer type. In addition, in the same line of code, we also change values from 1, 2, and 3 to 0, 1, and 2 respectively.

Partitioning the data

Next, we will partition this data into training and test datasets. To carry out data partitioning, we use the following code:

```
# Data partition
set.seed(1234)
 ind <- sample(2, nrow(data), replace = T, prob=c(.7, .3))
 training <- data[ind==1, 1:21]
 test <- data[ind==2, 1:21]
 trainingtarget <- data[ind==1, 22]
 testtarget <- data[ind==2, 22]
```

As you can see from the preceding code, to obtain the same samples in the training and test datasets for repeatability purposes, we use set.seed with a specific number, which in this case is 1234. This will ensure that the reader can also obtain the same samples in the training and test data. For data partitioning, a 70:30 split is used here, but any other ratio can be used too. In machine learning applications, this is a commonly used step to ensure that the prediction model works well with unseen data that is stored in the form of test data. Training data is used for developing the model and test data is used to assess the performance of the model. Sometimes, a prediction model may perform very well or even perfectly well with training data; however, when it is evaluated with test data that has not been seen by the model, the performance may turn out to be very disappointing. In machine learning, this problem is termed as over fitting the model. Test data helps to assess and ensure that the prediction model can be reliably implemented for making the appropriate decisions.

We use training and test names to store independent variables and we use trainingtarget and testtarget names to store target variables stored in the 22nd column of the dataset. After data partitioning, we will have 1,523 observations in the training data and the remaining 603 observations will be in the test data. Note that although we use a 70:30 split here, the actual ratio after data partitioning may not be exactly 70:30.

One-hot encoding

After data partitioning, we will carry out a one-hot encoding of the response variable. One-hot encoding helps to represent a categorical variable in zeros and ones. The code and output for one-hot encoding is as follows:

```
# One-hot encoding
 trainLabels <- to_categorical(trainingtarget)
 testLabels <- to_categorical(testtarget)
 print(testLabels[1:10,])

OUTPUT
##         [,1] [,2] [,3]
##   [1,]    1    0    0
##   [2,]    1    0    0
##   [3,]    1    0    0
##   [4,]    0    0    1
##   [5,]    0    0    1
##   [6,]    0    1    0
##   [7,]    1    0    0
##   [8,]    1    0    0
##   [9,]    1    0    0
##  [10,]    1    0    0
```

As you can see in the preceding code, with the help of the `to_categorical` function from the Keras package, we convert the target variable to a binary class matrix, where the presence or absence of a class is simply represented by 1 or 0 respectively. In this example, we have three classes for the target variable, which are converted to three dummy variables. This process is also called **one-hot encoding**. First, 10 rows from `testLabels` are printed. The first row indicates the normal category for the patient with (1,0,0), the sixth row indicates the suspect category for the patient with (0,1,0), and the fourth row provides an example of the pathologic category of a patient with (0,0,1).

Once we complete these steps for data preparation, we move to the next step, where we create the classification model to classify a patient as normal, suspect, or pathological.

Creating and fitting a deep neural network model

In this section, we will develop the model architecture, compile the model, and then fit the model.

Developing model architecture

The code used for developing the model is as follows:

```
# Initializing the model
 model <- keras_model_sequential()

# Model architecture
 model %>%
 layer_dense(units = 8, activation = 'relu', input_shape = c(21)) %>%
 layer_dense(units = 3, activation = 'softmax')
```

As shown in the preceding code, we start by creating a sequential model using the
`keras_model_sequential()` function, which allows a linear stack of layers to be added.
Next, we add layers to the model using the pipe operator, `%>%`. This pipe operator takes
information from the left as output and feeds that information as input to what is on the
right. We use a fully connected or densely connected neural network using
the `layer_dense` function and then specify various inputs. In this dataset, we have 21
independent variables, and as such, the `input_shape` function is specified as 21 neurons or
units in the neural network. This layer is also termed as the input layer in the network. The
first hidden layer has 8 units and the activation function that we use here is a rectified
linear unit, or `relu`, which is the most popular activation function used in these situations.
The first hidden layer is connected to the output layer with 3 units using the pipe operator.
We use 3 units since our target variable has 3 classes. The activation function used in the
output layer is `'softmax'`, which helps to keep the range of output values between 0 and
1. Keeping the range of output values between 0 and 1 will help us to interpret results in
the form of familiar probability values.

> For typing the pipe operator, `%>%`, in RStudio, you can use the *Shift +
> Command + M* shortcut for Mac, and for Windows, *Shift + Ctrl + M*.

To obtain a summary of the model architecture that we have created, we can run the
`summary` function, as shown in the following code:

```
# Model summary
 summary(model)

 OUTPUT
 ##

 ## Layer    (type) Output Shape Param #
 ##
 ================================================================================
```

```
## dense_1 (Dense)  (None, 8)        176
##

## dense_2 (Dense)  (None, 3)         27
##
## =================================================================
## Total params: 203
## Trainable params: 203
## Non-trainable params: 0
##
```

Since the input layer has 21 units that are connected to each of the 8 units in the first hidden layer, we end up with 168 weights (21 x 8). We also obtain one bias term for each unit in the hidden layer, with a total of 8 such terms. So, at the first and only hidden layer stage, we have a total of 176 parameters (168 + 8). Similarly, 8 units in the hidden layer are connected to 3 units in the output layer, yielding 24 weights (8 x 3). This way, we have 24 weights and 3 bias terms at the output layer that account for a total of 27 parameters. Finally, the total number of parameters for this neural network architecture will be 203.

Compiling the model

To configure the learning process for the neural network, we compile the model by specifying the loss, optimizer, and metrics, as shown in the following code:

```
# Compile model
model %>%
    compile(loss = 'categorical_crossentropy',
    optimizer = 'adam',
    metrics = 'accuracy')
```

We use loss for specifying the objective function that we want to optimize. As shown in the preceding code, for the loss, we use 'categorical_crossentropy', since our target variable has three categories. For situations where the target variable has two categories, we use binary_crossentropy. For the optimizer, we use the 'adam' optimization algorithm, which is a popular algorithm for deep learning. Its popularity is mainly due to the fact that it gives good results faster than other stochastic optimization methods, such as the **adaptive gradient algorithm (AdaGrad)** and **root mean square propagation (RMSProp)**. We specify the metrics for evaluating the model performance during training and testing. For metrics, we use accuracy to assess the classification performance of the model.

Now we are ready to fit the model, which we will do in the next section.

Fitting the model

To fit the model, we make use of the following code:

```
# Fit model
model_one <- model %>%
  fit(training,
    trainLabels,
    epochs = 200,
    batch_size = 32,
    validation_split = 0.2)

OUTPUT (last 3 epochs)
Epoch 198/200
1218/1218 [==============================] - 0s 43us/step - loss: 0.3662 -
acc: 0.8555 - val_loss: 0.5777 - val_acc: 0.8000
Epoch 199/200
1218/1218 [==============================] - 0s 41us/step - loss: 0.3654 -
acc: 0.8530 - val_loss: 0.5763 - val_acc: 0.8000
Epoch 200/200
1218/1218 [==============================] - 0s 40us/step - loss: 0.3654 -
acc: 0.8571 - val_loss: 0.5744 - val_acc: 0.8000
```

As seen from the preceding code, we see the following observations:

- To fit the model, we provide training data that has data for 21 independent variables and `trainLabels`, which contains data for the target variable.
- The number of iterations or epochs is specified as 200. An epoch is a single pass of the training data followed by model assessment using validation data.
- To avoid overfitting, we specified that the validation split is 0.2, which means that 20% of the training data will be used to assess the model performance as the training proceeds.
- Note that this 20% of data is the bottom 20% of the data points in the training data. We stored data on the loss and accuracy values for the training and validation data generated during the training of the model in `model_one` for later use.
- For `batch_size`, we used the default value of 32, which represents the number of samples that will be used per gradient.
- As the training of the model proceeds, we get a visual display of plots for loss and accuracy based on training and validation data after each epoch.

- For accuracy, we would like the model to have higher values, as accuracy is a `the-higher-the-better` type of metric, whereas for loss, which is a `the-lower-the-better` type of metric, we would like the model to have lower values.

- In addition, we also obtained the numeric summary of the loss output based on the last 3 epochs, as shown in the preceding code output. For each epoch, we saw that 1,218 samples out of 1,523 samples of the training data (about 80%) were used for fitting the model. The remaining 20% of the data was used for calculating accuracy and loss values for the validation data.

> A word of caution. When using `validation_split`, note that the validation data is not selected randomly from the training data—for example, when `validation_split = 0.2`, the last 20% of the training data is used for validation and the first 80% is used for training. Therefore, if the values of the target variable are not random, then `validation_split` may introduce bias in the classification model.

After the training process completes 200 epochs, we can plot the training progress in terms of loss and accuracy for training and validation data using the `plot` function, as shown in the following code:

```
plot(model_one)
```

The following graph provides a plot that has accuracy in the top window and loss in the lower window:

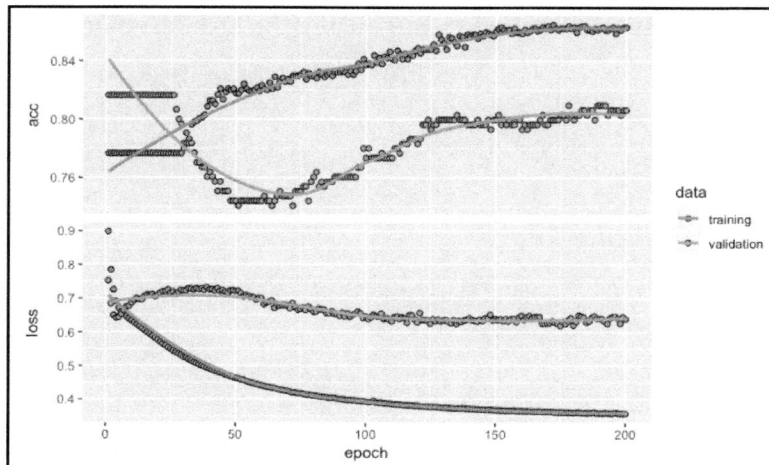

Accuracy and loss for training and validation data

From the preceding plot for loss and accuracy, we can make the following observations:

- From the plot for accuracy in the top graph, you can see that accuracy values increase significantly after about 25 epochs and then continue to increase gradually for the training data.
- For validation data, the progress is more uneven, with a drop in accuracy between the 25th and 50th epochs.
- A somewhat similar pattern is observed in the opposite direction for loss values.
- Note that if the training data accuracy increases with the number of epochs, but the validation data accuracy decreases, that would suggest an overfitting of the model. We do not see any major pattern suggesting model overfitting from this plot.

Model evaluation and predictions

In this section, we will use test data to evaluate the model performance. We can certainly calculate loss and accuracy values using the training data; however, the real test of a classification model is when it is used with unseen data. And since test data is kept separate from the model building process, we can now use it for model evaluation. We will first calculate loss and accuracy values with the test data and then develop a confusion matrix.

Loss and accuracy calculation

The code for obtaining loss and accuracy values using the test data along with the output is shown in the following:

```
# Model evaluation
 model %>%
 evaluate(test, testLabels)

OUTPUT
 ## $loss
 ## [1] 0.4439415
 ##
 ## $acc
 ## [1] 0.8424544
```

As you can see in the preceding code, using the `evaluate` function, we can obtain loss and accuracy values as `0.4439` and `0.8424` respectively. Using `colSums(testLabels)`, we can find that there are 460, 94, and 49 cases of normal, suspect, and pathological patients respectively in the test data. Converting these numbers to percentages using a total of 603 samples in the test data, we obtain 76.3%, 15.6%, and 8.1% respectively. The highest number of samples belongs to the normal category of patients, and we can use 76.3% as a benchmark for the model performance. If we do not use any model and simply classify all cases in the test data as belonging to the normal category of patients, then we will still be correct about 76.3% of the time since we will be right about all normal patients and incorrect about the other two categories.

In other words, the accuracy of our prediction will be as high as 76.3%; therefore, the model that we develop here should perform at least better than this benchmark number. If it functions below this number, then it is not likely to be of much practical use. Since we get an accuracy of 84.2% for the test data, we are definitely doing better than the benchmark value, but clearly we must also try to improve our model in order to perform even better. To do that, let's dig even deeper and learn about model performance for each category of the response variable with the help of a confusion matrix.

Confusion matrix

To obtain a confusion matrix, let's start by making a prediction for the test data and save it in `prec`. We use `predict_classes` to make this prediction and then use the `table` function to create a summary of predicted versus actual values for the test data to create a confusion matrix, as shown in the following code:

```
# Prediction and confusion matrix
pred <- model %>%
   predict_classes(test)
table(Predicted=pred, Actual=testtarget)

OUTPUT
        Actual
## Predicted   0    1    2
##          0 435  41   11
##          1  24  51   16
##          2   1   2   22
```

In the preceding confusion matrix, shown as output", values 0, 1, and 2 represent normal, suspect, and pathological categories respectively. From the confusion matrix, we can make the following observations:

- There were 435 patients in the test data who were actually normal and the model also predicted them as being normal.
- Similarly, there were 51 correct predictions for the suspect group and 22 correct predictions for the pathological group.
- If we add all the numbers on the diagonal of the confusion matrix, which are the correct classifications, we obtain 508 (435 + 51 + 22), or an accuracy level of 84.2% ((508 ÷ 603) x 100).
- In the confusion matrix, the off diagonal numbers indicate the number of patients who are misclassified. The highest number of misclassifications is 41, where the patients actually belong to the suspect group but the model incorrectly classified them in the normal category of patients.
- The instance of misclassification with the lowest number involved one patient who actually belonged to the normal category, but the model incorrectly classified this patient in the pathological category.

Let's also look at the predictions in terms of probabilities instead of only classes, which was the approach that we used previously. To predict probabilities, we can use the `predict_prob` function. We can then look at the first seven rows from the test data using the `cbind` function for comparison, as shown in the following code:

```
# Prediction probabilities
prob <- model %>%
    predict_proba(test)
cbind(prob, pred, testtarget)[1:7,]
```

```
OUTPUT
                                         pred testtarget
[1,] 0.993281245 0.006415705 0.000302993   0          0
[2,] 0.979825318 0.018759586 0.001415106   0          0
[3,] 0.982333243 0.014519051 0.003147765   0          0
[4,] 0.009040437 0.271216542 0.719743013   2          2
[5,] 0.008850170 0.267527819 0.723622024   2          2
[6,] 0.946622312 0.030137880 0.0232398603  0          1
[7,] 0.986279726 0.012411724 0.0013086179  0          0
```

In the preceding output, we have probability values for three categories based on the model and we also have the predicted category represented by `pred` and the actual category represented by `testtarget` in the test data. From the preceding output, we can make the following observations:

- For the first sample, the highest probability of 0.993 is for the normal category of patients, and that is the reason the predicted class is identified as 0. Since this prediction matches the actual result in the test data, we treat this as the correct classification.
- Similarly, since the fourth sample shows the highest probability of 0.7197 for the third category, the predicted class is labeled as 2, which turns out to be a correct prediction.
- However, the sixth sample has the highest probability of 0.9466 for the first category represented by 0, whereas the actual class is 1. In this case, our model misclassifies the sample.

Next, we will explore the option of improving the classification performance of the model to obtain better accuracy. Two key strategies that we can follow are to increase the number of hidden layers for building a deeper neural network and to change the number of units in the hidden layer. We will explore these options in the next section.

Performance optimization tips and best practices

In this section, we fine-tune the previous classification model to explore its functions and see whether its performance can be further improved.

Experimenting with an additional hidden layer

In this experiment, we will add an additional hidden layer to the previous model. The code and output of the summary of the model is given as follows:

```
# Model architecture
model <- keras_model_sequential()
model %>%
    layer_dense(units = 8, activation = 'relu', input_shape = c(21)) %>%
    layer_dense(units = 5, activation = 'relu') %>%
    layer_dense(units = 3, activation = 'softmax')
```

```
summary(model)
```

```
OUTPUT
```

Layer (type)	Output Shape	Param #
dense_1 (Dense)	(None, 8)	176
dense_2 (Dense)	(None, 5)	45
dense_3 (Dense)	(None, 3)	18

```
Total params: 239
Trainable params: 239
Non-trainable params: 0
```

As shown in the preceding code and output, we have added a second hidden layer with 5 units. In this hidden layer too, we use `relu` as the activation function. Note that as a result of this change, we have increased the total number of parameters from 203 in the previous model to 239 in this model.

Next, we compile and then fit the model using the following code:

```
# Compile and fit model
model %>%
 compile(loss = 'categorical_crossentropy',
 optimizer = 'adam',
 metrics = 'accuracy')
model_two <- model %>%
   fit(training,
       trainLabels,
       epochs = 200,
       batch_size = 32,
       validation_split = 0.2)
 plot(model_two)
```

As shown in the preceding code, we have compiled the model with same settings that we used earlier. We have also kept the setting for the `fit` function the same as earlier. The model-output-related information is stored in `model_two`. The following diagram provides the plot of accuracy and loss for `model_two`:

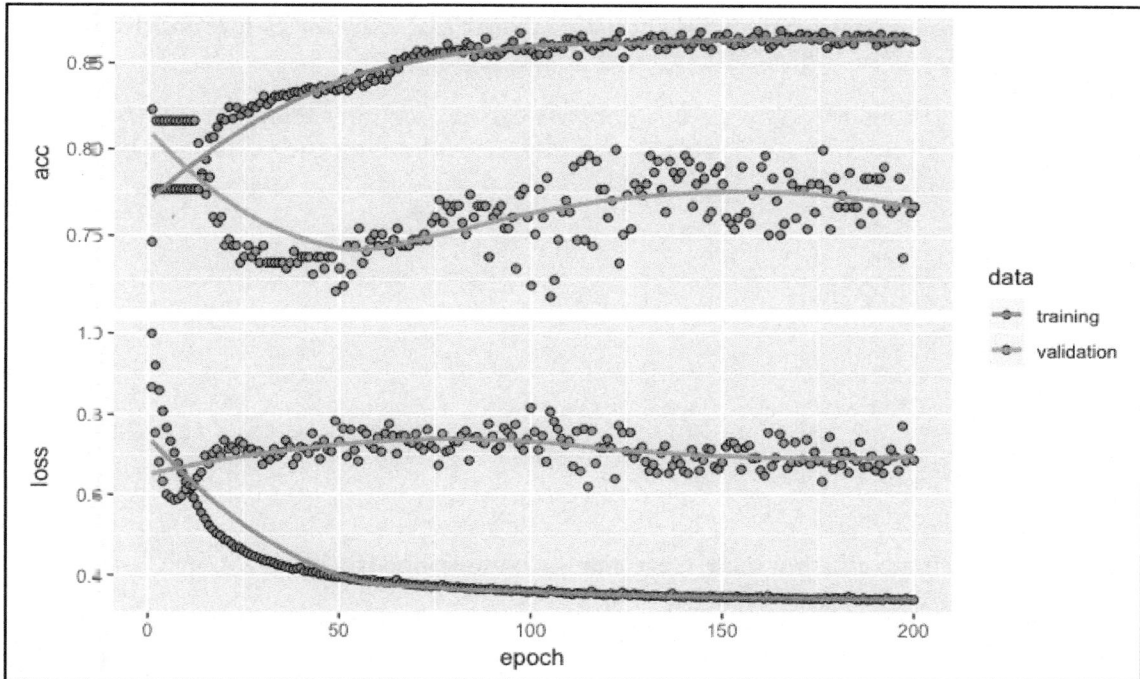

Accuracy and loss for training and validation data

From the preceding diagram, we can make the following observations:

- The accuracy values based on training and validation data remain relatively constant for the first few epochs.
- After about 20 epochs, the accuracy for the training data starts to increase and then continues to increase for the remaining epochs. The rate of increase, however, slows down after about 100 epochs.

- On the other hand, the accuracy based on validation data drops for approximately 50 epochs, then starts to increase, and then becomes more or less constant after about 125 epochs.
- Similarly, loss values initially drop significantly for training data, but after about 50 epochs, the rate of decrease drops.
- The loss values for the validation data drop during the initial few epochs and then increase and stabilize after about 25 epochs.

Using class predictions based on the test data, we can also obtain a confusion matrix to assess the performance of this classification model. The following code is used to obtain a confusion matrix:

```
# Prediction and confusion matrix
pred <- model %>%
    predict_classes(test)
table(Predicted=pred, Actual=testtarget)

OUTPUT
          Actual
## Predicted   0    1    2
##         0 429   38    4
##         1  29   54   33
##         2   2    2   12
```

From the preceding confusion matrix, we can make the following observations:

- By comparing correct classifications for 0, 1, and 2 classes with the previous model, we notice that improvement is only seen for class 1, whereas the correct classifications for classes 0 and 2 have, in fact, reduced.
- The overall accuracy for this model is 82.1%, which is below the accuracy value of 84.2% that we obtained earlier. So, our attempt to make our model slightly deeper did not improve accuracy, in this case.

Experimenting with a higher number of units in the hidden layer

Now, let's fine-tune the first model by changing the number of units in the first and only hidden layer using the following code:

```
# Model architecture
model <- keras_model_sequential()
model %>%
```

```
    layer_dense(units = 30, activation = 'relu', input_shape = c(21)) %>%
    layer_dense(units = 3, activation = 'softmax')

summary(model)
OUTPUT
```

Layer (type)	Output Shape	Param #
dense_1 (Dense)	(None, 30)	660
dense_2 (Dense)	(None, 3)	93

```
Total params: 753
Trainable params: 753
Non-trainable params: 0
```

```
# Compile model
 model %>%
   compile(loss = 'categorical_crossentropy',
           optimizer = 'adam',
           metrics = 'accuracy')

# Fit model
model_three <- model %>%
   fit(training,
       trainLabels,
       epochs = 200,
       batch_size = 32,
       validation_split = 0.2)
 plot(model_three )
```

As shown in the preceding code and output, we have increased the number of units in the first and only hidden layer from 8 to 30. The total number of parameters for this model is 753. We compile and fit the model with the same setting that we used earlier. We store the accuracy and loss values while fitting the model in `model_three`.

The following screenshot provides the plot for accuracy and loss for training and validation data based on the new classification model, as shown in the following graph:

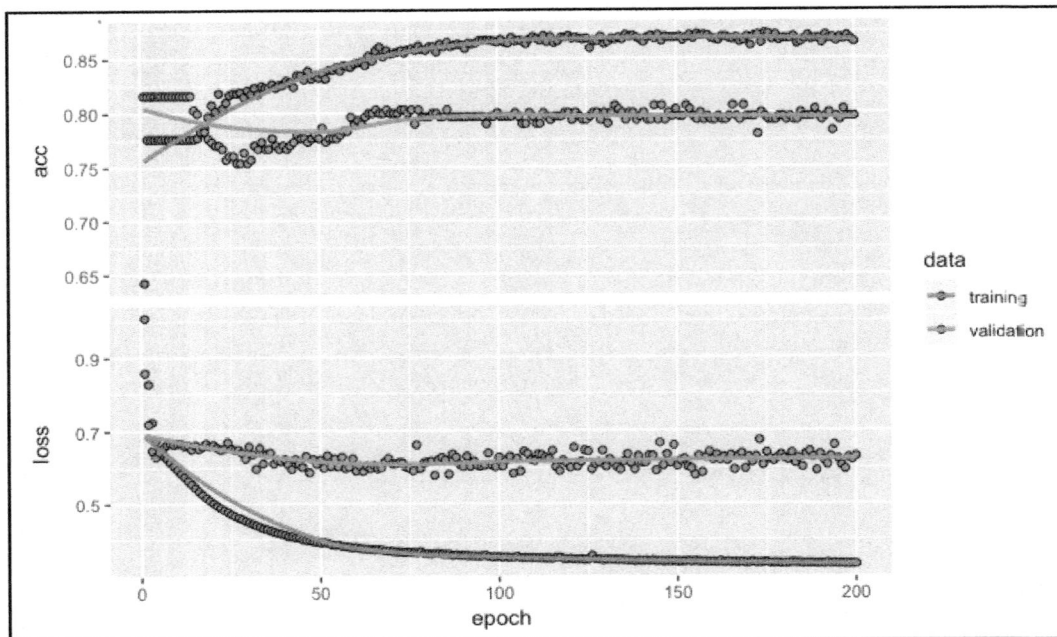

Accuracy and loss for training and validation data

We can make the following observations from the preceding plot:

- There is no evidence of overfitting.
- After about 75 epochs, we do not see any major improvement in the model performance.

The prediction of classes using the test data and confusion matrix is obtained using the following code:

```
# Prediction and confusion matrix
pred <- model %>%
    predict_classes(test)
table(Predicted=pred, Actual=testtarget)

OUTPUT
        Actual
## Predicted   0   1   2
##         0 424  35   5
```

```
##        1  28  55   5
##        2   8   4  39
```

From the preceding confusion matrix, we can make the following observations:

- We see improvements in the classification of 1 suspect and 2 pathological categories compared to the first model.
- The correct classifications for the 0, 1, and 2 categories are 424, 55, and 39 respectively.
- The overall accuracy using the test data comes to 85.9%, which is better than the first two models.

We can also obtain percentages that show how often this model correctly classifies each class by dividing the number of correct classifications in each column by the total of that column. We find that this classification model correctly classifies normal, suspect, and pathological cases with percentages of about 92.2%, 58.5%, and 79.6% respectively. So the model performance is at its highest when correctly classifying normal patients; however, the model accuracy drops to just 58.5% when correctly classifying patients in the suspect category. From the confusion matrix, we can see that the highest number of samples associated with misclassification is 35. Thus, there are 35 patients who actually belong to the suspect category, but the classification model incorrectly puts these patients in the normal category.

Experimenting using a deeper network with more units in the hidden layer

After building three different neural network models with 203, 239, and 753 parameters respectively, we will now build a deeper neural network model containing a larger number of units in the hidden layers. The code used for this experiment is as follows:

```
# Model architecture
model <- keras_model_sequential()
model %>%
        layer_dense(units = 40, activation = 'relu', input_shape = c(21))
%>%
        layer_dropout(rate = 0.4) %>%
        layer_dense(units = 30, activation = 'relu') %>%
        layer_dropout(rate = 0.3) %>%
        layer_dense(units = 20, activation = 'relu') %>%
        layer_dropout(rate = 0.2) %>%
        layer_dense(units = 3, activation = 'softmax')
summary(model)
```

```
OUTPUT
```

Layer (type)	Output Shape	Param #
dense_1 (Dense)	(None, 40)	880
dropout_1 (Dropout)	(None, 40)	0
dense_2 (Dense)	(None, 30)	1230
dropout_2 (Dropout)	(None, 30)	0
dense_3 (Dense)	(None, 20)	620
dropout_3 (Dropout)	(None, 20)	0
dense_4 (Dense)	(None, 3)	63

```
Total params: 2,793
Trainable params: 2,793
Non-trainable params: 0
```

```
# Compile model
 model %>%
   compile(loss = 'categorical_crossentropy',
           optimizer = 'adam',
           metrics = 'accuracy')

# Fit model
model_four <- model %>%
 fit(training,
 trainLabels,
 epochs = 200,
 batch_size = 32,
 validation_split = 0.2)
plot(model_four)
```

You can see from the preceding code and output that to try and improve the classification performance, this model has a total of 2,793 parameters. This model has three hidden layers with 40, 30, and 20 units in the three hidden layers. After each hidden layer, we have also added a dropout layer with dropout rates of 40%, 30%, and 20% to avoid overfitting—for example, with a dropout rate of 0.4 (or 40%) after the first hidden layer, 40% of the units in the first hidden layer are dropped to zero at random at the time of training. This helps to avoid any overfitting that may occur because of the higher number of units in the hidden layers. We compile the model and then run the model with same settings that we used earlier. We also store the loss and accuracy values after each epoch in `model_four`.

A plot for accuracy and loss values for training and validation data is shown in the following graph:

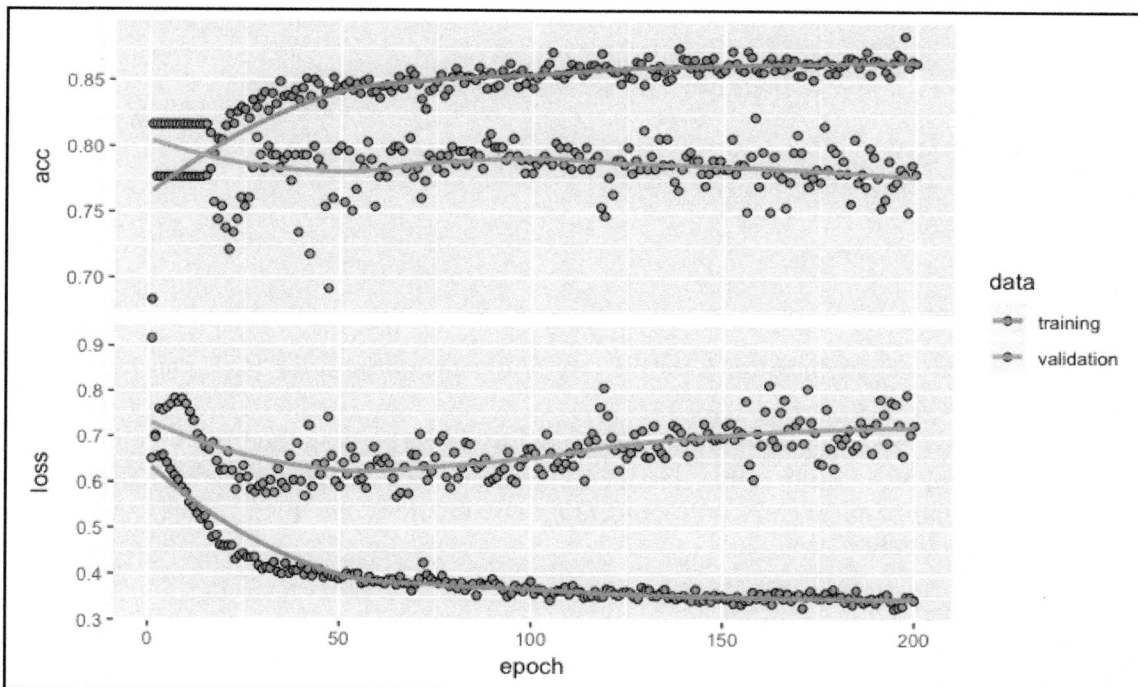

Accuracy and loss for training and validation data

From the preceding plot, we can make the following observations:

- Training loss and accuracy values stay approximately constant after about 150 epochs.
- Accuracy values for validation data are mainly flat after about 75 epochs.
- However, for loss, we see some divergence between training and validation data after about 75 epochs, with loss from validation data increasing gradually. This suggests the presence of overfitting after about 75 epochs.

Let's now make predictions using test data and review the resulting confusion matrix to assess model performance, as shown in the following code:

```
# Predictions and confusion matrix
pred <- model %>%
        predict_classes(test)
table(Predicted=pred, Actual=testtarget)

OUTPUT
         Actual
Predicted   0    1    2
        0 431   34    7
        1  20   53    2
        2   9    7   40
```

From the preceding confusion matrix, the following observations can be made:

- The correct classifications for the 0, 1, and 2 categories are 431, 53, and 40 respectively.
- The overall accuracy comes to 86.9%, which is better than the first three models.
- We can also find that this classification model correctly classifies normal, suspect, and pathological cases with percentages of about 93.7%, 56.4%, and 81.6% respectively.

Experimenting by addressing the class imbalance problem

In this dataset, the number of patients in the normal, suspect, and pathological categories is not the same. In the original dataset, the number of normal, suspect, and pathological patients are 1,655, 295, and 176, respectively.

We will make use of the following code to develop a bar plot:

```
# Bar plot
barplot(prop.table(table(data$NSP)),
        col = rainbow(3),
        ylim = c(0, 0.8),
        ylab = 'Proportion',
        xlab = 'NSP',
        cex.names = 1.5)
```

After running the preceding code, we obtain the following bar plot:

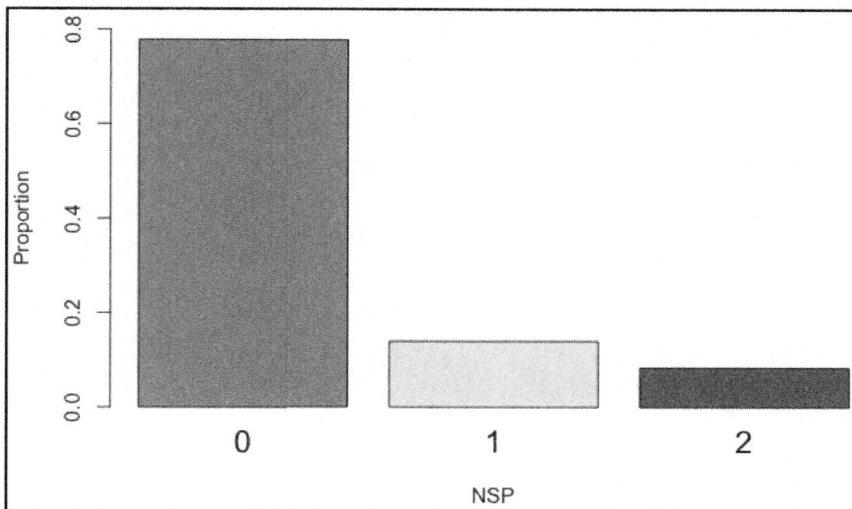

Proportion of samples in each of the three classes

In the preceding bar plot, the percentages of normal, suspect, and pathological patients are approximately 78%, 14%, and 8% respectively. When we compare these classes, we observe that the number of normal patients is about 5.6 times (1,655/295) greater than the number of suspect patients and about 9.4 times greater than the number of pathological patients. The dataset exhibiting a pattern where classes are not balanced but contain significantly different numbers of cases per class is described as having a class imbalance problem. The class that has a significantly higher number of cases may benefit from this at the time of training the model, but at the cost of the other classes.

As a result, a classification model may contain a bias toward the class that has a significantly higher number of cases, and provide results with higher classification accuracy for this class compared to the other classes. When data is influenced by such a class imbalance, it is important to address the issue to avoid bias in the final classification model. In such situations, we can make use of class weights to address the class imbalance issue in a dataset.

> Very often, datasets that are used for developing classification models have an unequal number of samples for each class. Such class imbalance issues can easily be handled using the `class_weight` function.

The code that includes `class_weight` to incorporate class imbalance information is shown in the following code:

```
# Fit model
model_five <- model %>%
  fit(training,
      trainLabels,
      epochs = 200,
      batch_size = 32,
      validation_split = 0.2,
      class_weight = list("0"=1,"1"=5.6, "2" = 9.4))
plot(model_five)
```

As you can see in the preceding code, we have specified a weight of 1 for the normal class, a weight of 5.6 for the suspect class, and a weight of 9.4 for the pathological class. Assigning these weights creates a level playing field for all three categories. We have kept all other settings the same as they were in the previous model. After training the network, the loss and accuracy values for each epoch are stored in `model_five`.

The loss and accuracy plot for this experiment is shown in the following screenshot:

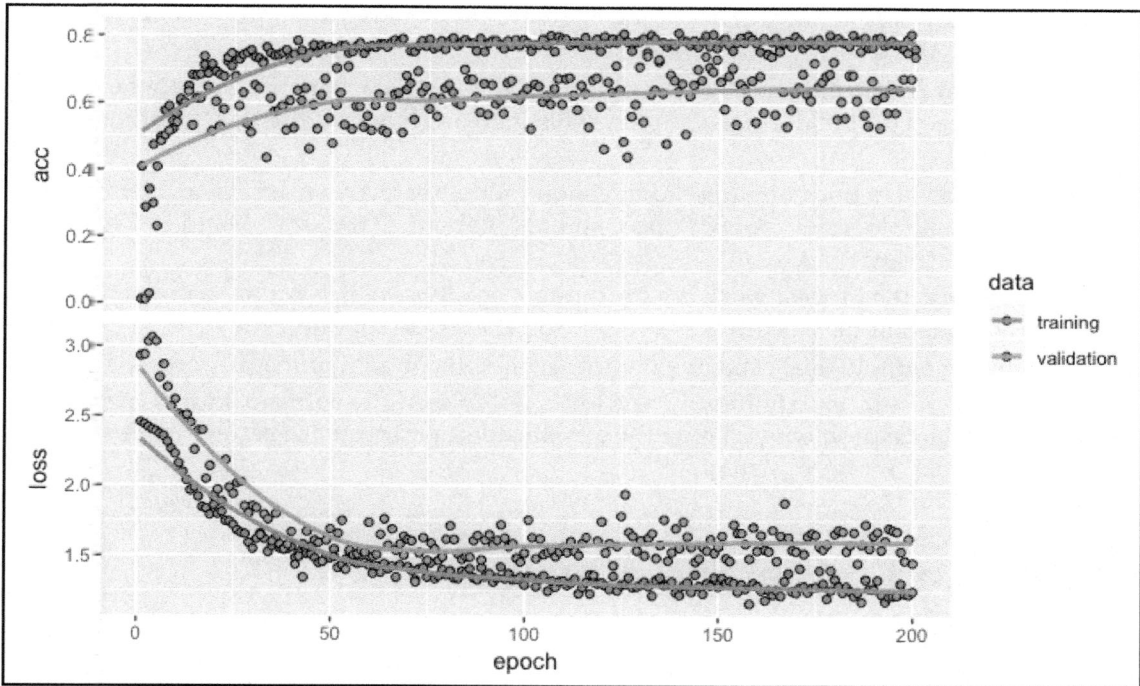

From the accuracy and loss plot based on training and validation data, we do not see any obvious pattern suggesting overfitting. After about 100 epochs, we do not see any major improvement in model performance in terms of loss and accuracy values.

The code for the predictions from the model and the resulting confusion matrix is as follows

```
# Prediction and confusion matrix
pred <- model %>%
  predict_classes(test)
table(Predicted=pred, Actual=testtarget)

OUTPUT
        Actual
Predicted   0   1   2
        0 358  12   3
        1  79  74   5
        2  23   8  41
```

From the preceding confusion matrix, we can make the following observations:

- The correct classifications for the 0, 1, and 2 categories are 358, 74, and 41 respectively.
- The overall accuracy is now reduced to 78.4%, which is mainly due to the drop in accuracy for the normal class, since we increased the weights for the other two classes.
- We can also find that this classification model correctly classifies normal, suspect, and pathological cases with percentages of about 77.8%, 78.7%, and 83.7% respectively.
- Clearly, the biggest gains are for the suspect class, which is now correctly classified at the rate of 78.7% versus the earlier rate of only 56.4%.
- In the pathological class, we do not see any major gain or loss in accuracy value.
- These results clearly indicate the influence of using weights to address class imbalance problems, as now the classification performance across the three classes is more consistent.

Saving and reloading a model

We know that each time we run a model in Keras, the model starts with different starting points due to random initial weights. Once we arrive at a model with an acceptable level of performance and would like to reuse the same model in the future, we can save the model using the save_model_hdf5 function. We can then load this same model using the load_model_hdf5 function:

```
# Save and reload model
save_model_hdf5(model,
  filepath,
  overwrite = TRUE,
  include_optimizer = TRUE)
model_x <- load_model_hdf5(filepath,
  custom_objects = NULL,
  compile = TRUE)
```

The preceding code will allow us to save the model architecture and the model weights, and, if needed, will allow us to resume the training of the model from the previous training session.

Summary

In this chapter, we saw how to develop a neural network model that helps to solve a classification type of problem. We started with a simple classification model and explored how to change the number of hidden layers and the number of units in the hidden layers. The idea behind exploring and fine-tuning a classification model was to illustrate how to explore and improve the performance of the classification model. We also saw how to dig deeper to understand the performance of a classification model with the help of a confusion matrix. We purposefully looked at a relatively smaller neural network model at the beginning of this chapter and finished with an example of a relatively deeper neural network model. Deeper networks involving several hidden layers can also lead to overfitting problems, where a classification model may have excellent performance with training data but doesn't do well with testing data. To avoid such situations, we can make use of dropout layers after each dense layer, as was illustrated previously. We also illustrated the use of class weights for situations where the class imbalance could cause a classification model to be more biased toward a specific class. Finally, we also saw how we can save the model details for future use when we don't need to rerun the model.

For the models that we used in this chapter, there were certain parameters that we kept constant during the various experiments—for example, when compiling a model, we always used `adam` as an optimizer. One of the reasons for the popularity of using `adam` is that it doesn't require much tuning, and provides good results in less time; however, the reader is encouraged to try out other optimizers, such as `adagrad`, `adadelta`, and `rmsprop`, and observe the impact on the classification performance of the model. Another setting that we kept constant in this chapter is the batch size of 32 at the time of training the network. The reader is also encouraged to experiment with higher (such as 64) and lower (such as 16) batch sizes and observe what impact this has on the classification performance.

As we go on to future chapters, we will gradually develop more and more complex and deeper neural network models. Having addressed a classification model where the response variables are categorical, in the next chapter, we will go over the steps for developing and improving the prediction model for the regression type of problems, where the target variable is numeric.

3
Deep Neural Networks for Regression

In the previous chapter, we worked with a dataset that had a categorical target variable, and we went over the steps for developing a classification model using Keras. In situations where the response variable is numeric, supervised learning problems are categorized as regression problems. In this chapter, we will develop a prediction model for numeric response variables. To illustrate the process of developing the prediction model, we will make use of the Boston Housing dataset, which is available within the `mlbench` package.

In this chapter, we will cover the following topics:

- Understanding the Boston Housing dataset
- Preparing the data
- Creating and fitting a deep neural network model for regression
- Model evaluation and prediction
- Performance optimization tips and best practices

Understanding the Boston Housing dataset

In this chapter, we will use six libraries. These libraries are as listed in the following code:

```
# Libraries
library(keras)
library(mlbench)
library(psych)
library(dplyr)
library(magrittr)
library(neuralnet)
```

The structure of the `BostonHousing` data is as follows:

```
# Data structure
data(BostonHousing)
str(BostonHousing)

OUTPUT
'data.frame':        506 obs. of  14 variables:
 $ crim   : num   0.00632 0.02731 0.02729 0.03237 0.06905 ...
 $ zn     : num   18 0 0 0 0 0 12.5 12.5 12.5 12.5 ...
 $ indus  : num   2.31 7.07 7.07 2.18 2.18 2.18 7.87 7.87 7.87 7.87 ...
 $ chas   : Factor w/ 2 levels "0","1": 1 1 1 1 1 1 1 1 1 1 ...
 $ nox    : num   0.538 0.469 0.469 0.458 0.458 0.458 0.524 0.524 0.524
0.524 ...
 $ rm     : num   6.58 6.42 7.18 7 7.15 ...
 $ age    : num   65.2 78.9 61.1 45.8 54.2 58.7 66.6 96.1 100 85.9 ...
 $ dis    : num   4.09 4.97 4.97 6.06 6.06 ...
 $ rad    : num   1 2 2 3 3 3 5 5 5 5 ...
 $ tax    : num   296 242 242 222 222 222 311 311 311 311 ...
 $ ptratio: num   15.3 17.8 17.8 18.7 18.7 18.7 15.2 15.2 15.2 15.2 ...
 $ b      : num   397 397 393 395 397 ...
 $ lstat  : num   4.98 9.14 4.03 2.94 5.33 ...
 $ medv   : num   24 21.6 34.7 33.4 36.2 28.7 22.9 27.1 16.5 18.9 ...
```

As you can see from the preceding output, this dataset has 506 observations and 14 variables. Out of the 14 variables, 13 are numeric and 1 variable (`chas`) is of the factor type. The last variable, `medv` (the median value of owner-occupied homes in thousand-USD units), is the dependent, or target, variable. The remaining 13 variables are independent. The following is a brief description of all the variables, drawn up in a table for easy reference:

Variables	Description
crim	Per-capita crime rate by town
zn	Proportion of residential land zoned for lots over 25,000 sq ft
indus	Proportion of nonretail business acres per town
chas	Charles River dummy variable (1 if the tract bounds a river; 0 otherwise)
nox	Nitric-oxides concentration (parts per 10 million)
rm	Average number of rooms per dwelling
age	Proportion of owner-occupied units built prior to 1940
dis	Weighted distances to five Boston employment centers
rad	Index of accessibility to radial highways
tax	Full-value property-tax rate per 10,000 USD
ptratio	Pupil–teacher ratio by town

lstat	Percentage of lower-income status members of the population
medv	Median value of owner-occupied homes in thousand-USD units

This data is based on the 1970 census. A detailed statistical study using this data was published by Harrison and Rubinfeld in 1978 (reference: http://citeseerx.ist.psu.edu/viewdoc/download?doi=10.1.1.926.5532rep=rep1type=pdf).

Preparing the data

We start by changing the name of the BostonHousing data to simply data for ease of use. Independent variables that are of the factor type are then converted to the numeric type using the lapply function.

> Note that for this data, the only factor variable is chas; however, for any other dataset with more factor variables, this code will work fine.

Take a look at the following code:

```
# Converting factor variables to numeric
data <- BostonHousing
data %>% lapply(function(x) as.numeric(as.character(x)))
data <- data.frame(data)
```

In the preceding code, after converting factor variables to the numeric type, we also change the format of data to data.frame.

Visualizing the neural network

To visualize a neural network with hidden layers, we will use the neuralnet function. For illustration, two hidden layers with 10 and 5 units will be used in this example. The input layer has 13 nodes based on 13 independent variables. The output layer has only one node for the target variable, medv. The code used is as follows:

```
# Neural network
n <-
neuralnet(medv~crim+zn+indus+chas+nox+rm+age+dis+rad+tax+ptratio+b+lstat,
               data = data,
               hidden = c(10,5),
               linear.output = F,
```

```
               lifesign = 'full',
               rep=1)

# Plot
plot(n, col.hidden = "darkgreen",
     col.hidden.synapse = 'darkgreen',
     show.weights = F,
     information = F,
     fill = "lightblue")
```

As shown in the preceding code, the result is saved in n, and it is then used for plotting the architecture of the neural network, as shown in the following diagram:

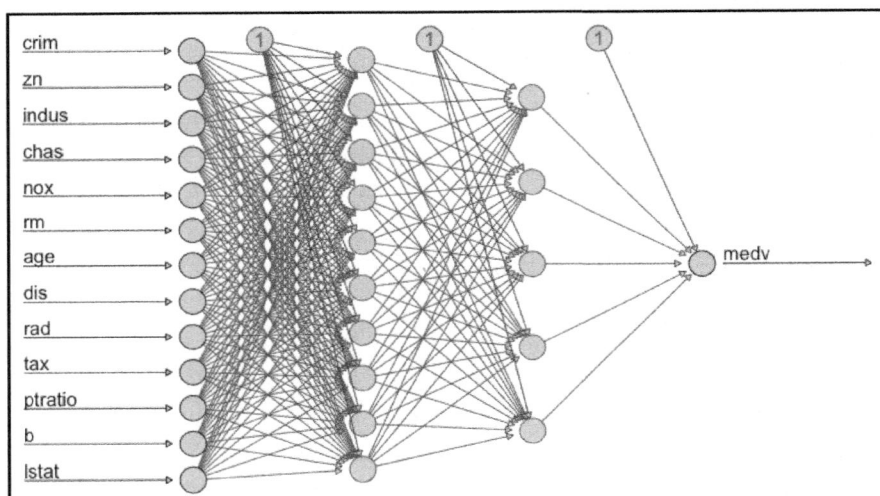

As you can see from the preceding diagram, the input layer has 13 nodes for 13 independent variables. There are two hidden layers: the first hidden layer has 10 nodes and the second hidden layer has 5 nodes. Each node in the hidden layer is connected to all the nodes in the previous and the following layer. The output layer has one node for the response variable, medv.

Data partitioning

Next, we change the data into a matrix format. We also set dimension names to NULL, which changes the names of the variables to the default names, V1, V2, V3, ..., V14:

```
data <- as.matrix(data)
dimnames(data) <- NULL
```

We then the partition data into training and test datasets using the following code:

```
# Data partitioning
set.seed(1234)
ind <- sample(2, nrow(data), replace = T, prob=c(.7, .3))
training <- data[ind==1, 1:13]
test <- data[ind==2, 1:13]
trainingtarget <- data[ind==1, 14]
testtarget <- data[ind==2, 14]
```

A data split of 70:30 is used in this example. To maintain the repeatability of the data split, we use a random seed of 1234. This will allow the same samples to be included in the training and test data each time data partitioning is carried out on any computer. The data for the independent variables are stored in training for the training data and in test for the test data. Similarly, the data for the dependent variable, medv, based on the corresponding split data, are stored in trainingtarget and testtarget.

Normalization

To normalize the data, the mean and standard deviations are obtained for all independent variables in the training data. Normalization is then carried out using the scale function:

> For both the train and test data, the mean and standard deviations are based on the training data used.

```
# Normalization
m <- colMeans(training)
sd <- apply(training, 2, sd)
training <- scale(training, center = m, scale = sd)
test <- scale(test, center = m, scale = sd)
```

This concludes the data preparation step for this data. It should be noted that different datasets may need extra steps that are unique to that dataset—for example, many large datasets may have very high amounts of missing data values, and they may require additional data preparation steps in the form of arriving at a strategy for handling missing values and inputting missing values wherever necessary.

In the next section, we will create a deep neural network architecture and then fit a model for the accurate prediction of the numeric target variable.

Creating and fitting a deep neural network model for regression

To create and fit a deep neural network model for a regression problem, we will make use of Keras. The code used for the model architecture is as follows:

> Note that the input layer having 13 units and the output layer having 1 unit is fixed based on the data; however, to arrive at a suitable number of hidden layers and the number of units in each layer, you need to experiment.

```
# Model architecture
model <- keras_model_sequential()
model %>%
    layer_dense(units = 10, activation = 'relu', input_shape = c(13)) %>%
    layer_dense(units = 5, activation = 'relu') %>%
    layer_dense(units = 1)
summary(model)
```

OUTPUT

Layer (type)	Output Shape	Param #
dense_1 (Dense)	(None, 10)	140
dense_2 (Dense)	(None, 5)	55
dense_3 (Dense)	(None, 1)	6

Total params: 201
Trainable params: 201
Non-trainable params: 0

As you can see from the preceding code, we use the `keras_model_sequential` function to create a sequential model. The structure of the neural network is defined using the `layer_dense` function. Since there are 13 independent variables, `input_shape` is used to specify 13 units. The first hidden layer has `10` units and the rectified linear unit, or `relu`, is used as the activation function in this first hidden layer. The second hidden layer has 5 units, with `relu` as the activation function. The last, `layer_dense`, has 1 unit, which represents one dependent variable, `medv`. Using the `summary` function, you can print a model summary, which shows 201 total parameters.

Calculating the total number of parameters

Let's now see how a total of 201 parameters are obtained for this model. The `dense_1` layer shows `140` parameters. These parameters are based on there being 13 units in the input layer that connect with each of the 10 units in the first hidden layer, meaning that there are 130 parameters (13 x 10). The remaining 10 parameters come from the bias term for each of the 10 units in the first hidden layer. Similarly, 50 parameters (10 x 5) are from the connections between two hidden layers and the remaining 5 parameters come from the bias term from each of the 5 units in the second hidden layer. Finally, `dense_3` has 6 parameters ((5 x 1) + 1). Thus, in all, there are 201 parameters based on the architecture of the neural network model that was chosen in this example.

Compiling the model

After the model architecture is defined, the model is compiled to configure the learning process using the following code:

```
# Compile model
model %>% compile(loss = 'mse',
    optimizer = 'rmsprop',
    metrics = 'mae')
```

As shown in the preceding code, we define the loss function as the mean square error, or `mse`. At this step, the `rmsprop` optimizer and mean absolute error, or `mae`, metric is also defined. We choose these because our response variable is numeric.

Fitting the model

Next, the model is trained using the `fit` function. Note that, as the training of the model proceeds, we get a visual as well as a numerical summary after each epoch. The output from the last three epochs is shown in the following code. We get the mean absolute error and loss values for both the training and the validation data. Note that, as pointed out in `Chapter 1`, *Revisiting Deep Learning Architecture and Techniques*, each time we train a network, the training and validation errors can vary because of the random initialization of network weights. Such an outcome is expected even when the data is partitioned using the same random seed. To obtain repeatable results, it is always a good idea to save the model using the `save_model_hdf5` function and then reload it when needed.

The code used for training the network is as follows:

```
# Fit model
model_one <- model %>%
    fit(training,
    trainingtarget,
    epochs = 100,
    batch_size = 32,
    validation_split = 0.2)

OUTPUT from last 3 epochs
Epoch 98/100
284/284 [==============================] - 0s 74us/step - loss: 24.9585 -
mean_absolute_error: 3.6937 - val_loss: 86.0545 - val_mean_absolute_error:
8.2678
Epoch 99/100
284/284 [==============================] - 0s 78us/step - loss: 24.6357 -
mean_absolute_error: 3.6735 - val_loss: 85.4038 - val_mean_absolute_error:
8.2327
Epoch 100/100
284/284 [==============================] - 0s 92us/step - loss: 24.3293 -
mean_absolute_error: 3.6471 - val_loss: 84.8307 - val_mean_absolute_error:
8.2015
```

As you can see from the preceding code, the model is trained in small batches of size 32, and 20% of the data is reserved for validation to avoid overfitting. Here, 100 epochs or iterations are run to train the network. Once the training process is completed, information related to the training process is saved in `model_one`, which can then be used to plot the loss and mean absolute error based on the training and validation data for all epochs:

```
plot(model_one)
```

The preceding line of code will return the following output. Let's have a look at the loss and mean absolute error for training and validation data (`model_one`) plot:

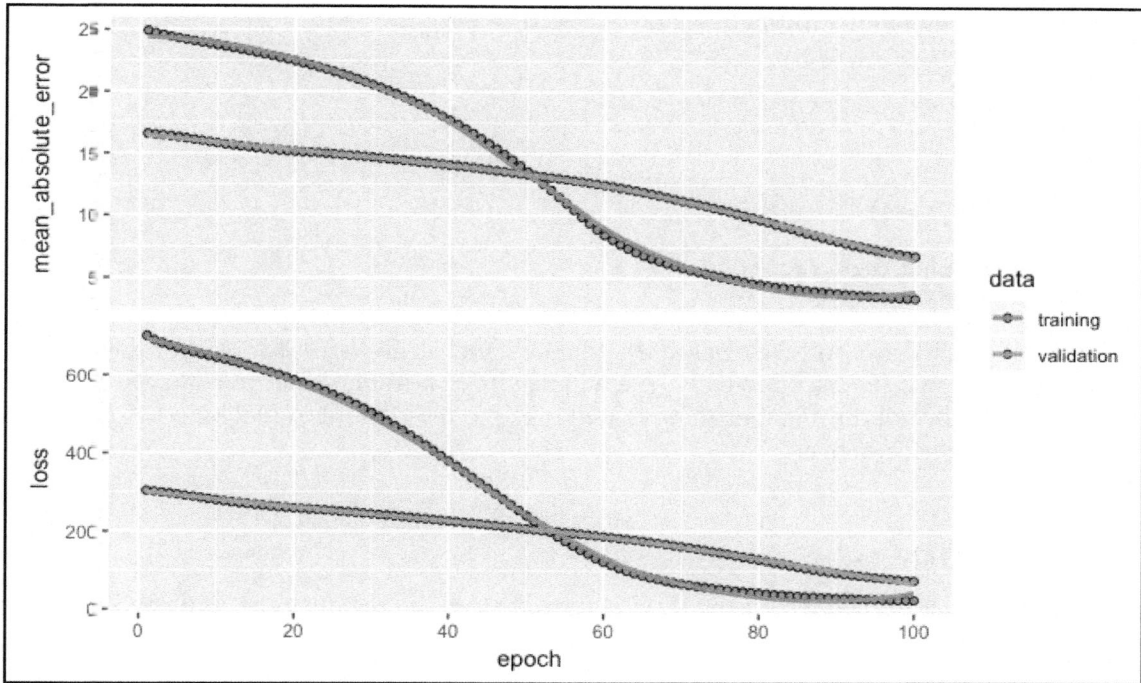

From the preceding plot, we can make the following observations:

- The `mae` and `loss` values decrease for both the training and validation data as the training proceeds.
- The rate of decrease in errors for the training data reduces after about 60 epochs.

After developing the prediction model, we can assess its performance by evaluating the prediction quality of the model, which we will look at in the next section.

Model evaluation and prediction

Model evaluation is an important step in the process of arriving at a suitable prediction model. A model may show good performance with training data that was used for developing the model; however, the real test of a model is with data that the model has not yet seen. Let's look at the model performance based on the test data.

Evaluation

The performance of the model is evaluated using the `evaluate` function with the help of the test data shown in the following code:

```
# Model evaluation
model %>%  evaluate(test, testtarget)

OUTPUT
 ## $loss
 ## [1]  31.14591
 ##
 ## $mean_absolute_error
 ## [1]  3.614594
```

From the preceding output, we can see that the loss and mean absolute error for the test data are 31.15 and 3.61 respectively. We will use these numbers later to compare and assess whether or not the changes that we will make to the current model help to improve the prediction performance.

Prediction

Let's predict the `medv` values for the `test` data and store the results in `pred` using the following code:

```
# Prediction
pred <- model %>%  predict(test)
cbind(pred[1:10], testtarget[1:10])

OUTPUT
           [,1]   [,2]
  [1,] 33.18942  36.2
  [2,] 18.17827  20.4
  [3,] 17.89587  19.9
  [4,] 13.07977  13.9
  [5,] 14.17268  14.8
  [6,] 19.09264  18.4
  [7,] 19.81316  18.9
  [8,] 21.00356  24.7
  [9,] 30.50263  30.8
 [10,] 19.75816  19.4
```

We can take a look at the first 10 predicted and actual values using the `cbind` function. The first column in the output shows the predicted values based on the model and the second column shows the actual values. We can make the following observations from the output:

- The prediction for the first sample in the test data is about `33.19` and the actual value is `36.2`. The model underestimates the response by about 3 points.
- For the second sample, the model underestimates the response by over 2 points.
- For the tenth sample, the predicted and actual values are very close.
- For the sixth sample, the model overestimates the response.

To get an overall picture of the prediction performance, we can develop a scatter plot of the predicted versus the actual values. We will use the following code:

```
plot(testtarget, pred,
     xlab = 'Actual',
     ylab = 'Prediction')
 abline(a=0,b=1)
```

The scatter plot shows the predicted versus the actual response values based on the test data:

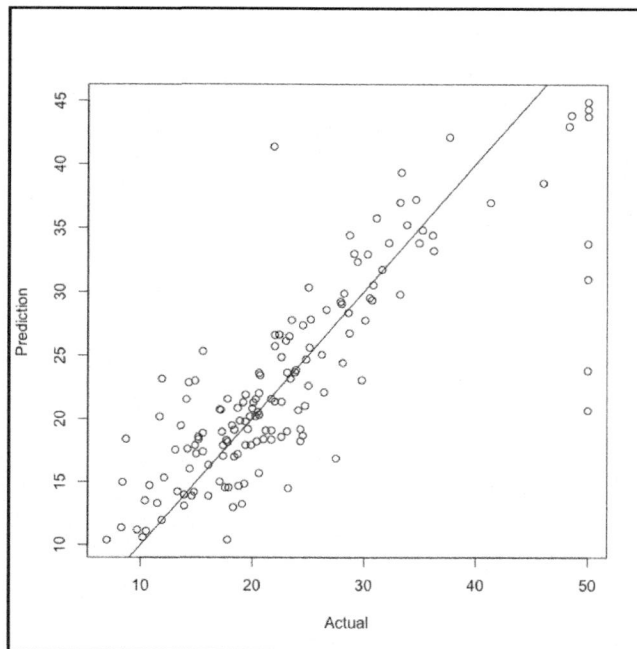

From the preceding graph, we can see the overall performance of the prediction model. The relationship between the actual and predicted values is positive and approximately linear. Although we can see that the model has decent performance, clearly there is scope for further improvement that makes data points closer to the ideal line that has zero intercepts and a slope of 1. We will further explore making improvements to the model by developing a deeper neural network model.

Improvements

In the modified new model, we will build a deeper network by adding more layers. The additional layers are expected to show patterns in the data that the smaller network we used earlier was not able to show.

Deeper network architecture

The code used for this experiment is as follows:

```
# Model Architecture
model <- keras_model_sequential()
model %>%
  layer_dense(units = 100, activation = 'relu', input_shape = c(13)) %>%
  layer_dropout(rate = 0.4) %>%
  layer_dense(units = 50, activation = 'relu') %>%
  layer_dropout(rate = 0.3) %>%
  layer_dense(units = 20, activation = 'relu') %>%
  layer_dropout(rate = 0.2) %>%
  layer_dense(units = 1)
summary(model)

OUTPUT
##
```

## Layer (type)	Output Shape	Param #
## dense_4 (Dense)	(None, 100)	1400
## dropout_1 (Dropout)	(None, 100)	0
## dense_5 (Dense)	(None, 50)	5050

```
## dropout_2 (Dropout)          (None, 50)              0
##

## dense_6 (Dense)              (None, 20)           1020
##

## dropout_3 (Dropout)          (None, 20)              0
##

## dense_7 (Dense)              (None, 1)              21
##
## ===============================================================
## Total params: 7,491
## Trainable params: 7,491
## Non-trainable params: 0
##
```

```
# Compile model
model %>% compile(loss = 'mse',
                  optimizer = 'rmsprop',
                  metrics = 'mae')

# Fit model
model_two <- model %>%
    fit(training,
        trainingtarget,
        epochs = 100,
        batch_size = 32,
        validation_split = 0.2)
plot(model_two)
```

From the preceding code, we can observe that we now have three hidden layers with 100, 50, and 20 units respectively. We have also added a dropout layer after each hidden layer with rates of 0.4, 0.3, and 0.2 respectively. As an example of what a dropout layer's rate means, a rate of 0.4 means that 40% of the units in the first hidden layer are dropped to zero at the time of training, which helps to avoid overfitting. The total number of parameters in this model has now increased to 7,491. Note that, in the previous model, the total number of parameters was 201, and clearly we are going for a significantly bigger neural network. Next, we compile the model with the same settings that we used earlier, and subsequently, we will fit the model and store the results in model_two.

Results

The following figure provides the loss and mean absolute error for `model_two` over 100 epochs:

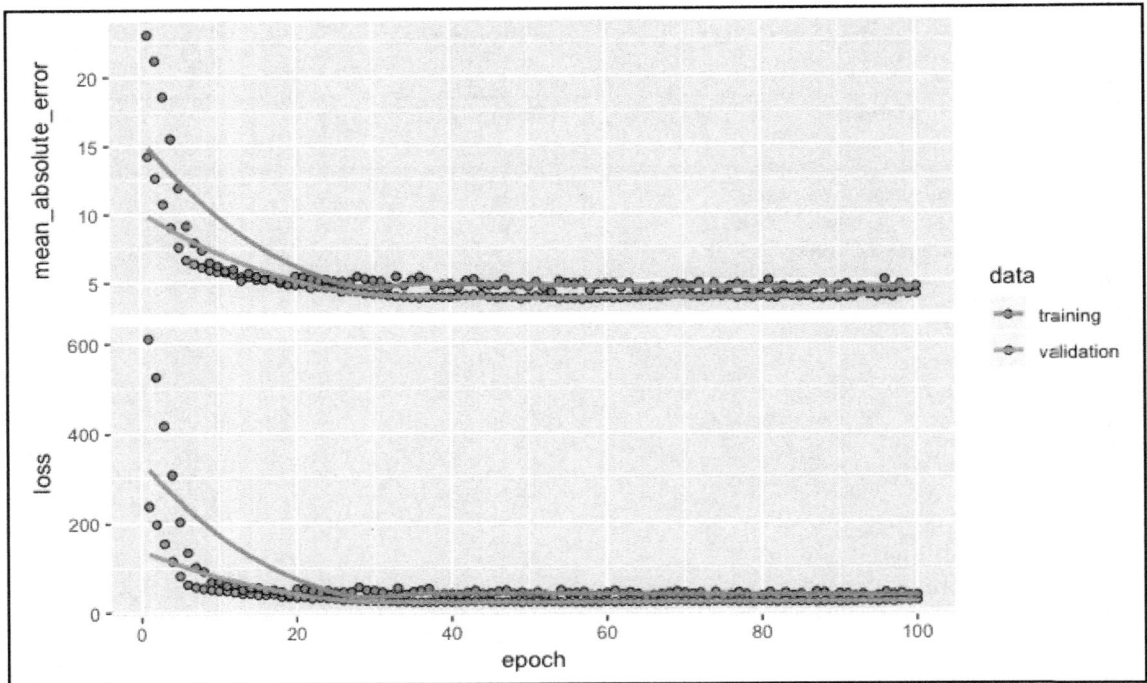

From the preceding figure, we can make the following observations:

- The mean absolute error and loss values for the training and validation data drop very quickly to low values, and after about 30 epochs, we do not see any major improvement.
- There is no evidence of overfitting as the training and validation errors seem closer to each other.

We can obtain the loss and mean absolute error values for the test data using the following code:

```
# Model evaluation
model %>%  evaluate(test, testtarget)

OUTPUT
 ## $loss
```

```
## [1] 24.70368
##
## $mean_absolute_error
## [1] 3.02175

pred <- model %>% predict(test)
plct(testtarget, pred,
     xlab = 'Actual',
     ylab = 'Prediction')
abline(a=0,b=1)
```

The loss and mean absolute error values using the test data and model_two are obtained as 24.70 and 3.02 respectively. This is a significant improvement compared to the results that we obtained from model_one.

We can visually see this improvement using the scatter plot for the predicted values versus the actual response values in the following graph:

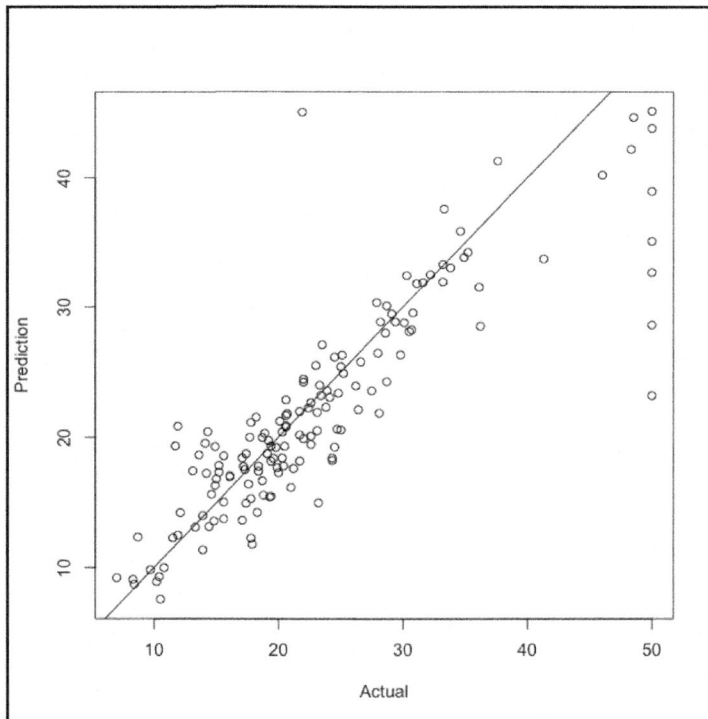

From the preceding graph, we can see that the spread in the scatter plot of actual versus predicted values is visibly less than that of the earlier scatter plot. This indicates better prediction performance compared to the previous model. Although `model_two` performs better than the previous model, at higher values, we can see the occurrence of significant underestimation of the target values. So, although we have developed a better model, we can also further explore the potential for the further improvement of this prediction model.

Performance optimization tips and best practices

Improving model performance can involve different strategies. Here, we will discuss two main strategies. One strategy is to make changes to the model architecture and observe the results to get any useful insights or indications of improvement. Another strategy could involve exploring the transformation of the target variable. In this section, we will try a combination of both of these strategies.

Log transformation on the output variable

To overcome the issue of significant underestimation of the target variable at higher values, let's try log transformation on the target variable and see whether or not this helps us to further improve the model. Our next model has some minor changes to the architecture as well. In `model_two`, we did not notice any major issue or evidence related to overfitting, and as a result, we can increase the number of units a little and also slightly reduce the percentages for dropout. The following is the code for this experiment:

```
# log transformation and model architecture
trainingtarget <- log(trainingtarget)
 testtarget <- log(testtarget)
 model <- keras_model_sequential()
 model %>%
   layer_dense(units = 100, activation = 'relu', input_shape = c(13)) %>%
   layer_dropout(rate = 0.4) %>%
   layer_dense(units = 50, activation = 'relu') %>%
   layer_dropout(rate = 0.2) %>%
   layer_dense(units = 25, activation = 'relu') %>%
   layer_dropout(rate = 0.1) %>%
   layer_dense(units = 1)
 summary(model)

OUTPUT
```

```
##
```

## Layer (type)	Output Shape	Param #
## dense_8 (Dense)	(None, 100)	1400
## dropout_4 (Dropout)	(None, 100)	0
## dense_9 (Dense)	(None, 50)	5050
## dropout_5 (Dropout)	(None, 50)	0
## dense_10 (Dense)	(None, 25)	1275
## dropout_6 (Dropout)	(None, 25)	0
## dense_11 (Dense)	(None, 1)	26

```
## Total params: 7,751
## Trainable params: 7,751
## Non-trainable params: 0
##
```

We will increase the number of units in the third hidden layer from 20 to 25. Dropout rates for the second and third hidden layers are also reduced to 0.2 and 0.1 respectively. Note that the overall number of parameters has now increased to 7751.

We next compile the model and then fit the model. The model results are stored in model_three, which we use for plotting the graph, as shown in the following code:

```
# Compile model
model %>% compile(loss = 'mse',
                  optimizer = optimizer_rmsprop(lr = 0.005),
                  metrics = 'mae')

# Fit model
 model_three <- model %>%
   fit(training,
```

```
            trainingtarget,
            epochs = 100,
            batch_size = 32,
            validation_split = 0.2)
    plot(model_three)
```

The following shows the output of the loss and mean absolute error for training and validation data (model_three):

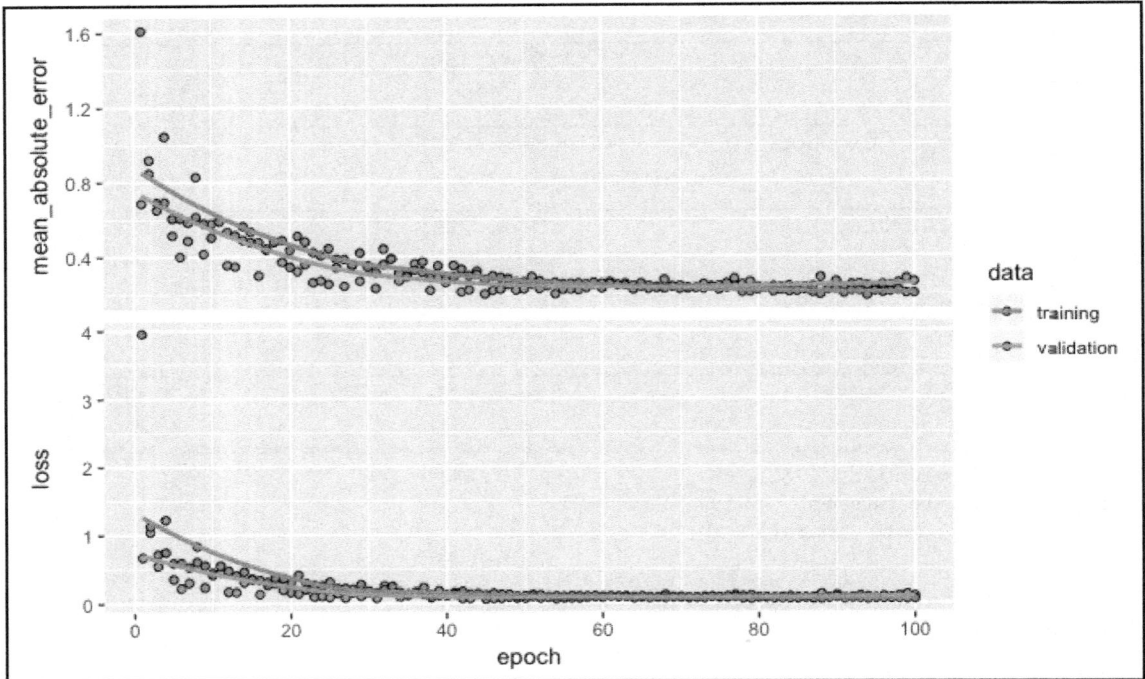

We can see from the preceding plot that although the values in the plot are not directly comparable to earlier figures because of the log transformation, we can see that the overall errors decrease and become stable after about 50 epochs for both the mean absolute error and the loss.

Model performance

We also obtain `loss` and `mae` values for this new model, but again, the numbers obtained are not directly comparable to the earlier two models for the log scale:

```
# Model evaluation
model %>%  evaluate(test, testtarget)

OUTPUT
## $loss
 ## [1] 0.02701566
 ##
 ## $mean_absolute_error
 ## [1] 0.1194756

pred <- model %>%  predict(test)
 plot(testtarget, pred)
```

We obtain a scatter plot of the actual values (log transformed) versus the predicted values based on the test data. We also get a scatter plot of the actual versus predicted values in the original scale for comparison with earlier plots. The scatter plots for predicted versus actual response values (`model_three`) are as shown in the following graph:

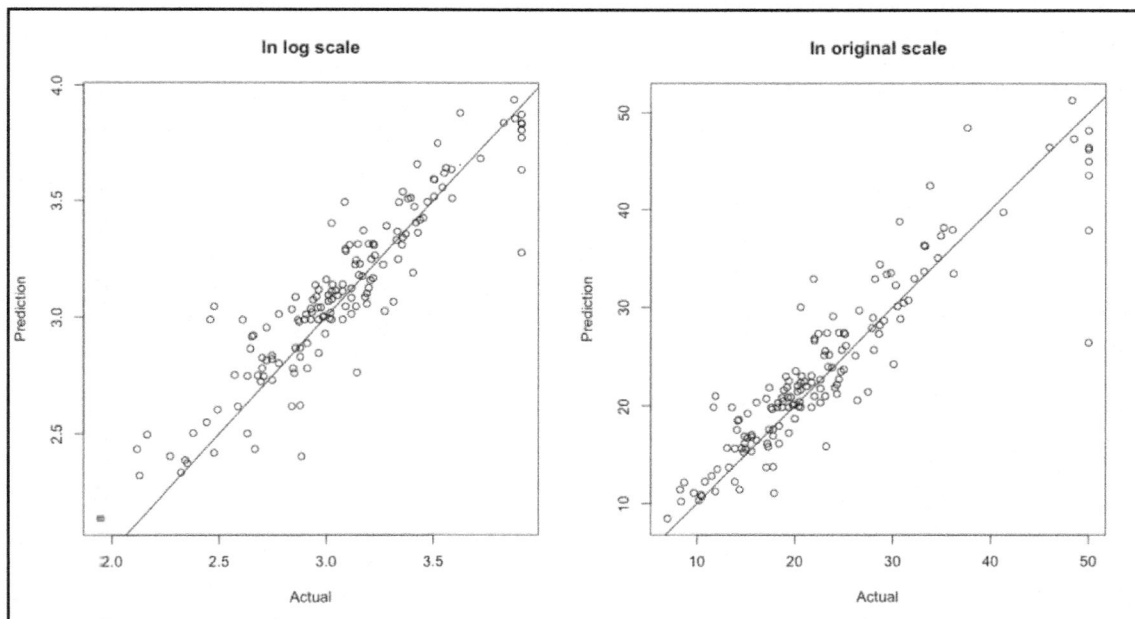

From the preceding graph, we can see that the significant underestimation pattern observed in earlier models shows improvement, both in the log scale and in the original scale. In the original scale, the data points at higher values are relatively closer to the diagonal line, indicating improved prediction performance by the model.

Summary

In this chapter, we went through the steps for developing a prediction model when the response variable is of a numeric type. We started with a neural network model that had 201 parameters and then developed deep neural network models with over 7,000 parameters. You may have noticed that, in this chapter, we made use of comparatively deeper and more complex neural network models compared to the previous chapter, where we developed a classification model for the target variable that was of a categorical nature. In both Chapter 2, *Deep Neural Networks for Multiclass Classification*, and Chapter 3, *Deep Neural Networks for Regression*, we developed models based on data that was structured. In the next chapter, we move on to problems where the data type is unstructured. More specifically, we'll deal with the image type of data and go over the problem of image classification and recognition using deep neural network models.

In the next chapter, we will cover the steps required to develop an image recognition and prediction model using deep neural networks.

Section 3: Deep Learning for Computer Vision

This section explains how to deal with image data and how to use popular deep learning methods. It consists of five chapters that illustrate the use of convolutional neural networks, autoencoder networks, transfer learning, and generative adversarial networks for computer vision applications.

This section contains the following chapters:

- Chapter 4, *Image Classification and Recognition*
- Chapter 5, *Image Classification Using Convolutional Neural Networks*
- Chapter 6, *Applying Autoencoder Neural Networks Using Keras*
- Chapter 7, *Image Classification for Small Data Using Transfer Learning*
- Chapter 8, *Creating New Images Using Generative Adversarial Networks*

4
Image Classification and Recognition

In the previous chapters, we looked at the process of developing deep neural network models for classification and regression problems. In both cases, we were dealing with structured data and the models were of the supervised learning type, where target variables were available. Images or pictures belong to the unstructured category of data. In this chapter, we will illustrate the use of deep learning neural networks for image classification and recognition using the Keras package with the help of an easy-to-follow example. We will get started with a small sample size to illustrate the steps involved in developing an image-classification model. We will apply this model to a supervised learning situation involving the labeling of images or pictures.

Keras contains several built-in datasets for image classification, such as CIFAR10, CIFAR100, MNIST, and fashion-MNIST. CIFAR10 contains 50,000 32 x 32 color training images and 10,000 testing images with 10 label categories. CIFAR100, on the other hand, contains 50,000 32 x 32 color training images and 10,000 testing images with as many as 100 label categories. The MNIST dataset has 60,000 28 x 28 grayscale images for training and 10,000 images for testing with 10 different digits. The fashion-MNIST dataset has 60,000 28 x 28 grayscale images for training and 10,000 images for testing with 10 fashion categories. These datasets are already in a format that can be used straightaway to develop deep neural network models with a minimal need for data-preparation-related steps. However, to get a better handle on dealing with image data, we will start by reading raw images from our computer into RStudio and go over all the steps needed to make image data ready for building a classification model.

The steps involved include exploring image data, resizing and reshaping images, one-hot encoding, developing a sequential model, compiling the model, fitting the model, evaluating the model, making predictions, and model-performance assessment using a confusion matrix.

More specifically, in this chapter, we will cover the following topics:

- Handling image data
- Data preparation
- Creating and fitting the model
- Model evaluation and prediction
- Performance optimization tips and best practices

Handling image data

In this section, we will read image data into R and explore it further to understand the various characteristics of image data. The code for reading and displaying images is as follows:

```
# Libraries
library(keras)
library(EBImage)

# Reading and plotting images
setwd("~/Desktop/image18")
temp = list.files(pattern="*.jpg")
mypic <- list()
for (i in 1:length(temp)) {mypic[[i]] <- readImage(temp[i])}
par(mfrow = c(3,6))
for (i in 1:length(temp)) plot(mypic[[i]])
par(mfrow = c(1,1))
```

As you can see from the preceding code, we will make use of the keras and EBImage libraries. The EBImage library is useful for handling and exploring image data. We will start by reading 18 JPEG image files that are stored in the image18 folder of my computer. These images each contain 6 pictures of bicycles, cars, and airplanes that were downloaded from the internet. These image files are read using the readImage function and are stored in mypic.

All 18 images are shown in the following screenshot:

From the preceding screenshot, we can see the six images of bicycles, cars, and airplanes. You might have noticed that not all of the pictures are of the same size. For example, the fifth and sixth bicycles noticeably vary in size. Similarly, the fourth and fifth airplanes are clearly of different sizes, too. Let's take a closer look at the data for the fifth bicycle using the following code:

```
# Exploring 5th image data
print(mypic[[5]])

OUTPUT
Image
  colorMode      : Color
  storage.mode   : double
  dim            : 299 169 3
  frames.total   : 3
  frames.render: 1

imageData(object)[1:5,1:6,1]
      [,1] [,2] [,3] [,4] [,5] [,6]
[1,]    1    1    1    1    1    1
[2,]    1    1    1    1    1    1
[3,]    1    1    1    1    1    1
[4,]    1    1    1    1    1    1
[5,]    1    1    1    1    1    1

hist(mypic[[5]])
```

Using the `print` function, we can look at how the image of a bicycle (unstructured data) has been converted into numbers (structured data). The dimensions for the fifth bicycle are 299 x 169 x 3, which leads to a total of 151,593 data points, or pixels, obtained by multiplying the three numbers. The first number, 299, represents the image width in terms of pixels and the second number, 169, represents the image height in terms of pixels. Note that a colored image consists of three channels representing the colors red, blue, and green. The small table extracted from the data shows the first five rows of data in the x-dimension, and the first six rows of data in the y-dimension, and the value for the z-dimension is one. Although all values in the body of the table are 1, they are expected to vary between 0 and 1.

TIP

A color image has red, green, and blue channels. A grayscale image has only one channel.

These data points for the fifth bicycle are used for creating a histogram, as shown in the following screenshot:

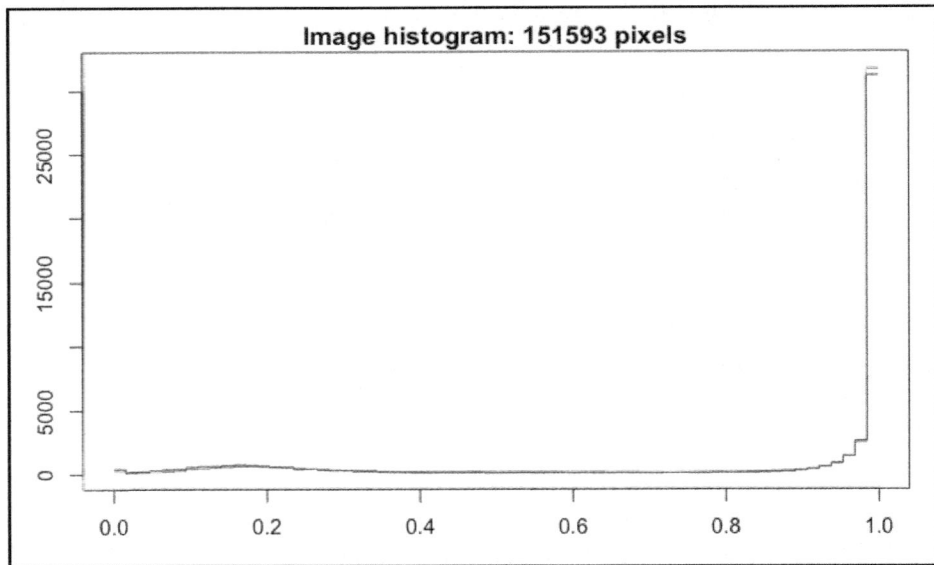

The preceding histogram shows the distribution of intensity values for the fifth image's data. It can be seen that most of the data points have high-intensity values for this image.

Let's now look at the following histogram of data based on the 16th image (that of an airplane) for comparison:

Image histogram: 151686 pixels

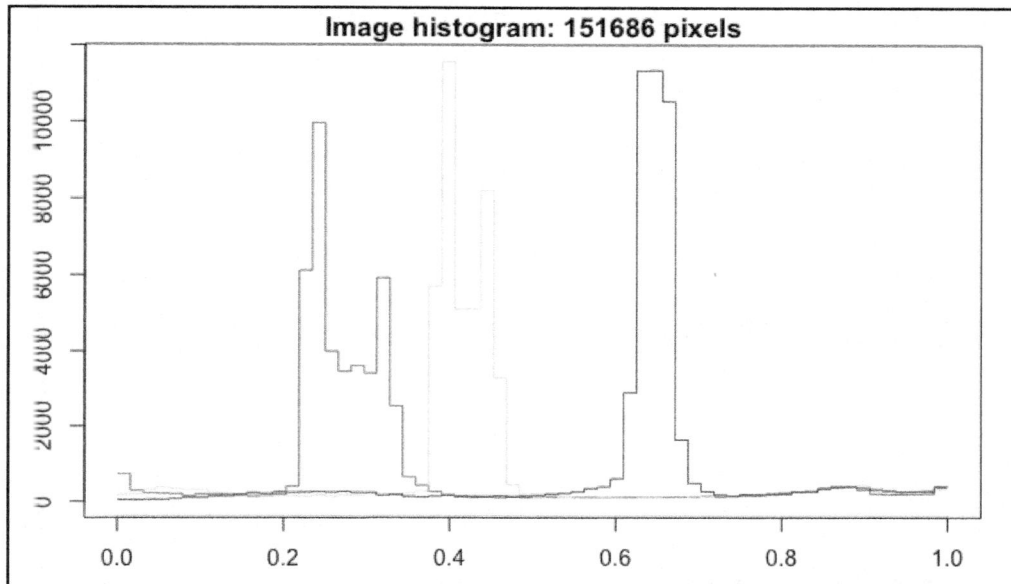

From the preceding histogram, we can see that this image has different intensity values for the red, green, and blue colors. In general, intensity values lie between zero and one. Data points that are closer to zero represent a darker color in the image and those closer to one indicate a brighter color in the image.

Let's take a look at data related to the 16th image, of an airplane, using the following code:

```
# Exploring 16th image data
print(mypic[[16]])

OUTPUT

Image
 colorMode : Color
 storage.mode : double
 dim : 318 159 3
 frames.total : 3
 frames.render: 1

imageData(object)[1:5,1:6,1]
  [,1]   [,2]   [,3]   [,4]   [,5]   [,6]
[1,] 0.2549020 0.2549020 0.2549020 0.2549020 0.2549020 0.2549020
```

```
[2,] 0.2549020 0.2549020 0.2549020 0.2549020 0.2549020 0.2549020
[3,] 0.2549020 0.2549020 0.2549020 0.2549020 0.2549020 0.2549020
[4,] 0.2588235 0.2588235 0.2588235 0.2588235 0.2588235 0.2588235
[5,] 0.2588235 0.2588235 0.2588235 0.2588235 0.2588235 0.2588235
```

From the output provided in the preceding code, we can see that the two images have different dimensions. The dimensions for the 16th image are 318 x 159 x 3, which results in a total of 151,686 data points or pixels.

In order to prepare this data for developing an image classification model, we will start by resizing all images to the same dimensions.

Data preparation

In this section, we will go over the steps for making our image data ready for developing an image classification model. These steps will involve resizing images to obtain the same size for all images, followed by reshaping, data partitioning, and the one-hot encoding of the response variables.

Resizing and reshaping

To prepare the data for developing a classification model, we start by resizing the dimensions of all 18 images to the same size using the following code:

```
# Resizing
for (i in 1:length(temp)) {mypic[[i]] <- resize(mypic[[i]], 28, 28)}
```

As can be seen from the preceding code, all images are now resized to 28 x 28 x 3. Let's plot all the images again to see the impact of resizing using the following code:

```
# Plot images
par(mfrow = c(3,6))
for (i in 1:length(temp)) plot(mypic[[i]])
par(mfrow = c(1,1))
```

When we reduce the dimensions of a picture, it will lead to a lower number of pixels, which in turn will cause pictures to have lower quality, as can be seen in the following screenshot:

Next, we will reshape the dimensions of 28 x 28 x 3 into a single dimension of 28 x 28 x 3 (or 2,352 vectors) using the following code:

```
# Reshape
for (i in 1:length(temp)) {mypic[[i]] <- array_reshape(mypic[[i]], c(28,
28,3))}
str(mypic)

OUTPUT

List of 18
 $ : num [1:28, 1:28, 1:3] 1 1 1 1 1 1 1 1 1 1 ...
 $ : num [1:28, 1:28, 1:3] 1 1 1 1 1 ...
 $ : num [1:28, 1:28, 1:3] 1 1 1 1 1 1 1 1 1 1 ...
 $ : num [1:28, 1:28, 1:3] 1 1 1 1 1 1 1 1 1 1 ...
 $ : num [1:28, 1:28, 1:3] 1 1 1 1 1 1 1 1 1 1 ...
 $ : num [1:28, 1:28, 1:3] 1 1 1 1 1 1 1 1 1 1 ...
 $ : num [1:28, 1:28, 1:3] 0.953 0.953 0.953 0.953 0.953 ...
 $ : num [1:28, 1:28, 1:3] 1 1 1 1 1 1 1 1 1 1 ...
 $ : num [1:28, 1:28, 1:3] 1 1 1 1 1 1 1 1 1 1 ...
 $ : num [1:28, 1:28, 1:3] 1 1 1 1 1 1 1 1 1 1 ...
 $ : num [1:28, 1:28, 1:3] 1 1 1 1 1 1 1 1 1 1 ...
 $ : num [1:28, 1:28, 1:3] 1 1 1 1 1 1 1 1 1 1 ...
 $ : num [1:28, 1:28, 1:3] 1 1 1 1 1 1 1 1 1 1 ...
 $ : num [1:28, 1:28, 1:3] 1 1 1 1 0.328 ...
 $ : num [1:28, 1:28, 1:3] 0.26 0.294 0.312 0.309 0.289 ...
 $ : num [1:28, 1:28, 1:3] 0.49 0.49 0.49 0.502 0.502 ...
 $ : num [1:28, 1:28, 1:3] 1 1 1 1 1 1 1 1 1 1 ..
```

By observing the structure of the preceding data using `str(mypic)`, we can see that there are 18 different items in the list that correspond to the 18 images that we started with.

Next, we will create training, validation, and test data.

Training, validation, and test data

We will use the first three images of the bicycles, cars, and airplanes respectively for training, the fourth image of each type for validation, and the remaining two images of each type for testing. Thus, the training data will have nine images, the validation data will have three images, and the test data will have six images. The following is the code to achieve this:

```
# Training Data
a <- c(1:3, 7:9, 13:15)
trainx <- NULL
for (i in a) {trainx <- rbind(trainx, mypic[[i]]) }
str(trainx)

OUTPUT

num [1:9, 1:2352] 1 1 1 1 0.953 ...

# Validation data
b <- c(4, 10, 16)
validx <- NULL
for (i in b) {validx <- rbind(validx, mypic[[i]]) }
str(validx)

OUTPUT

num [1:3, 1:2352] 1 1 0.26 1 1 ...

# Test Data
c <- c(5:6, 11:12, 17:18)
testx <- NULL
for (i in c) {testx <- rbind(testx, mypic[[i]])}
str(testx)

OUTPUT

num [1:6, 1:2352] 1 1 1 1 0.49 ...
```

As you can see from the preceding code, we will use the `rbind` function to combine the rows of data that we have for each image when creating training, validation, and `test` data. After combining the rows of data from the nine images, the structure of `trainx` indicates that there are 9 rows and 2,352 columns. Similarly, for the validation data, we have 3 rows and 2,352 columns, and for the test data, we have 6 rows and 2,352 columns.

One-hot encoding

For the one-hot encoding of the response variables, we use the following code:

```
# Labels
trainy <- c(0,0,0,1,1,1,2,2,2)
validy <- c(0,1,2)
testy <- c(0,0,1,1,2,2)

# One-hot encoding
trainLabels <- to_categorical(trainy)
validLabels <- to_categorical(validy)
testLabels <- to_categorical(testy)
trainLabels

OUTPUT
      [,1] [,2] [,3]
 [1,]   1    0    0
 [2,]   1    0    0
 [3,]   1    0    0
 [4,]   0    1    0
 [5,]   0    1    0
 [6,]   0    1    0
 [7,]   0    0    1
 [8,]   0    0    1
 [9,]   0    0    1
```

From the preceding code, we can see the following:

- We have stored target values for each image in trainy , validy, and testy, where 0, 1, and 2 indicate bicycle, car, and airplane images respectively.
- We carry out one-hot encoding of trainy , validy, and testy by using the to_categorical function. One-hot encoding here helps to convert a factor variable into a combination of zeros and ones.

Now we have the data in a format that can be used for developing a deep neural network classification model, and that is what we will do in the next section.

Creating and fitting the model

In this section, we will develop an image classification model to classify the images of the bicycles, cars, and airplanes. We will first specify a model architecture, then we will compile the model, and then fit the model using training and validation data.

Developing the model architecture

When developing the model architecture, we start by creating a sequential model and then add various layers. The following is the code:

```
# Model architecture
model <- keras_model_sequential()
model %>%
    layer_dense(units = 256, activation = 'relu', input_shape = c(2352)) %>%
    layer_dense(units = 128, activation = 'relu') %>%
    layer_dense(units = 3, activation = 'softmax')
summary(model)
```

OUTPUT

Layer (type)	Output Shape	Param #
dense_1 (Dense)	(None, 256)	602368
dense_2 (Dense)	(None, 128)	32896
dense_3 (Dense)	(None, 3)	387

Total params: 635,651
Trainable params: 635,651
Non-trainable params: 0

As can be seen from the preceding code, the input layer has 2352 units (28 x 28 x 3). For the initial model, we use two hidden layers with 256 and 128 units respectively. For both hidden layers, we will use the relu activation function. For the output layer, we will use 3 units since the target variable has 3 classes, representing a bicycle, car, and airplane. The total number of parameters for this model is 635,651.

Compiling the model

After developing the model architecture, we can compile the model using the following code:

```
# Compile model
model %>% compile(loss = 'categorical_crossentropy',
  optimizer = 'adam',
  metrics = 'accuracy')
```

We compile the model by using `categorical_crossentropy` for loss, since we are doing multiclass classification. We have specified `adam` and `accuracy` for the optimizer and metrics, respectively.

Fitting the model

Now we are ready to train the model. The following is the code for this:

```
# Fit model
model_one <- model %>% fit(trainx,
                           trainLabels,
                           epochs = 30,
                           batch_size = 32,
                           validation_data =  list(validx, validLabels))
plot(model_one)
```

From the preceding code, we can see the following facts:

- We can fit the model using `independent` variables stored in `trainx` and `target` variables stored in `trainLabels`. To safeguard against overfitting, we will use `validation_data`.

  Note that, in the previous chapters, we made use of `validation_split` by specifying a certain percentage, such as 20%; however, if we used `validation_split` with a 20% rate, it would have used the last 20% of the training data (all airplane images) for validation.

- This would have created a situation where the training data had no sample from the airplane images and the classification model would have been based on bicycle and car images only.

- Therefore, the resulting image classification model would be biased and would have performed well only with bicycle and car images. Therefore, instead of using the `validation_split` function, in this situation, we make use of `validation_data`, where we have made sure that we have a sample of each type represented in both the training and validation data.

The following graphs show the loss and accuracy for 30 epochs separately for training and validation data:

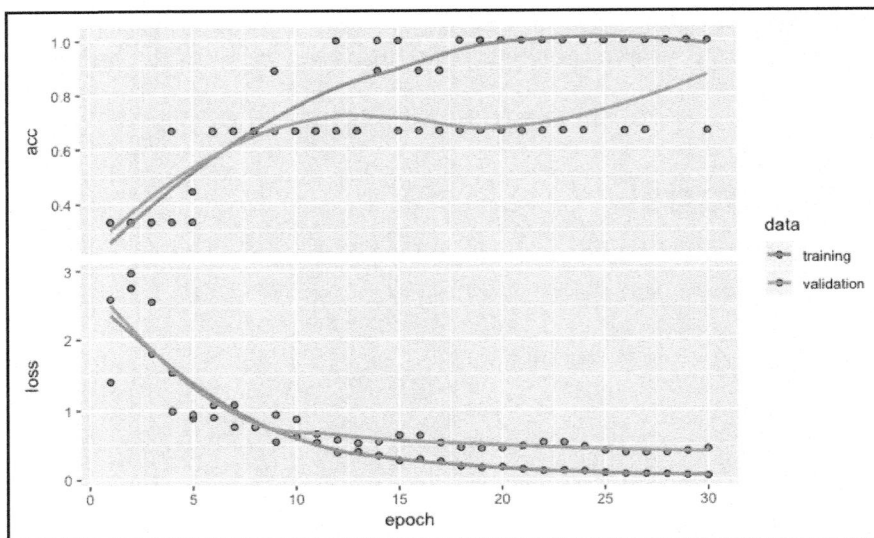

We can make the following observations from the preceding plots:

- From the parts of the graphs dealing with accuracy, we can see that from the eighteenth epoch onward, the accuracy values for the training data attain the highest value of 1.
- On the other hand, the accuracy based on the validation data is mainly around two thirds, or 66.7%. Since we have data from three images that is used for validation, if all three images' from validation data is correctly classified, the reported accuracy will be 1. In this case, two out of three images are correctly classified, and that leads to accuracy of 66.7%.
- From the parts of the graphs dealing with loss, we can see that for the training data, the loss values drop significantly from about 3 to less than 1 after 8 epochs. They continue to reduce from then on; however, the rate of decrease in the loss values slows down.

- An approximately similar pattern can be seen based on the validation data.
- In addition, since the loss uses probability values in its calculation, we observe a clearer trend for the loss-related plot compared to the accuracy-related plot.

Next, let's evaluate the model's image classification performance in greater detail to understand its behavior.

Model evaluation and prediction

In this section, we will carry out model evaluation and create a confusion matrix with the help of predictions, both for training and test data. Let's start by evaluating the image classification performance of the model using training data.

Loss, accuracy, and confusion matrices for training data

We will now obtain loss and accuracy values for the training data and then create a confusion matrix using the following code:

```
# Model evaluation
model %>% evaluate(trainx, trainLabels)

OUTPUT
12/12 [==============================] - 0s 87us/step
$loss
[1] 0.055556579307

$acc
[1] 1

# Confusion matrix
pred <- model %>%   predict_classes(trainx)
table(Predicted=pred, Actual=trainy)

OUTPUT
         Actual
Predicted 0 1 2
        0 3 0 0
        1 0 3 0
        2 0 0 3
```

As you can see from the preceding output, the loss and accuracy values are 0.056 and 1 respectively. The confusion matrix based on the training data indicates that all nine images are correctly classified into three categories, and therefore the resulting accuracy is 1.

Prediction probabilities for training data

We can now look at the probabilities of the three classes for all nine images in the training data that this model provides. The following is the code:

```
# Prediction probabilities
prob <- model %>%  predict_proba(trainx)
cbind(prob, Predicted_class = pred, Actual = trainy)
```

OUTPUT

			Predicted_class	Actual
[1,] 0.9431666135788	0.007227868307	0.049605518579	0	0
[2,] 0.8056846261024	0.005127847660	0.189187481999	0	0
[3,] 0.9556384682655	0.001881886506	0.042479615659	0	0
[4,] 0.0018005876336	0.988727569580	0.009471773170	1	1
[5,] 0.0002136278927	0.998095452785	0.001690962003	1	1
[6,] 0.0008950306219	0.994426369667	0.004678600468	1	1
[7,] 0.0367377623916	0.010597365908	0.952664911747	2	2
[8,] 0.0568452328444	0.011656147428	0.931498587132	2	2
[9,] 0.0295505002141	0.011442330666	0.959007143974	2	2

In the preceding output, the first three columns show the probability of an image being a bicycle, car, or airplane, and the total of these three probabilities is 1. We can make the following observations from the output:

- The probabilities for the first image in the training data are 0.943, 0.007, and 0.049 for bicycle, car, and airplane respectively. Since the highest probability is for the first class, the predicted class based on the model is 0 (for bicycle), and this is also the actual class of the image.
- Although all 9 images are correctly classified, the probability of correct classification varies from 0.806 (image 2) to 0.998 (image 5).
- For the car images (rows 4 to 6), the probability of correct classification ranges from 0.989 to 0.998 and is consistently high for all three images. Therefore, this classification model gives its best performance when classifying car images.
- For bicycle images (rows 1 to 3), the probability of correct classification ranges from 0.806 to 0.956, which indicates some difficulty in correctly classifying bicycle images.

- For the second sample, which represents a bicycle image, the second-highest probability is 0.189 of being an airplane image. Clearly, this model is little bit confused when it comes to deciding whether this image is a bicycle or an airplane.
- For the airplane images (rows 7 to 9), the probability of correct classification ranges from 0.931 to 0.959, which is also consistently high for all three images.

Looking at prediction probabilities allows us to dig deeper into the classification performance of the model, which cannot be obtained only by looking at the accuracy value. However, while good performance with training data is necessary, it is not sufficient to arrive at a reliable image-classification model. When a classification model suffers from an overfitting problem, we have difficulty replicating good results based on training data on test data that the model has not seen. Therefore, a real test of a good classification model is when it performs well with the test data. Let's now review the image-classification performance of the model for test data.

Loss, accuracy, and confusion matrices for test data

We can now obtain loss and accuracy values for the test data and then create a confusion matrix using the following code:

```
# Loss and accuracy
model %>% evaluate(testx, testLabels)

OUTPUT
6/6 [==============================] - 0s 194us/step
$loss
[1] 0.5517520905

$acc
[1] 0.8333333

# Confusion matrix
pred <- model %>%   predict_classes(testx)
table(Predicted=pred, Actual=testy)

OUTPUT
        Actual
Predicted 0 1 2
        0 2 0 0
        1 0 1 0
        2 0 1 2
```

As you can see from the preceding output, the loss and accuracy values for the images in the test data are 0.552 and 0.833 respectively. These results are slightly inferior to the numbers that we saw for the training data; however, some amount of performance deterioration is expected when a model is assessed based on unseen data. The confusion matrix indicates one incorrectly classified image, where an image of a car is mistaken for an image of an airplane. Therefore, with five out of six correct classifications, the model accuracy based on the test data is 83.3%. Let's now look more deeply into the model's prediction performance by investigating the probability values based on images in the test data.

Prediction probabilities for test data

We can now review the probabilities for the three classes for all six images in the test data. The following is the code:

```
# Prediction probabilities
prob <- model %>%   predict_proba(testx)
cbind(prob, Predicted_class = pred, Actual = testy)

OUTPUT
```

				Predicted_class	Actual
[1,]	0.587377548218	0.02450981364	0.38811263442	0	0
[2,]	0.532718658447	0.04708640277	0.42019486427	0	0
[3,]	0.115497209132	0.18486714363	0.69963568449	2	1
[4,]	0.001700860681	0.98481327295	0.01348586939	1	1
[5,]	0.230999588966	0.03030913882	0.73869132996	2	2
[6,]	0.112148292363	0.02054920420	0.86730253696	2	2

Looking at these predicted probabilities, we can make the following observations:

- Bicycle images are predicted correctly, as shown by the first two samples. However, prediction probabilities are relatively lower at 0.587 and 0.533.
- The results for car images (rows 3 and 4) are mixed, with the fourth sample, correctly predicted with a high probability of 0.985, but the third car image is misclassified as an airplane with about 0.7 probability.
- Airplane images are represented by the fifth and sixth samples. The prediction probabilities for these two images are 0.739 and 0.867 respectively.
- Although five out of six images are correctly classified, many prediction probabilities are relatively low when compared to the model's performance on training data.

Therefore, overall, we can say that there is definitely some scope to improve the model's performance further. In the next section, we will explore improving the model's performance.

Performance optimization tips and best practices

In this section, we will explore a deeper network for improving the performance of the image-classification model. We will look at the results for comparison.

Deeper networks

The code used for experimenting with a deeper network in this section are as follows:

```
# Model architecture
model <- keras_model_sequential()
model %>%
  layer_dense(units = 512, activation = 'relu', input_shape = c(2352)) %>%
  layer_dropout(rate = 0.1) %>%
  layer_dense(units = 256, activation = 'relu') %>%
  layer_dropout(rate = 0.1) %>%
  layer_dense(units = 3, activation = 'softmax')
summary(model)
```

OUTPUT

Layer (type)	Output Shape	Param #
dense_1 (Dense)	(None, 512)	1204736
dropout_1 (Dropout)	(None, 512)	0
dense_2 (Dense)	(None, 256)	131328
dropout_2 (Dropout)	(None, 256)	0
dense_3 (Dense)	(None, 3)	771

Total params: 1,336,835
Trainable params: 1,336,835
Non-trainable params: 0

```
# Compile model
model %>% compile(loss = 'categorical_crossentropy',
  optimizer = 'adam',
  metrics = 'accuracy')

# Fit model
model_two <- model %>% fit(trainx,
  trainLabels,
  epochs = 30,
  batch_size = 32,
  validation_data = list(validx, validLabels))
plot(model_two)
```

From the preceding code, we can see the following:

- We are increasing the number of units in the first and second hidden layers to 512 and 256 respectively.
- We are also adding dropout layers after each hidden layer with a 10% dropout rate.
- The total number of parameters with this change has now gone up to 1336835.
- This time, we will also run the model for 50 epochs. We do not make any other changes to the model.

The following graphs provide accuracy and loss values for the training and validation data for 50 epochs:

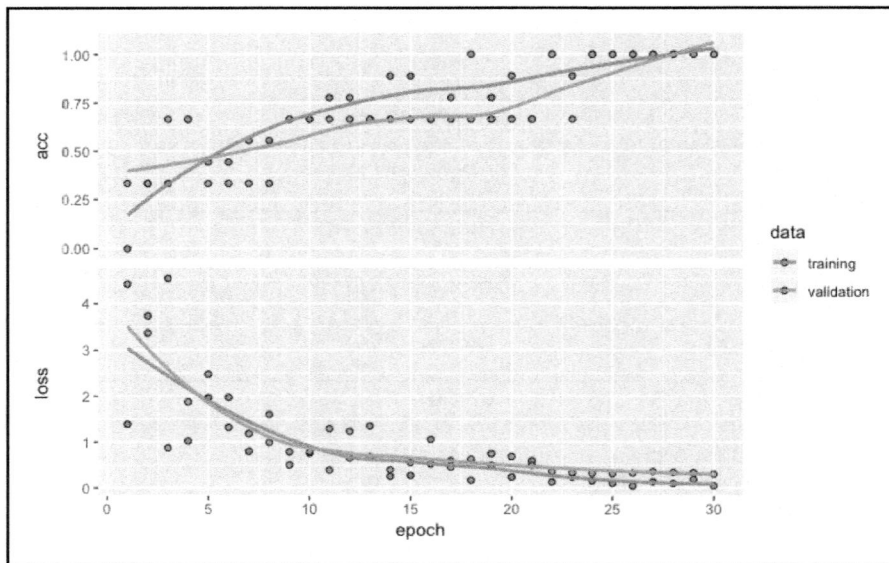

From the preceding graphs, we can see the following:

- There are some major changes observed in the accuracy and loss values compared to the earlier model.
- The accuracy for both the training and validation data after 50 epochs is 100%.
- In addition, the closeness of the training- and validation-related curves for loss and accuracy indicate that this image-classification model is not likely to suffer from an overfitting problem.

Results

To further explore any changes in the image-classification performance of the model that may not be obvious from a graphical summary, let's look at some numerical summaries:

1. We will look at the results based on the training data first, and will make use of the following code:

```
# Loos and accuracy
model %>% evaluate(trainx, trainLabels)
OUTPUT
12/12 [==============================] - 0s 198us/step
$loss
[1] 0.03438224643

$acc
[1] 1

# Confusion matrix
pred <- model %>%   predict_classes(trainx)
table(Predicted=pred, Actual=trainy)

OUTPUT
          Actual
Predicted 0 1 2
        0 3 0 0
        1 0 3 0
        2 0 0 3
```

From the preceding output, we can see that the loss value has now reduced to `0.034` and the accuracy is maintained at `1.0`. We obtain the same confusion matrix results for the training data as we did earlier as all nine images are correctly classified by the model, which gives an accuracy level of 100%.

2. To look more deeply at the classification performance of the model, we make use of the following code and output:

```
# Prediction probabilities
prob <- model %>%   predict_proba(trainx)
cbind(prob, Predicted_class = pred, Actual = trainy)
```

OUTPUT

			Predicted_class	
Actual				
[1,] 0.97638195753098	0.0071088117547	0.01650915294886	0	0
[2,] 0.89875286817551	0.0019298568368	0.09931717067957	0	0
[3,] 0.98671281337738	0.0004396488657	0.01284754090011	0	0
[4,] 0.00058794603683	0.9992876648903	0.00012432398216	1	1
[5,] 0.00005639552546	0.9999316930771	0.00001191849515	1	1
[6,] 0.00020669832884	0.9997472167015	0.00004611289114	1	1
[7,] 0.03771930187941	0.0022936603054	0.95998704433441	2	2
[8,] 0.08463590592146	0.0022607713472	0.91310334205627	2	2
[9,] 0.03016609139740	0.0019471622072	0.96788680553436	2	2

From the preceding prediction probabilities that we obtain as an output of the training data, we can make the following observations:

- Correct classifications are now made with higher probability values than the earlier model.
- The lowest correct classification probability based on the second row is 0.899.
- Therefore, this model seems to be more sure when correctly classifying images compared to what was observed with the previous model.

3. Now let's see whether this improvement is also seen with the test data. We will use the following codes and output:

```
# Loss and accuracy
model %>% evaluate(testx, testLabels)
```

OUTPUT

```
6/6 [==============================] - 0s 345us/step
$loss
[1] 0.40148338683

Sacc
[1] 0.8333333

# Confusion matrix
pred <- model %>%   predict_classes(testx)
```

```
table(Predicted=pred, Actual=testy)
```

OUTPUT
```
          Actual
Predicted 0 1 2
        0 2 0 0
        1 0 1 0
        2 0 1 2
```

As indicated in the preceding output, the test data loss and accuracy values are
0.401 and 0.833 respectively. We do see some improvement in loss values;
however, the accuracy value is again the same as it was earlier. Looking at the
confusion matrix, we can see that this time, an image of a car is misclassified as an
airplane. Therefore, we do not see any major differences based on the confusion
matrix.

4. Next, let's review the prediction probabilities using the following code and its
   output:

```
# Prediction probabilities
prob <- model %>%   predict_proba(testx)
cbind(prob, Predicted_class = pred, Actual = testy)
```

OUTPUT

				Predicted_class
			Actual	
[1,]	0.7411330938339	0.015922509134	0.242944419384	0
			0	
[2,]	0.7733710408211	0.021422179416	0.205206796527	0
			0	
[3,]	0.3322730064392	0.237866103649	0.429860889912	2
			1	
[4,]	0.0005808877177	0.999227762222	0.000191345287	1
			1	
[5,]	0.2163420319557	0.009395645000	0.774262309074	2
			2	
[6,]	0.1447975188494	0.002772571286	0.852429926395	2
			2	

Using the prediction probabilities for the test data, we can make the following two
observations:

- We see a consistently similar pattern to the one that we observed based on the
  results from the training data. This model correctly classifies images in the test
  data with higher probabilities (0.74 to 0.99) than the earlier model (0.53 to
  0.98).

- For the fourth sample in the test data, the model seems to be confused between the image of a bicycle and an airplane, when in reality, this image is of a car.

Therefore, overall, we have observed that by developing a deeper neural network, we are able to improve the model's performance. The improvement in the performance was not obvious from the accuracy calculation; however, the calculation of prediction probabilities allowed us to develop better insights and compare model performance.

Summary

In this chapter, we explored image data and a deep neural network image-classification model. We used data from 18 images of bicycles, cars, and airplanes, and carried out appropriate data processing to make the data ready to use with the Keras library. We partitioned image data into training, validation, and test data, and subsequently developed a deep neural model using training data and evaluated its performance by looking at the loss, accuracy, confusion matrix, and probability values for both the training and test data. We also made modifications to the model to improve its classification performance. In addition, we observed that when the confusion matrix provides the same level of performance, prediction probabilities may be able to help in extracting finer differences between the two models.

In the next chapter, we will go over the steps to develop a deep neural network image-classification model using **convolutional neural networks (CNNs)**, which are becoming very popular when it comes to image classification applications. CNNs are regarded as the gold standard for image-classification problems, and are very effective for large-scale image-classification applications.

5
Image Classification Using Convolutional Neural Networks

Convolutional neural networks (CNNs) are popular deep neural networks and are considered to be the gold standard for large-scale image classification tasks. Applications involving CNNs include image recognition and classification, natural language processing, medical image classification, and many others. In this chapter, we will continue with supervised learning situations where a response variable exists. This chapter provides steps for applying image classification and recognition using convolutional neural networks with an easy-to-follow practical example involving fashion-related **Modified National Institute of Standards and Technology (MNIST)** data. We also make use of images of fashion items downloaded from the internet to explore the generalization potential of the classification model that we develop.

More specifically in this chapter, we cover the following topics:

- Data preparation
- Layers in convolutional neural networks
- Fitting the model
- Model evaluation and prediction
- Performance optimization tips and best practices
- Summary

Data preparation

In this chapter, we will make use of the Keras and EBImage libraries:

```
# Libraries
library(keras)
library(EBImage)
```

Let's get started by looking at some images downloaded from the internet. There are 20 images that include fashion articles such as shirts, bags, sandals, dresses, and others. These images were obtained using a Google search. We will try to develop an image recognition and classification model that recognizes these images and classifies them in appropriate categories. And to develop such a model, we will make use of the fashion-MNIST database of fashion articles:

```
# Read data
setwd("~/Desktop/image20")
temp = list.files(pattern = "*.jpg")
mypic <- list()
for (i in 1:length(temp))  {mypic[[i]] <- readImage(temp[[i]])}
par(mfrow = c(5,4))
for (i in 1:length(temp)) plot(mypic[[i]])
```

The 20 images of fashion items downloaded from the internet are shown as follows:

Next, let's look at the fashion-MNIST data that contains a much larger collection of images of such fashion items.

Fashion-MNIST data

We can access fashion-MNIST data from Keras using the dataset_fashion_mnist function. Take a look at the following code and its output:

```
# MNIST data
mnist <- dataset_fashion_mnist()
str(mnist)

OUTPUT
List of 2
 $ train:List of 2
  ..$ x: int [1:60000, 1:28, 1:28] 0 0 0 0 0 0 0 0 0 0 ...
  ..$ y: int [1:60000(1d)] 9 0 0 3 0 2 7 2 5 5 ...
 $ test :List of 2
  ..$ x: int [1:10000, 1:28, 1:28] 0 0 0 0 0 0 0 0 0 0 ...
  ..$ y: int [1:10000(1d)] 9 2 1 1 6 1 4 6 5 7 ...
```

Looking at the structure of the preceding data, we see that it contains train data with 60,000 images and test data with 10,000 images. All these images are 28 x 28 grayscale images. We know from the previous chapter that images can be represented as numeric data based on color and intensity. The independent variable x contains the intensity values, and the dependent variable y contains labels from 0 to 9.

The 10 different fashion items in the fashion-MNIST dataset are labelled from 0 to 9, as shown in the following table:

Label	Description
0	T-shirt/Top
1	Trouser
2	Pullover
3	Dress
4	Coat
5	Sandal
6	Shirt
7	Sneaker
8	Bag
9	Ankle Boot

Looking at the preceding table, we may observe that developing a classification model for these images will be challenging as some categories will be difficult to differentiate.

Train and test data

We extract train image data, store it in `trainx`, and store the respective labels in `trainy`. In a similar fashion, we create `testx` and `testy` from the test data. The table based on `trainy` indicates that there are exactly 6,000 images each for the 10 different fashion articles in the train data, while in the test data, there are exactly 1,000 images of each fashion article:

```
#train and test data
trainx <- mnist$train$x
trainy <- mnist$train$y
testx <- mnist$test$x
testy <- mnist$test$y
table(mnist$train$y, mnist$train$y)

      0    1    2    3    4    5    6    7    8    9
0  6000    0    0    0    0    0    0    0    0    0
1     0 6000    0    0    0    0    0    0    0    0
2     0    0 6000    0    0    0    0    0    0    0
3     0    0    0 6000    0    0    0    0    0    0
4     0    0    0    0 6000    0    0    0    0    0
5     0    0    0    0    0 6000    0    0    0    0
6     0    0    0    0    0    0 6000    0    0    0
7     0    0    0    0    0    0    0 6000    0    0
8     0    0    0    0    0    0    0    0 6000    0
9     0    0    0    0    0    0    0    0    0 6000
table(mnist$test$y,mnist$test$y)
      0    1    2    3    4    5    6    7    8    9
0  1000    0    0    0    0    0    0    0    0    0
1     0 1000    0    0    0    0    0    0    0    0
2     0    0 1000    0    0    0    0    0    0    0
3     0    0    0 1000    0    0    0    0    0    0
4     0    0    0    0 1000    0    0    0    0    0
5     0    0    0    0    0 1000    0    0    0    0
6     0    0    0    0    0    0 1000    0    0    0
7     0    0    0    0    0    0    0 1000    0    0
8     0    0    0    0    0    0    0    0 1000    0
9     0    0    0    0    0    0    0    0    0 1000
```

We next plot the first 64 images in the train data. Note that these are grayscale image data and that each image has a black background. Since our image classification model will be based on this data, the color images that we started with will have to be converted into grayscale images too. In addition, images of shirts, coats, and dresses are somewhat challenging to differentiate and this may impact the accuracy of our model. Let's have a look at the following lines of code:

```
# Display images
par(mfrow = c(8,8), mar = rep(0, 4))
for (i in 1:84) plot(as.raster(trainx[i,,], max = 255))
par(mfrow = c(1,1))
```

We get the output of the first 64 images in the train data as shown:

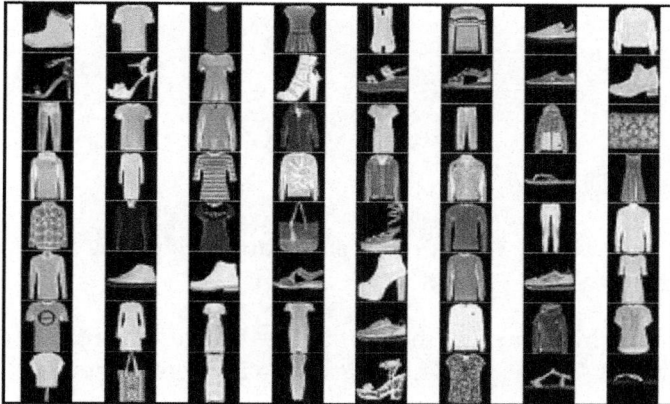

A histogram based on the first image (an ankle boot) in the train data is shown in the following graph:

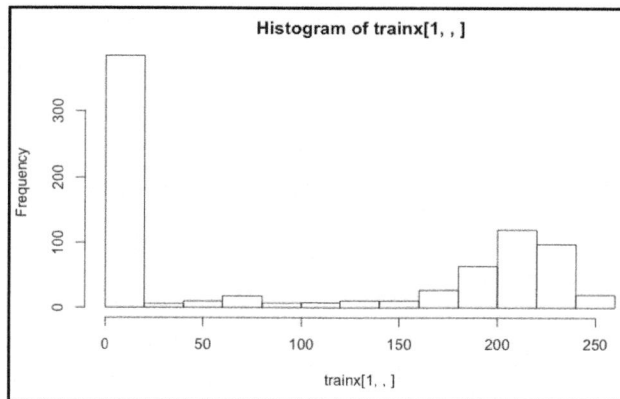

The highest bar on the left is from the low intensity data points that capture the black background in the image. The higher intensity values representing the lighter color of the ankle boot are reflected in the higher bars toward the right. These intensity values in the histogram range from 0 to 255.

Reshaping and resizing

Next, we reshape, train, and test data. We also divide the train and the test data by 255 to change the range of values from 0-255 to 0-1. The codes used are as follows:

```
# Reshape and resize
trainx <- array_reshape(trainx, c(nrow(trainx), 784))
testx <- array_reshape(testx, c(nrow(testx), 784))
trainx <- trainx / 255
testx <- testx / 255
str(trainx)

OUTPUT

num [1:60000, 1:784] 0 0 0 0 0 0 0 0 0 0 ...
```

The structure of the preceding `trainx` shows that after reshaping the train data, we now have data with 60,000 rows and 784 (28 x 28) columns.

We get the output of the histogram based on the first image (an ankle boot) in the train data after dividing the data by 255, as shown in the following screenshot:

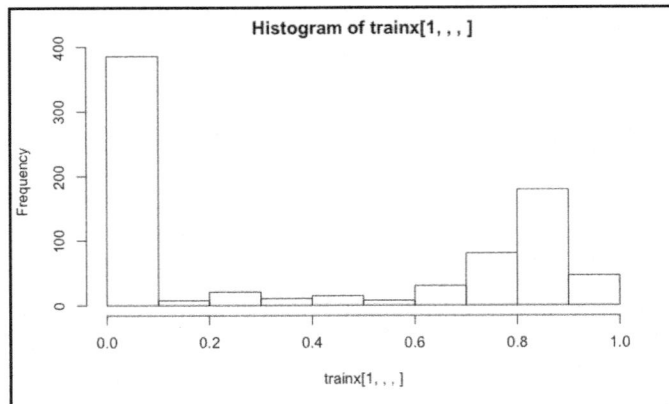

The preceding histogram shows that the range of data points has now changed to values between 0 and 1. However, the shape observed in the previous histogram has not changed.

One-hot encoding

Next, we do one-hot encoding of labels stored in `trainy` and `testy` using the following code:

```
# One-hot encoding
trainy <- to_categorical(trainy, 10)
testy <- to_categorical(testy, 10)
head(trainy)
     [,1] [,2] [,3] [,4] [,5] [,6] [,7] [,8] [,9] [,10]
[1,]    0    0    0    0    0    0    0    0    0     1
[2,]    1    0    0    0    0    0    0    0    0     0
[3,]    1    0    0    0    0    0    0    0    0     0
[4,]    0    0    0    1    0    0    0    0    0     0
[5,]    1    0    0    0    0    0    0    0    0     0
[6,]    0    0    1    0    0    0    0    0    0     0
```

After one-hot encoding, the first row for the train data indicates a value of 1 for the tenth category (ankle boot). Similarly, the second row for the train data indicates a value of 1 for the first category (t-shirt/top). After completing the changes mentioned previously, now the fashion-MNIST data is ready for developing an image recognition and classification model.

Layers in the convolutional neural networks

In this section, we will develop model architecture and then compile the model. We will also carry out calculations to compare the convolutional network with a fully connected network. Let's get started by specifying the model architecture.

Model architecture and related calculations

We start by creating a model using the `keras_model_sequential` function. The codes used for the model architecture are given as follows:

```
# Model architecture
model <- keras_model_sequential()
model %>%
        layer_conv_2d(filters = 32,
                kernel_size = c(3,3),
                activation = 'relu',
                input_shape = c(28,28,1)) %>%
        layer_conv_2d(filters = 64,
                kernel_size = c(3,3),
                activation = 'relu') %>%
```

```
layer_max_pooling_2d(pool_size = c(2,2)) %>%
layer_dropout(rate = 0.25) %>%
layer_flatten() %>%
layer_dense(units = 64, activation = 'relu') %>%
layer_dropout(rate = 0.25) %>%
layer_dense(units = 10, activation = 'softmax')
```

As shown in the preceding code, we add various layers to develop a CNN model. The input layer in this network has 28 x 28 x 1 dimensions based on the height and width of the images, which are 28 each. And since we are using grayscale images, the color channel is one. We use two-dimensional convolutional layers here as we are building a deep learning model with gray-scale images.

> **TIP**
>
> Note that when developing an image recognition and classification model with gray scale image data, we make use of a 2D convolutional layer, and with color images, we make use of a 3D convolutional layer.

Let's look at some calculations involving the first convolutional layer of the network, which will help us to appreciate the use of such layers compared to a densely connected layer. In a CNN, neurons in a layer are not connected to all the neurons in the next layer.

Here, the input layer has an image with dimensions of 28 x 28 x 1. To obtain the output shape, we subtract three (from `kernel_size`) from 28 (height of the input image) and add one. This gives us 26. The final dimension for the output shape becomes 26 x 26 x 32, where 32 is the number of output filters. Thus, the output shape has reduced height and width, but it has a greater depth. To arrive at the number of parameters, we use 3 x 3 x 1 x 32 + 32 = 320, where 3 x 3 is the `kernel_size`, 1 is the number of channels for the image, 32 is the number of output filters, and to this we add 32 bias terms.

If we compare this to a fully connected neural network, we will obtain a much larger number of parameters. In a fully connected network, 28 x 28 x 1 = 784 neurons will be connected to 26 x 26 x 32 = 21,632 neurons. So, the total number of parameters will be 784 x 21,632 + 21,632 = 16,981,120. This is more than 53,000 times the number of parameters for a densely connected layer compared to what we get for a convolutional layer. This, in turn, helps to significantly reduce the processing time and thereby the processing cost.

The number of parameters for each layer is indicated in the following code:

```
# Model summary
summary(model)
```

Layer (type	Output Shape	Param #
===		
conv2d_1 (Conv2D)	(None, 26, 26, 32)	320

conv2d_2 (Conv2D)	(None, 24, 24, 64)	18496
max_pooling2d_1 (MaxPooling2D)	(None, 12, 12, 64)	0
dropout_1 (Dropout)	(None, 12, 12, 64)	0
flatten_1 (Flatten)	(None, 9216)	0
dense_1 (Dense)	(None, 64)	589888
dropout_2 (Dropout)	(None, 64)	0
dense_2 (Dense)	(None, 10)	650

```
=================================================================
Total params: 609,354
Trainable params: 609,354
Non-trainable params: 0
```

The output shape for the second convolutional network is 24 x 24 x 64, where 64 is the number of output filters. Here too, the output shape has a reduced height and width, but it has a greater depth. To arrive at a number of parameters, we use 3 x 3 x 32 x 64 + 64 = 18,496, where 3 x 3 is the `kernel_size`, 32 is the number of filters in the previous layer, and 64 is the number of output filters, and to this, we add 64 bias terms.

The next layer is the pooling layer, which is usually placed after the convolutional layer and performs a down-sampling operation. This helps to reduce processing time and also helps to reduce overfitting. To obtain output shape, we can divide 24 by 2, where 2 comes from the pool size that we have specified. The output shape here is 12 x 12 x 64 and no new parameters are added. The pooling layer is followed by a dropout layer with the same output shape and, once again, no new parameters are added.

In the flattened layer, we go from 3 dimensions (12 x 12 x 64) to one dimension by multiplying the three numbers to obtain 9,216. This is followed by a densely connected layer with 64 units. The number of parameters here can be obtained as 9216 x 64 + 64 = 589,888. This is followed by another dropout layer to avoid the overfitting problem and no parameters are added here. And finally, we have the last layer, which is a densely connected layer with 10 units representing 10 fashion items. The number of parameters here is 64 x 10 + 10 = 650. The total number of parameters is thus 609,354. In the CNN architecture that we have, we are using the relu activation function for the hidden layers and softmax for the output layer.

Compiling the model

Next, we compile the model using the following code:

```
# Compile model
model %>% compile(loss = 'categorical_crossentropy',
                  optimizer = optimizer_adadelta(),
                  metrics = 'accuracy')
```

In the preceding code, loss is specified as `categorical_crossentropy` as there are 10 categories of fashion items. For the optimizer, we make use of `optimizer_adadelta` with its recommended default settings. Adadelta is an adaptive learning rate method for gradient descent. As the name suggests, it dynamically adapts over time and doesn't require manual tuning of the learning rate. We have also specified `accuracy` for the metrics.

In the next section, we will fit the model for image recognition and classification.

Fitting the model

For fit the model, we will continue with the format that we have been using in the earlier chapters. The following code is used to fit the model:

```
# Fit model
model_one <- model %>% fit(trainx,
                           trainy,
                           epochs = 15,
                           batch_size = 128,
                           validation_split = 0.2)
plot(model_one)
```

Here, we are using 20 epochs, a batch size of 128, and 20% of the training data is reserved for validation. Since the neural network used here is more complex than the previous chapters, each run is likely to take relatively more time.

Accuracy and loss

After fitting the model, accuracy and loss values for the 15 epochs are plotted as follows:

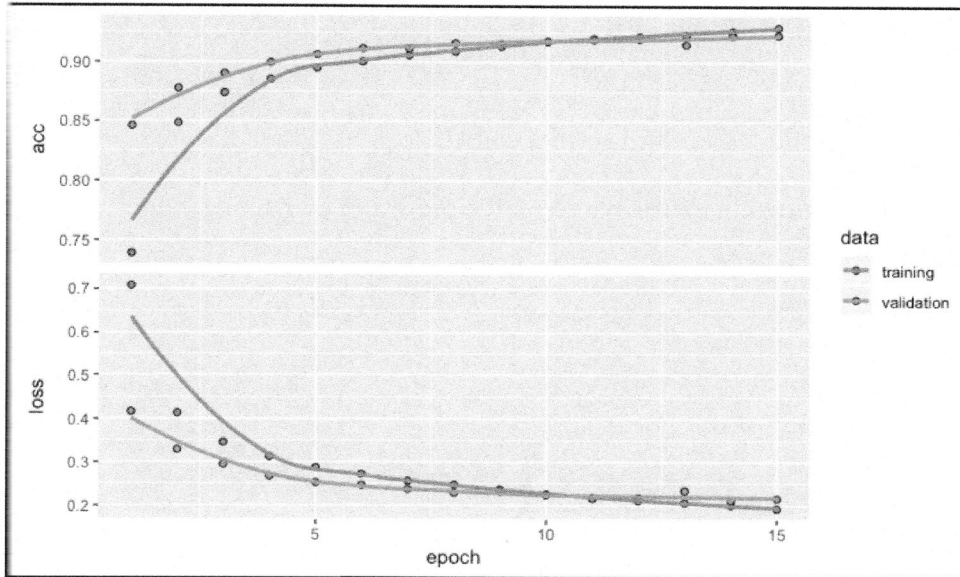

We can observe from the preceding plot that training accuracy continues to increase, whereas validation accuracy for the last few epochs is more or less flat. A similar pattern in the opposite direction is observed for the loss values. However, we do not observe any major overfitting problem.

Let's now evaluate this model and see how predictions with this model perform.

Model evaluation and prediction

After fitting the model, we will evaluate its performance in terms of loss and accuracy. We will also create a confusion matrix to assess classification performance across all 10 types of fashion items. We will perform a model evaluation and prediction for both train and test data. We will also obtain images of fashion items that do not belong to the MNIST fashion data and explore how well the performance of the model can be generalized to new images.

Training data

Loss and accuracy based on training data are obtained as 0.115 and 0.960, respectively, as shown in the following code:

```
# Model evaluation
model %>% evaluate(trainx, trainy)

$loss   0.1151372
$acc    0.9603167
```

Next, we create a confusion matrix based on the predicted and actual values:

```
# Prediction and confusion matrix
pred <- model %>%   predict_classes(trainx)
table(Predicted=pred, Actual=mnist$train$y)

OUTPUT
```

	Actual									
Predicted	0	1	2	3	4	5	6	7	8	9
0	5655	1	53	48	1	0	359	0	2	0
1	1	5969	2	8	1	0	3	0	0	0
2	50	0	5642	23	219	0	197	0	2	0
3	42	23	20	5745	50	0	50	0	3	0
4	7	1	156	106	5566	0	122	0	4	0
5	0	0	0	0	0	5971	0	6	1	12
6	230	3	121	68	159	0	5263	0	11	0
7	0	0	0	0	0	22	0	5958	3	112
8	15	3	6	2	4	4	6	0	5974	0
9	0	0	0	0	0	3	0	36	0	5876

From the preceding confusion matrix, we can make the following observations:

- The correct classifications shown on the diagonal for all 10 categories have large values, with the lowest being 5,263 out of 6,000 for item 6 (shirt).
- The best classification performance is seen for item 8 (bag), where this model correctly classifies 5,974 bag images out of 6,000.
- Among off-diagonal numbers representing misclassifications by the model, the highest value is 359, where item 6 (shirt) is mistaken for item 0 (t-shirt/top). There are 230 occasions when item-0 (t-shirt/top) is misclassified as item 6 (shirt). So, this model certainly has some difficulty differentiating between item 0 and item 6.

Let's also look deeper by calculating prediction probabilities for the first five items, as shown in the following code:

```
# Prediction probabilities
prob <- model %>%  predict_proba(trainx)
prob <- round(prob, 3)
cbind(prob, Predicted_class = pred, Actual = mnist$train$y)[1:5,]
```

```
OUTPUT
                                             Predicted_class Actual
[1,] 0.000 0.000 0.000 0.000 0 0 0.000 0.001 0 0.999               9      9
[2,] 1.000 0.000 0.000 0.000 0 0 0.000 0.000 0 0.000               0      0
[3,] 0.969 0.000 0.005 0.003 0 0 0.023 0.000 0 0.000               0      0
[4,] 0.023 0.000 0.000 0.968 0 0 0.009 0.000 0 0.000               3      3
[5,] 0.656 0.001 0.000 0.007 0 0 0.336 0.000 0 0.000               0      0
```

We can observe from the preceding output that all five fashion items are correctly classified. The correct classification probabilities range from 0.656 (item 0 in the fifth row) to 1.000 (item 0 in the second row). These probabilities are significantly high to effect correct classification without any confusion.

Now, let's see whether this performance is replicated with test data.

Test data

We start by looking at loss and accuracy values based on the test data:

```
# Model evaluation
model %>% evaluate(testx, testy)

$loss   0.240465
$acc    0.9226
```

We observe that loss is higher and accuracy is lower compared to the values obtained from the train data. This is as expected considering a similar situation with validation data that we observed earlier.

Confusion matrix for test data is provided as follows:

```
# Prediction and confusion matrix
pred <- model %>% predict_classes(testx)
table(Predicted=pred, Actual=mnist$test$y)

OUTPUT
          Actual
Predicted   0   1   2   3   4   5   6   7   8   9
```

```
0  878    0   14   15    0    0   91    0    0    0
1    1  977    0    2    1    0    1    0    2    0
2   22    1  899    9   55    0   65    0    2    0
3   12   14    6  921   14    0   20    0    3    0
4    2    5   34   26  885    0   57    0    0    0
5    1    0    0    0    0  988    0    8    1    6
6   74    1   43   23   43    0  755    0    2    0
7    0    0    0    0    0    6    0  969    3   26
8   10    2    4    4    2    0   11    0  987    1
9    0    0    0    0    0    6    0   23    0  967
```

From the preceding confusion matrix, we can make the following observations:

- This model is most confused regarding item 6 (shirt), with 91 instances where it classifies fashion items as item-0 (t-shirt/top).
- The best image recognition and classification performance is for item-5 (sandal), with 988 correct predictions out of 1,000.
- Overall, the confusion matrix exhibits a similar pattern to the one we observed with the training data.

Looking at prediction probabilities for the first five items in the test data, we observe that all five predictions are correct. Prediction probability for all five items is quite high:

```
# Prediction probabilities
prob <- model %>% predict_proba(testx)
prob <- round(prob, 3)
cbind(prob, Predicted_class = pred, Actual = mnist$test$y)[1:5,]
```

```
OUTPUT
                                          Predicted_class Actual
[1,]  0.000 0 0.000 0 0.000 0 0.000 0 0 1        9          9
[2,]  0.000 0 1.000 0 0.000 0 0.000 0 0 0        2          2
[3,]  0.000 1 0.000 0 0.000 0 0.000 0 0 0        1          1
[4,]  0.000 1 0.000 0 0.000 0 0.000 0 0 0        1          1
[5,]  0.003 0 0.001 0 0.004 0 0.992 0 0 0        6          6
```

Now, with sufficiently high classification performances with both the training and testing data in terms of accuracy, let's see if we can do the same with the 20 images of fashion items with which we started this chapter.

20 fashion items from the internet

We read the 20 colored images from the desktop and change them to gray to maintain compatibility with the data and model that we have used so far. Take a look at the following code:

```
setwd("~/Desktop/image20")
temp = list.files(pattern = "*.jpg")
mypic <- list()
for (i in 1:length(temp))  {mypic[[i]] <- readImage(temp[[i]])}
for (i in 1:length(temp))  {mypic[[i]] <- channel(mypic[[i]], "gray")}
for (i in 1:length(temp)) {mypic[[i]] <- 1-mypic[[i]]}
for (i in 1:length(temp)) {mypic[[i]] <- resize(mypic[[i]], 28, 28)}
par(mfrow = c(5,4), mar = rep(0, 4))
for (i in 1:length(temp)) plot(mypic[[i]])
```

As seen previously, we also resize all 20 images to 28 x 28, and the resulting 20 images to be classified are as follows:

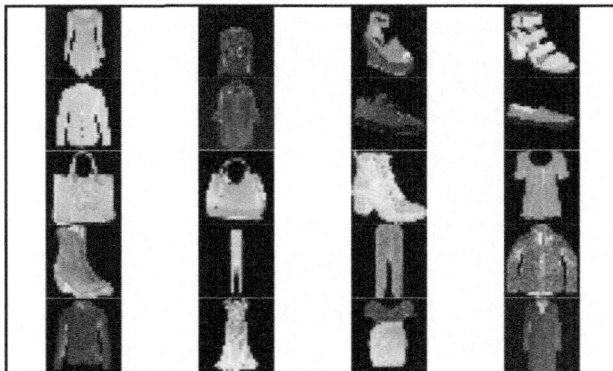

As we can observe from the preceding plot, there are two fashion items belonging to each of the 10 categories of the fashion-MNIST data:

```
# Reshape and row-bind
for (i in 1:length(temp)) {mypic[[i]] <- array_reshape(mypic[[i]],
c(1,28,28,1))}
new <- NULL
for (i in 1:length(temp)) {new <- rbind(new, mypic[[i]])}
str(new)

OUTPUT

num [1:20, 1:784] 0.0458 0.0131 0 0 0 ...
```

We reshape images in the required dimensions and then row-bind them. Looking at the structure of new, we see a 20 x 784 matrix. However, to get an appropriate, structure we will reshape it further to 20 x 28 x 28 x 1, as shown in the following code:

```
# Reshape
newx <- array_reshape(new, c(nrow(new),28,28,1))
newy <- c(0,4,5,5,6,6,7,7,8,8,9,0,9,1,1,2,2,3,3,4)
```

We reshape new to get the appropriate format, and save the result in newx. We use newy to store the actual labels for the 20 fashion items.

Now, we are ready to use the prediction model, and create a confusion matrix as shown in the following code:

```
# Confusion matrix for 20 images
pred <- model %>%   predict_classes(newx)
table(Predicted=pred, Actual=newy)
```

OUTPUT

	Actual									
Predicted	0	1	2	3	4	5	6	7	8	9
0	1	0	0	0	0	0	0	0	0	0
1	0	1	0	0	0	0	0	0	0	0
2	0	0	1	0	0	0	0	0	0	0
3	1	1	0	2	0	0	0	0	0	2
4	0	0	1	0	1	0	0	0	0	0
5	0	0	0	0	0	0	0	1	0	0
6	0	0	0	0	0	0	2	0	0	0
8	0	0	0	0	1	2	0	1	2	0

We observe from the numbers on the diagonal that only 10 items are correctly classified out of 20. This translates to a low accuracy of only 50%, compared to over 90% accuracy observed for the train and test data.

Next, we summarize these predictions in the form of a plot that includes the prediction probabilities, predicted class, and actual class, using the following code:

```
# Images with prediction probabilities, predicted class, and actual class
setwd("~/Desktop/image20")
temp = list.files(pattern = "*.jpg")
mypic <- list()
for (i in 1:length(temp))   {mypic[[i]] <- readImage(temp[[i]])}
for (i in 1:length(temp))   {mypic[[i]] <- channel(mypic[[i]], "gray")}
for (i in 1:length(temp)) {mypic[[i]] <- 1-mypic[[i]]}
for (i in 1:length(temp)) {mypic[[i]] <- resize(mypic[[i]], 28, 28)}
predictions <-  predict_classes(model, newx)
probabilities <- predict_proba(model, newx)
```

```
probs <- round(probabilities, 2)
par(mfrow = c(5, 4), mar = rep(0, 4))
for(i in 1:length(temp)) {plot(mypic[[i]])
        legend("topleft", legend = max(probs[i,]),
              bty = "n",text.col = "white",cex = 2)
        legend("top", legend = predictions[i],
              bty = "n",text.col = "yellow", cex = 2)
        legend("topright", legend = newy[i],
              bty = "",text.col = "darkgreen", cex = 2) }
```

The preceding plot summarizes the performance of the classification model with the help of prediction probabilities, predicted class, and actual class (model-one):

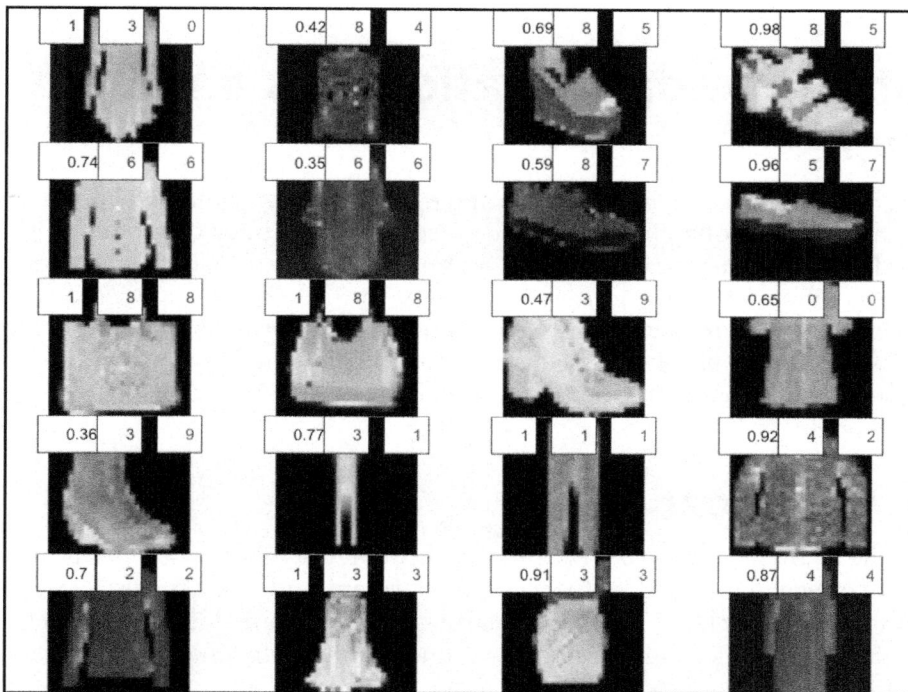

In the preceding plot, the first number in the top-left position is the prediction probability, the second number in the top-middle position is the predicted class, and the third number in the top-right position is the actual class. Looking at some of these misclassifications, what stands out is the fact that surprisingly, all images of the sandal (item 5), sneakers (item 7), and ankle boots (item 9) are incorrectly classified. These categories of images were classified with high accuracy in the training as well as test data. These six misclassifications have contributed to the significantly low accuracy value.

Two key aspects of what we have done so far can now be summarized as follows:

- The first one is what we would generally expect—model performance with the test data is usually lower compared to what is observed with the training data.
- The second one is a bit of an unexpected outcome. The 20 fashion item images that were downloaded from the internet had significantly reduced accuracy with the same model.

Let's see whether we can devise a strategy or make changes to the model to obtain better performance. We plan to have a closer look at the data and find a way to translate the performance that we saw with training and test data, if possible, to the 20 new images.

Performance optimization tips and best practices

In any data analysis task, it is important to understand how the data was collected. With the model that we developed in the previous section, the accuracy dropped from over 90% for the test data to 50% for the 20 fashion item images that were downloaded from the internet. If this difference is not addressed, it will be difficult for this model to generalize well with any fashion items that are not part of the training or test data, and therefore will not be of much practical use. In this section, we will explore improvements to the classification performance of the model.

Image modification

Looking at the 64 images at the beginning of this chapter reveals some clues as to what's going on. We notice that images of the sandals, sneakers, and ankle boots seem to have a specific pattern. In all pictures involving these fashion items, the toe has always been pictured pointing in the left direction. On the other hand, in the images downloaded from the internet for the three footwear fashion items, we notice that the toe has been pictured pointing in the right direction. To address this, let's modify images of the 20 fashion items with a `flop` function that will make the toes point in the left direction, and then we can again assess the classification performance of the model:

```
# Images with prediction probabilities, predicted class, and actual class
setwd("~/Desktop/image20")
temp = list.files(pattern = "*.jpg")
mypic <- list()
for (i in 1:length(temp)) {mypic[[i]] <- readImage(temp[[i]])}
```

```r
for (i in 1:length(temp)) {mypic[[i]] <- flop(mypic[[i]])}
for (i in 1:length(temp)) {mypic[[i]] <- channel(mypic[[i]], "gray")}
for (i in 1:length(temp)) {mypic[[i]] <- 1-mypic[[i]]}
for (i in 1:length(temp)) {mypic[[i]] <- resize(mypic[[i]], 28, 28)}
predictions <- predict_classes(model, newx)
probabilities <- predict_proba(model, newx)
probs <- round(probabilities, 2)
par(mfrow = c(5, 4), mar = rep(0, 4))
for(i in 1:length(temp)) {plot(mypic[[i]])
 legend("topleft", legend = max(probs[i,]),
 bty = "",text.col = "black",cex = 1.2)
 legend("top", legend = predictions[i],
 bty = "",text.col = "darkred", cex = 1.2)
 legend("topright", legend = newy[i],
 bty = "",text.col = "darkgreen", cex = 1.2) }
```

The following screenshot shows the prediction probabilities, predicted class, and actual class after applying the flop (model-one) function:

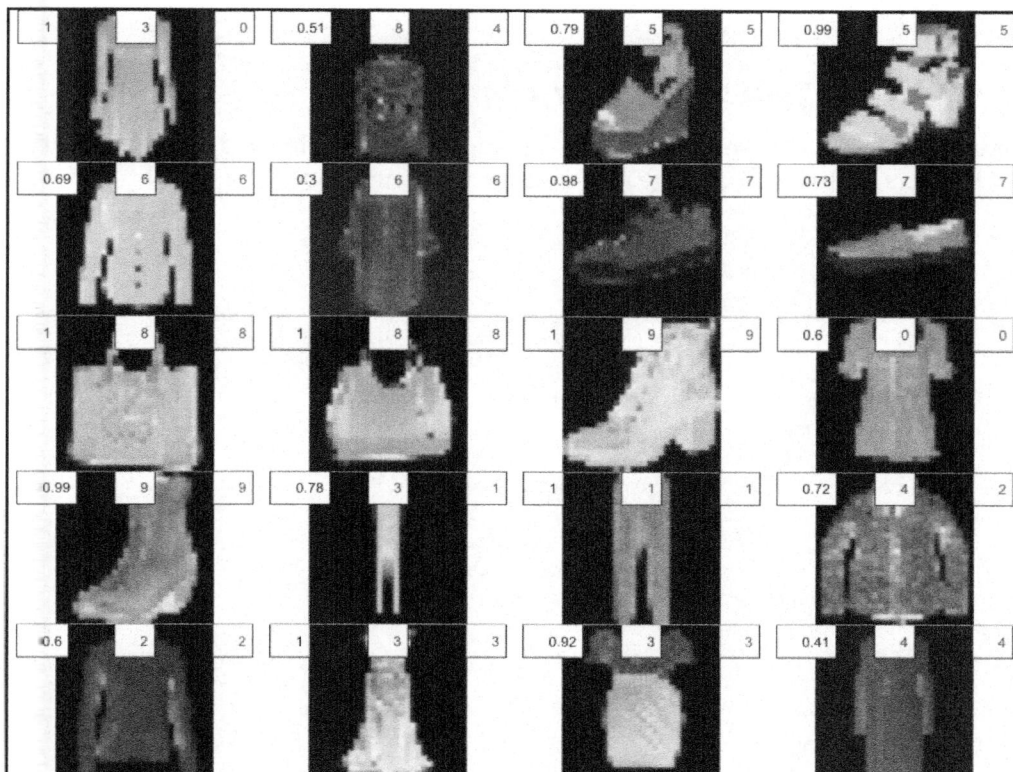

As observed from the preceding plot, after changing the orientation of the images of the fashion items, we now get correct classifications by the model for sandals, sneakers, and ankle boots. With 16 correct classifications out of 20, the accuracy improves to 80%, compared to a figure of 50% that we obtained earlier. Note that this improvement in accuracy comes from the same model. The only thing that we did here was to observe how the original data was collected and then maintain consistency with the new image data being used. Next, let's work on the modification of the deep network architecture and see whether we can improve results further.

> Before prediction models are used for generalizing the results to new data, it is a good idea to review how data was originally collected and then maintain consistency in terms of the format for the new data.

We encourage you to experiment a bit further to explore and see what happens if certain percentages of images in the fashion-MNIST data are changed to their mirror images. Can this help to generalize even better without a need to make changes to the new data?

Changes to the architecture

We modify the architecture of the CNN by adding more convolutional layers to illustrate how such layers can be added. Take a look at the following code:

```
# Model architecture
model <- keras_model_sequential()
model %>%
        layer_conv_2d(filters = 32, kernel_size = c(3,3),
                    activation = 'relu', input_shape = c(28,28,1)) %>%
        layer_conv_2d(filters = 32, kernel_size = c(3,3),
                    activation = 'relu') %>%
        layer_max_pooling_2d(pool_size = c(2,2)) %>%
        layer_dropout(rate = 0.25) %>%
        layer_conv_2d(filters = 64, kernel_size = c(3,3),
                    activation = 'relu') %>%
        layer_conv_2d(filters = 64, kernel_size = c(3,3),
                    activation = 'relu') %>%
        layer_max_pooling_2d(pool_size = c(2,2)) %>%
        layer_dropout(rate = 0.25) %>%
        layer_flatten() %>%
        layer_dense(units = 512, activation = 'relu') %>%
        layer_dropout(rate = 0.5) %>%
        layer_dense(units = 10, activation = 'softmax')

# Compile model
```

```
model %>% compile(loss = 'categorical_crossentropy',
                  optimizer = optimizer_adadelta(),
                  metrics = 'accuracy')

# Fit model
model_two <- model %>% fit(trainx,
                  trainy,
                  epochs = 15,
                  batch_size = 128,
                  validation_split = 0.2)
plot(model_two)
```

In the preceding code, for the first two convolutional layers, we use 32 filters each, and for the next set of convolutional layers, we use 64 filters each. After each pair of convolutional layers, as done earlier, we add pooling and dropout layers. Another change carried out here is the use of 512 units in the dense layer. Other settings are similar to the earlier network.

The following screenshot shows accuracy and loss for training and validation data (model_two):

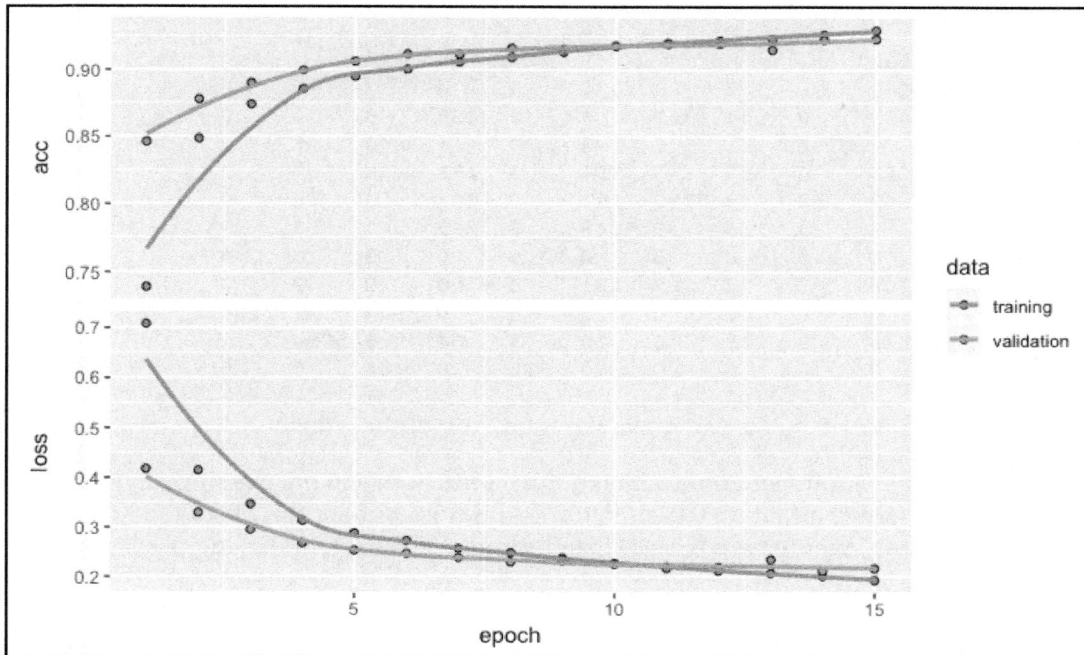

The plot based on `model_two` shows closer performance between training and validation data for loss and accuracy compared to `model_one`. In addition, a flattening of the lines toward the fifteenth epoch also suggests that increasing the number of epochs is not likely to help much in improving the classification performance further.

Loss and accuracy values for the training data are obtained as follows:

```
# Loss and accuracy
model %>% evaluate(trainx, trainy)

$loss 0.1587473
$acc 0.94285
```

The loss and accuracy values based on this model do not show a major improvement, with the loss value being slightly higher and accuracy values being slightly lower.

The following confusion matrix summarizes the predicted and actual classes:

```
# Confusion matrix for training data
pred <- model %>%   predict_classes(trainx)
table(Predicted=pred, Actual=mnist$train$y)

OUTPUT
          Actual
Predicted   0     1     2     3     4     5     6     7     8     9
        0 5499     0    58    63     3     0   456     0     4     0
        1    2  5936     1     5     3     0     4     0     1     0
        2   83     0  5669    13   258     0   438     0     7     0
        3   69    52    48  5798   197     0   103     0     6     0
        4    3     3   136    49  5348     0   265     0     5     0
        5    0     0     0     0     0  5879     0     3     0     4
        6  309     6    73    67   181     0  4700     0     2     0
        7    0     0     0     0     0    75     0  5943     1   169
        8   35     3    15     5    10     3    34     0  5974     2
        9    0     0     0     0     0    43     0    54     0  5825
```

From the confusion matrix, we can make the following observations:

- It shows that the model has maximum confusion (456 misclassifications) between item 6 (shirt) and item 0 (t-shirt/top). And this confusion is observed in both directions, where item 6 is confused for item 0, and item-0 being confused for item 6.
- Item 8 (bag) has been classified most accurately, with 5,974 instances out of a total of 6,000 (about 99.6% accuracy).
- Item-6 (shirt) has been classified with the lowest accuracy out of 10 categories, with 4,700 instances out of 6,000 (about 78.3% accuracy).

For the test data loss, the accuracy and confusion matrices are provided as follows:

```
# Loss and accuracy for the test data
model %>% evaluate(testx, testy)

$loss 0.2233179
$acc 0.9211

# Confusion matrix for test data
pred <- model %>% predict_classes(testx)
table(Predicted=pred, Actual=mnist$test$y)

OUTPUT
        Actual
Predicted   0    1    2    3    4    5    6    7    8    9
        0 875    1   18    8    0    0  104    0    3    0
        1   0  979    0    2    0    0    0    0    0    0
        2  19    0  926    9   50    0   78    0    1    0
        3  10   14    9  936   35    0   19    0    3    0
        4   2    0   30   12  869    0   66    0    0    0
        5   0    0    0    0    0  971    0    2    1    2
        6  78    3   16   29   45    0  720    0    1    0
        7   0    0    0    0    0   18    0  988    1   39
        8  16    3    1    4    1    0   13    0  989    1
        9   0    0    0    0    0   11    0   10    1  958
```

From the preceding output, we observe that loss is lower than we obtained with the earlier model, while accuracy is slightly lower than the earlier performance. From the confusion matrix, we can make the following observations:

- It shows that the model has the maximum confusion (104 misclassifications) between item 6 (shirt) and item 0 (t-shirt/top).
- Item 8 (bag) has been classified most accurately, with 989 instances out of a total of 1,000 (about 98.9% accuracy).
- Item 6 (shirt) has been classified with the lowest accuracy out of 10 categories, with 720 instances out of 1,000 (about 72.0% accuracy).

Thus, overall, we observe a similar performance to the one that we observed with the training data.

For the 20 images of fashion items downloaded from the internet, the following screenshot summarizes the performance of the model:

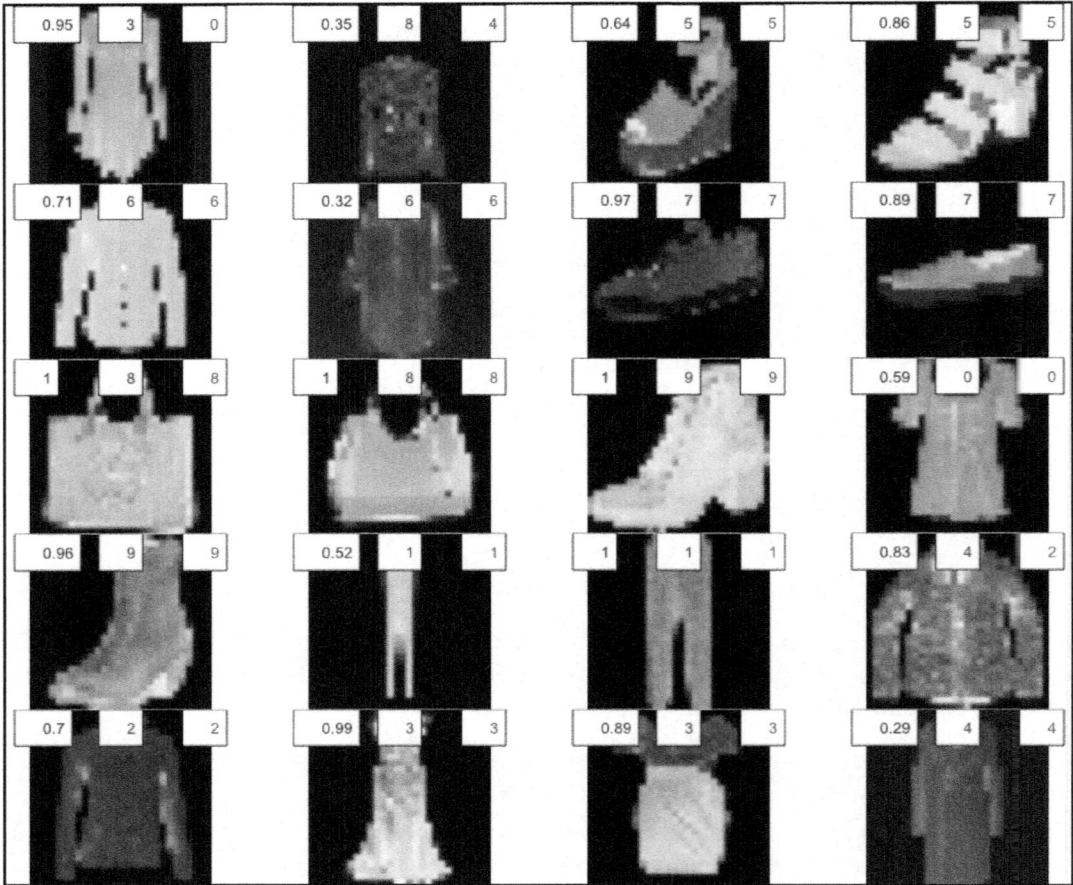

As seen from the preceding plot, this time, we have 17 out 20 images correctly classified. Although this is a slightly better performance, it is still a little lower than the figure in the region of 92% accuracy for the test data. In addition, note that due to a much smaller sample, the accuracy values can fluctuate significantly.

In this section, we made modifications to the 20 new images and made some changes to the CNN model architecture to obtain a better classification performance.

Summary

In this chapter, we showed how to use a **convolutional neural network (CNN)** deep learning model for image recognition and classification. We made use of the popular fashion-MNIST data for training and testing the image classification model. We also went over calculations involving a number of parameters, and were able to contrast this with the number of parameters that would have been needed by a densely connected neural network. CNN models help to significantly reduce the number of parameters needed and thus result in significant savings in computing time and resources. We also used images of fashion items downloaded from the internet to see whether a classification model based on fashion-MNIST data can be generalized to similar items. We did notice that it is important to maintain consistency in the way images are laid out in the training data. Additionally, we also showed how we can add more convolutional layers in the model architecture to develop a deeper CNN model.

So far, we have gradually progressed from not-so-deep neural network models to more complex and deeper neural network models. We also mainly covered such applications that are categorized under supervised learning methods. In the next chapter, we will go over another interesting class of deep neural network models called autoencoders. We will cover applications involving autoencoder networks that can be classified under unsupervised learning approaches.

6
Applying Autoencoder Neural Networks Using Keras

Autoercoder networks belong to the unsupervised learning category of methods, where labeled target values are not available. However, since autoencoders often use targets that are some form of input data, they can also be called self-supervised learning methods. In this chapter, we will learn how to apply autoencoder neural networks using Keras. We will cover three applications of autoencoders: dimension reduction, image denoising, and image correction. The examples in this chapter will use images of fashion items, images of numbers, and pictures containing people.

More specifically, in this chapter, we will cover the following topics:

- Types of autoencoders
- Dimension reduction autoencoders
- Denoising autoencoders
- Image correction autoencoders

Types of autoencoders

Autoencoder neural networks consist of two main parts:

- The first part is called the encoder, which reduces the dimensions of the input data. Generally, this is an image. When data from an input image is passed through a network that leads to a lower dimension, the network is forced to extract only the most important features of the input data.
- The second part of the autoencoder is called the decoder and it tries to reconstruct the original data from whatever is available from the output of the encoder. The autoencoder network is trained by specifying what output this network should try to match.

Let's consider some examples where we will use image data. If the output that's specified is the same image that was given as input, then after training, the autoencoder network is expected to provide an image with a lower resolution that retains the key features of the input image but misses some finer details that were part of the original input image. This type of autoencoder can be used for dimension reduction applications. Since autoencoders are based on neural networks that are able to capture non-linearity in data, they have superior performance compared to methods that only use linear functions. The following diagram shows the encoder and decoder parts of autoencoder networks:

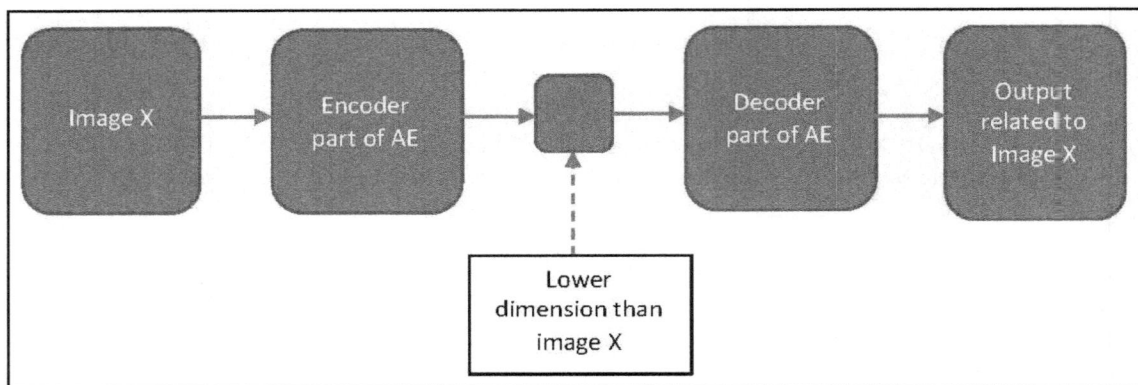

If we train autoencoders so that the input image contains some noise or non-clarity and the output as the same image but without any noise, then we can create denoising autoencoders. Similarly, if we train autoencoders with such input/output images where we have images with and without glasses, or with and without a mustache, and so on, we can create networks that help with image correction/modification.

Next, we will look at three separate examples of how to use an autoencoder: using dimension reduction, image denoising, and image correction. We will start by using autoencoders for dimension reduction.

Dimension reduction autoencoders

In this section, we will use fashion-MNIST data, specify the autoencoder model architecture, compile the model, fit the model, and then reconstruct the images. Note that fashion-MNIST is part of the Keras library.

MNIST fashion data

We will continue to use the Keras and EBImage libraries. The code for reading the fashion-MNIST data is as follows:

```
# Libraries
library(keras)
library(EBImage)

# Fashion-MNIST data
mnist <- dataset_fashion_mnist()
str(mnist)
List of 2
 $ train:List of 2
  ..$ x: int [1:60000, 1:28, 1:28] 0 0 0 0 0 0 0 0 0 0 ...
  ..$ y: int [1:60000(1d)] 9 0 0 3 0 2 7 2 5 5 ...
 $ test :List of 2
  ..$ x: int [1:10000, 1:28, 1:28] 0 0 0 0 0 0 0 0 0 0 ...
  ..$ y: int [1:10000(1d)] 9 2 1 1 6 1 4 6 5 7 ...
```

Here, the training data has 60,000 images and the test data has 10,000 images of fashion items. Since we will be using an unsupervised learning approach for this example, we will not use the labels that are available for the train and test data.

We store the training image data in trainx and test image data in testx, as shown in the following code:

```
# Train and test data
trainx <- mnist$train$x
testx <- mnist$test$x

# Plot of 64 images
par(mfrow = c(8,8), mar = rep(0, 4))
for (i in 1:64) plot(as.raster(trainx[i,,], max = 255))
```

The first 64 images of fashion items can be seen in the following image:

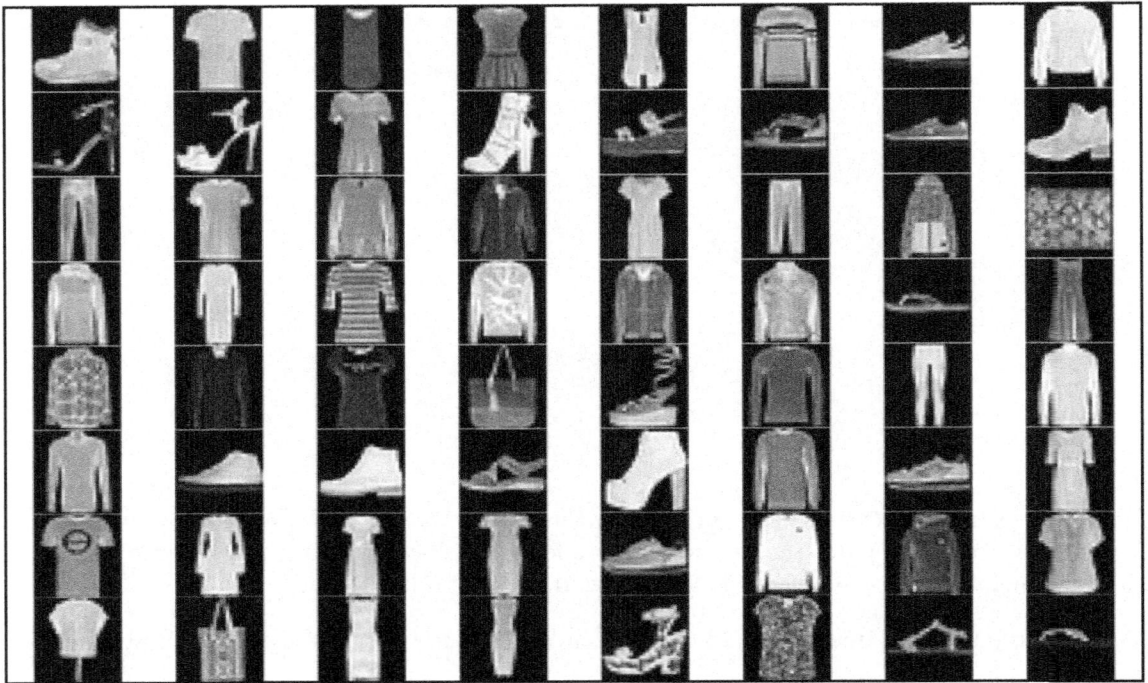

Next, we will reshape the image data into a suitable format, as shown in the following code:

```
# Reshape images
trainx <- array_reshape(trainx, c(nrow(trainx), 28, 28, 1))
testx <- array_reshape(testx, c(nrow(testx), 28, 28, 1))
trainx <- trainx / 255
testx <- testx / 255
```

Here, we have also divided `trainx` and `testx` by 255 to change the range of values that are between 0-255 to a range between 0 and 1.

Encoder model

To specify the encoder model architecture, we will use the following code:

```
# Encoder
input_layer <-
        layer_input(shape = c(28,28,1))
encoder <-  input_layer %>%
        layer_conv_2d(filters = 8,
                      kernel_size = c(3,3),
                      activation = 'relu',
                      padding = 'same') %>%
        layer_max_pooling_2d(pool_size = c(2,2),
                             padding = 'same') %>%
        layer_conv_2d(filters = 4,
                      kernel_size = c(3,3),
                      activation = 'relu',
                      padding = 'same') %>%
        layer_max_pooling_2d(pool_size = c(2,2),
                             padding = 'same')
summary(encoder)
Output
Tensor("max_pooling2d_10/MaxPool:0", shape=(?, 7, 7, 4), dtype=float32)
```

Here, for the input to the encoder, we specify the input layer so that it's 28 x 28 x 1 in size. Two convolutional layers, one with 8 filters and another with 4 filters, are used. Activation functions for both of these layers use **rectified linear units (relus)**. The convolutional layer includes padding = 'same', which retains the height and width of the input at the time of the output. For example, after the first convolution layer, the output has 28 x 28 as its height and width. Each convolution layer is followed by pooling layers. After the first pooling layer, the height and width change to 14 x 14, and, after the second pooling layer, it changes to 7 x 7. The output of the encoder network in this example is 7 x 7 x 4.

Decoder model

To specify the decoder model architecture, we will use the following code:

```
# Decoder
decoder <- encoder %>%
        layer_conv_2d(filters = 4,
                      kernel_size = c(3,3),
                      activation = 'relu',
                      padding = 'same') %>%
        layer_upsampling_2d(c(2,2)) %>%
        layer_conv_2d(filters = 8,
```

```
                              kernel_size = c(3,3),
                              activation = 'relu',
                              padding = 'same') %>%
                layer_upsampling_2d(c(2,2)) %>%
                layer_conv_2d(filters = 1,
                              kernel_size = c(3,3),
                              activation = 'sigmoid',
                              padding = 'same')
summary(decoder)
Output
Tensor("conv2d_25/Sigmoid:0", shape=(?, 28, 28, 1), dtype=float32)
```

Here, the encoder model has become the input for the decoder model. For the decoder network, we use a similar structure, with the first convolutional layer having 4 filters and the second convolutional layer having 8 filters. In addition, instead of pooling layers, we now use up-sampling layers. The first upsampling layer changes the height and width to 14 x 14 and the second upsampling layer restores it to the original height and width of 28 x 28. In the last layer, we make use of the sigmoid activation function, which ensures that the output values remain between 0 and 1.

Autoencoder model

The autoencoder model and the summary of the model showing the output shape and the number of parameters for each layer is as follows:

```
# Autoencoder
ae_model <- keras_model(inputs = input_layer, outputs = decoder)
summary(ae_model)
```

Layer (type)	Output Shape	Param #
input_5 (InputLayer)	(None, 28, 28, 1)	0
conv2d_21 (Conv2D)	(None, 28, 28, 8)	80
max_pooling2d_9 (MaxPooling2D)	(None, 14, 14, 8)	0
conv2d_22 (Conv2D)	(None, 14, 14, 4)	292
max_pooling2d_10 (MaxPooling2D)	(None, 7, 7, 4)	0
conv2d_23 (Conv2D)	(None, 7, 7, 4)	148
up_sampling2d_9 (UpSampling2D)	(None, 14, 14, 4)	0

conv2d_24 (Conv2D)	(None, 14, 14, 8)	296
up_sampling2d_10 (UpSampling2D)	(None, 28, 28, 8)	0
conv2d_25 (Conv2D)	(None, 28, 28, 1)	73

```
=================================================================
Total params: 889
Trainable params: 889
Non-trainable params: 0
```

Here, the autoencoder model has five convolutional layers, two maximum pooling layers, and two upsampling layers, apart from the input layer. Here, the total number of parameters in this autoencoder model is 889.

Compiling and fitting the model

Next, we will compile and fit the model using the following code:

```
# Compile model
ae_model %>% compile( loss='mean_squared_error',
        optimizer='adam')

# Fit model
model_one <- ae_model %>% fit(trainx,
                    trainx,
                    epochs = 20,
                    shuffle=TRUE,
                    batch_size = 32,
                    validation_data = list(testx,testx))
```

Here, we compile the model using mean squared error as the loss function and specify adam as the optimizer. For training the model, we will make use of trainx as the input and output. We'll use textx for validation. We fit the model with a batch size of 32 and use 20 epochs.

The following output shows the plot of the loss values for the train and validation data:

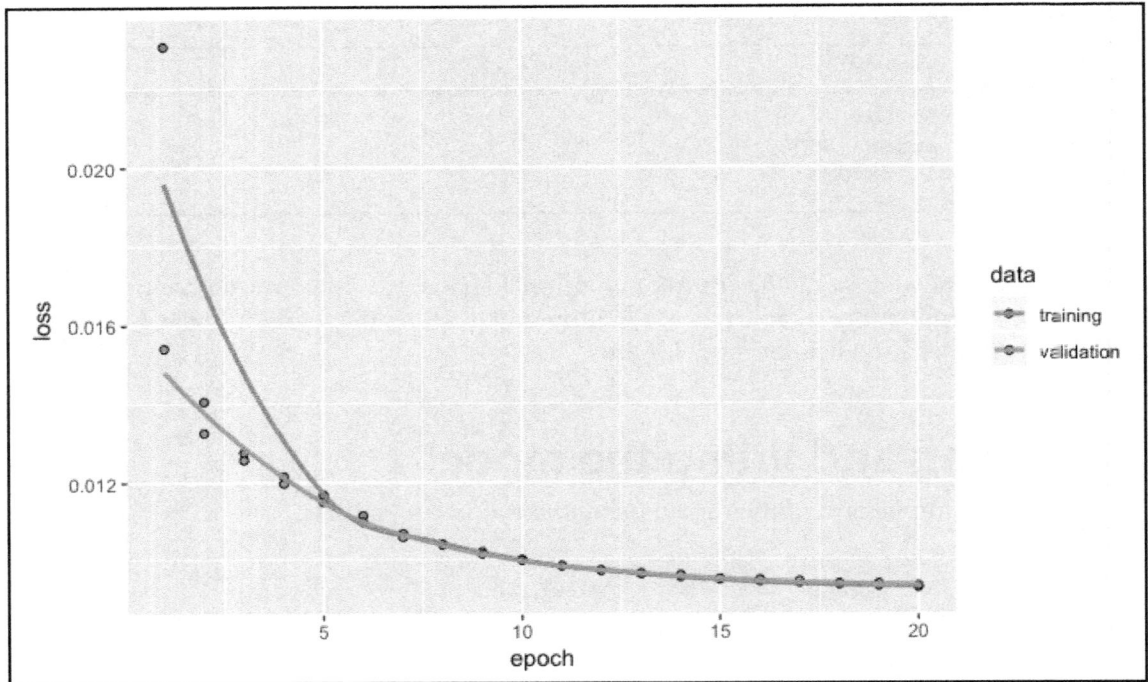

The preceding plot shows good convergence and doesn't show any signs of overfitting.

Reconstructed images

To obtain reconstructed images, we use `predict_on_batch` to predict the output using the autoencoder model. We do this with the following code:

```
# Reconstruct and plot images - train data
rc <-    ae_model %>%     keras::predict_on_batch(x = trainx)
par(mfrow = c(2,5), mar = rep(0, 4))
for (i in 1:5) plot(as.raster(trainx[i,,,]))
for (i in 1:5) plot(as.raster(rc[i,,,]))
```

The first five fashion images from the training data (first row) and the corresponding reconstructed images (second row) are as follows:

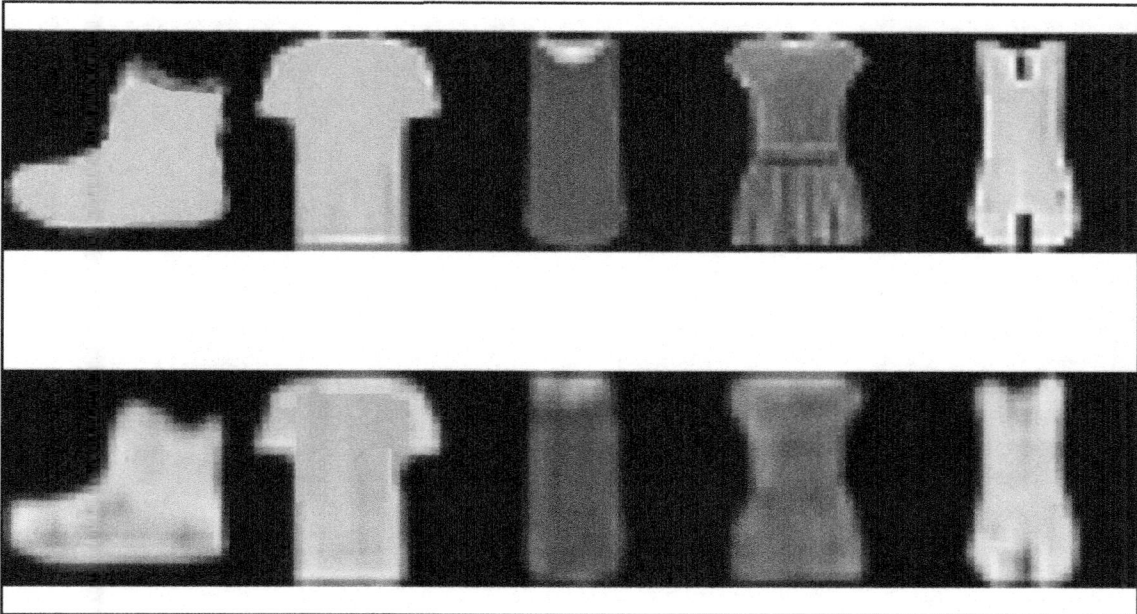

Here, as expected, the reconstructed images are seen to capture key features of the training images. However, it ignores certain finer details. For example, the logos that are more clearly visible in the original training images are blurred in the reconstructed images.

We can also take a look at the plot of the original and reconstructed images using images from the test data. For this, we can use the following code:

```
# Reconstruct and plot images - train data
rc <- ae_model %>% keras::predict_on_batch(x = testx)
par(mfrow = c(2,5), mar = rep(0, 4))
for (i in 1:5) plot(as.raster(testx[i,,,]))
for (i in 1:5) plot(as.raster(rc[i,,,]))
```

The following image shows the original images (first row) and reconstructed images (second row) using the test data:

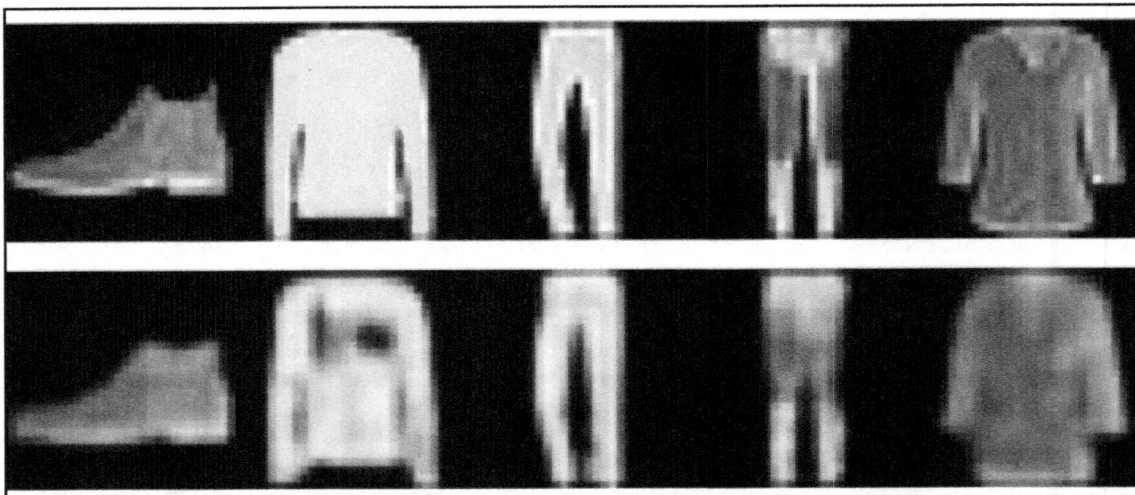

Here, the reconstructed images behave as they did previously for the training data.

In this example, we have used MNIST fashion data to build an autoencoder network that helps reduce the dimensions of the images by keeping the main features and removing the features that involve finer details. Next, we will look at another variant of the autoencoder model that helps remove noise from images.

Denoising autoencoders

In situations where input images contain unwanted noise, autoencoder networks can be trained to remove such noise. This is achieved by providing images with noise as input and providing a clean version of the same image as output. The autoencoder network is trained so that the output of the autoencoder is as close to the output image as possible.

MNIST data

We will make use of MNIST data that's available in the Keras package to illustrate the steps that are involved in creating a denoising autoencoder network. MNIST data can be read using the following code:

```
# MNIST data
mnist <- dataset_mnist()
str(mnist)
List of 2
 $ train:List of 2
  ..$ x: int [1:60000, 1:28, 1:28] 0 0 0 0 0 0 0 0 0 0 ...
  ..$ y: int [1:60000(1d)] 5 0 4 1 9 2 1 3 1 4 ...
 $ test :List of 2
  ..$ x: int [1:10000, 1:28, 1:28] 0 0 0 0 0 0 0 0 0 0 ...
  ..$ y: int [1:10000(1d)] 7 2 1 0 4 1 4 9 5 9 ...
```

The structure of the MNIST data indicates that it contains train and test data, along with the respective labels. The training data has 60,000 images of digits from 0 to 9. Similarly, the test data has 10,000 images of digits from 0 to 9. Although each image has a corresponding label identifying the image, in this example, the data for labels isn't required and so we will ignore this information.

We will be storing training images in trainx and the test images in testx. To do this, we will use the following code:

```
# Train and test data
trainx <- mnist$train$x
testx <- mnist$test$x

# Plot
par(mfrow = c(8,8), mar = rep(0, 4))
for (i in 1:64) plot(as.raster(trainx[i,,], max = 255))
```

The following image shows a plot of 64 images in 8 rows and 8 columns based on images of digits between 0 and 9 from MNIST:

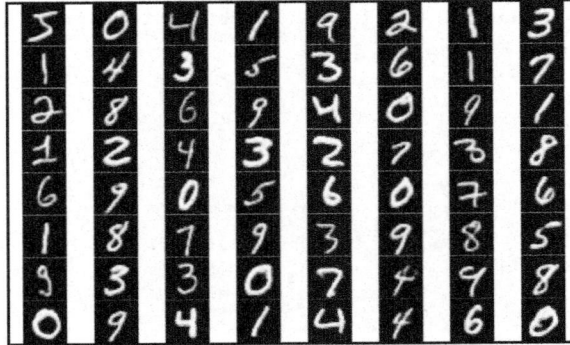

The preceding plot shows handwritten digits in various writing styles. We will reshape this image data in the required format and add random noise to it.

Data preparation

Next, we will reshape images in the required format using the following code:

```
# Reshape
trainx <- array_reshape(trainx, c(nrow(trainx),28,28,1))
testx <- array_reshape(testx, c(nrow(testx),28,28,1))
trainx <- trainx / 255
testx <- testx / 255
```

Here, we've reshaped the training data so that it's 60,000 x 28 x 28 x 1 in size and reshaped the test data so that it's 10,000 x 28 x 28 x 1 in size. We also divided the pixel values that are between 0 and 255 by 255 to obtain a new range that is between 0 and 1.

Adding noise

To add noise to the training images, we need to obtain 60,000 x 28 x 28 random numbers between 0 and 1 using uniform distribution using the following code:

```
# Random numbers from uniform distribution
n <- runif(60000*28*28,0,1)
n <- array_reshape(n, c(60000,28,28,1))

# Plot
```

```
par(mfrow = c(8,8), mar = rep(0, 4))
for (i in 1:64) plot(as.raster(n[i,,,]))
```

Here, we're reshaping the random numbers that were generated using uniform distribution to match the dimensions of the matrix that we have for the training images. The results are plotted in the form of images that show resulting images containing noise.

The following image shows the images containing noise:

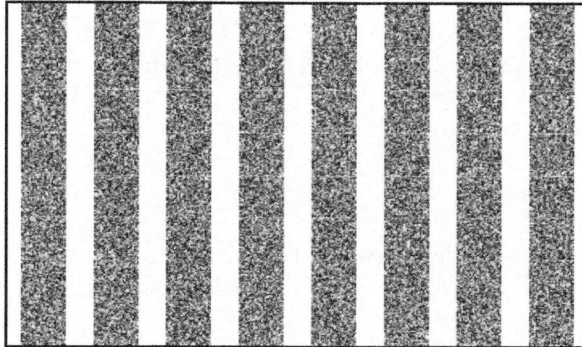

The images depicting noise are added to the images that are stored in `trainx`. We need to divide this by 2 to keep the resulting `trainn` values between 0 and 1. We can use the following code to do this:

```
# Adding noise to handwritten images - train data
trainn <- (trainx + n)/2
par(mfrow = c(8,8), mar = rep(0, 4))
for (i in 1:64) plot(as.raster(trainn[i,,,]))
```

The first 64 training images, along with their noise, are shown in the following image:

Although noise is added to the original handwritten digits, the digits are still readable. The main objective of using a denoising autoencoder is to train a network that retains the handwritten digits and removes noise from the images.

We will repeat the same steps for the test data using the following code:

```
# Adding noise to handwritten images - test data
n1 <- runif(10000*28*28,0,1)
n1 <- array_reshape(n1, c(10000,28,28,1))
testn <- (testx +n1)/2
```

Here, we have added noise to test images and stored them in `testn`. Now, we can specify the encoder architecture.

Encoder model

The code that's used for the encoder network is as follows:

```
# Encoder
input_layer <-
        layer_input(shape = c(28,28,1))
encoder <-  input_layer %>%
        layer_conv_2d(filters = 32,
                      kernel_size = c(3,3),
                      activation = 'relu',
                      padding = 'same') %>%
        layer_max_pooling_2d(pool_size = c(2,2),
                             padding = 'same') %>%
        layer_conv_2d(filters = 32,
                      kernel_size = c(3,3),
                      activation = 'relu',
                      padding = 'same') %>%
        layer_max_pooling_2d(pool_size = c(2,2),
                             padding = 'same')
summary(encoder)
OutputTensor("max_pooling2d_6/MaxPool:0", shape=(?, 7, 7, 32),
dtype=float32)
```

Here, the input layer is specified to be 28 x 28 x 1 in size. We use two convolution layers with 32 filters each and a rectifier linear unit as the activation function. Each convolution layer is followed by pooling layers. After the first pooling layer, the height and width change to 14 x 14, and after the second pooling layer, this changes to 7 x 7. The output of the encoder network in this example has 7 x 7 x 32 dimensions.

Decoder model

For the decoder network, we keep the same structure, except that, instead of pooling layers, we use upsampling layers. We can use the following code to do this:

```
# Decoder
decoder <- encoder %>%
        layer_conv_2d(filters = 32,
                      kernel_size = c(3,3),
                      activation = 'relu',
                      padding = 'same') %>%
        layer_upsampling_2d(c(2,2)) %>%
        layer_conv_2d(filters = 32,
                      kernel_size = c(3,3),
                      activation = 'relu',
                      padding = 'same') %>%
        layer_upsampling_2d(c(2,2)) %>%
        layer_conv_2d(filters = 1,
                      kernel_size = c(3,3),
                      activation = 'sigmoid',
                      padding = 'same')
summary(decoder)
Output
Tensor("conv2d_15/Sigmoid:0", shape=(?, 28, 28, 1), dtype=float32)
```

In the preceding code, the first upsampling layer changes the height and width to 14 x 14 and the second upsampling layer restores it to the original height and width of 28 x 28. In the last layer, we use a sigmoid activation function, which ensures that the output values remain between 0 and 1.

Autoencoder model

Now, we can specify the autoencoder network. The autoencoder's model and summary is as follows:

```
# Autoencoder
ae_model <- keras_model(inputs = input_layer, outputs = decoder)
summary(ae_model)
```

Layer (type)	Output Shape	Param #
input_3 (InputLayer)	(None, 28, 28, 1)	0
conv2d_11 (Conv2D)	(None, 28, 28, 32)	320
max_pooling2d_5 (MaxPooling2D)	(None, 14, 14, 32)	0
conv2d_12 (Conv2D)	(None, 14, 14, 32)	9248
max_pooling2d_6 (MaxPooling2D)	(None, 7, 7, 32)	0
conv2d_13 (Conv2D)	(None, 7, 7, 32)	9248
up_sampling2d_5 (UpSampling2D)	(None, 14, 14, 32)	0
conv2d_14 (Conv2D)	(None, 14, 14, 32)	9248
up_sampling2d_6 (UpSampling2D)	(None, 28, 28, 32)	0
conv2d_15 (Conv2D)	(None, 28, 28, 1)	289

```
Total params: 28,353
Trainable params: 28,353
Non-trainable params: 0
```

From the preceding summary of the autoencoder network, we can see that there are 28,353 parameters in total. Next, we will compile this model using the following code:

```
# Compile model
ae_model %>% compile( loss='binary_crossentropy', optimizer='adam')
```

> For denoising autoencoders, the `bianary_crossentropy` loss function performs better than other options.

When compiling the autoencoder model, we will use `binary_crossentropy` for the loss function since the input values are between 0 and 1. For the optimizer, we will use `adam`. After compiling the model, we are ready to fit it.

Fitting the model

To train the model, we use images with noise stored in `trainn` as input and images without noise stored in `trainx` as output. The code that's used to fit the model is as follows:

```
# Fit model
model_two <- ae_model %>% fit(trainn,
                         trainx,
                         epochs = 100,
                         shuffle = TRUE,
                         batch_size = 128,
                         validation_data = list(testn,testx))
```

Here, we also use `testn` and `testx` to monitor validation errors. We will run 100 epochs with a batch size of 128. After network training is completed, we obtain the loss values for the train and test data using the following code:

```
# Loss for train data
ae_model %>% evaluate(trainn, trainx)
      loss
0.07431865

# Loss for test data
ae_model %>% evaluate(testn, testx)
      loss
0.07391542
```

The loss for the training and test data is 0.0743 and 0.0739, respectively. The closeness of the two numbers indicates the lack of an overfitting problem.

Image reconstruction

After fitting the model, we can reconstruct images using the following code:

```
# Reconstructing images - train data
rc <- ae_model %>%   keras::predict_on_batch(x = trainn)

# Plot
```

```
par(mfrow = c(8,8), mar = rep(0, 4))
for (i in 1:64) plot(as.raster(rc[i,,]))
```

In the preceding code, we have used `ae_model` to reconstruct the images by providing images with noise contained in `trainn`. As shown in the following image, we have plotted the first 64 reconstructed images to see if the noisy images become clearer:

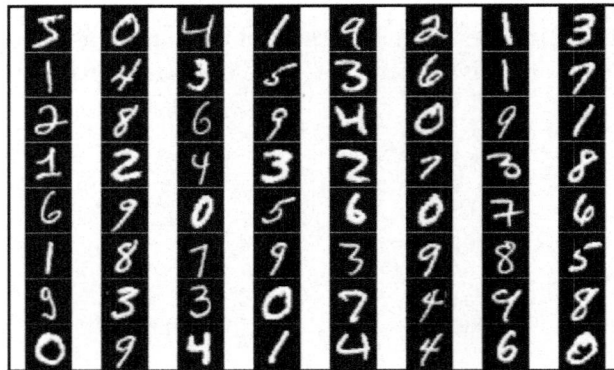

From the preceding plot, we can observe that the autoencoder network has successfully removed noise. We can also reconstruct the images for the test data with the help of `ae_model` using the following code:

```
# Reconstructing images - test data
rc <- ae_model %>% keras::predict_on_batch(x = testn)
par(mfrow = c(8,8), mar = rep(0, 4))
for (i in 1:64) plot(as.raster(rc[i,,]))
```

The resulting images for the first 64 handwritten digits in the test data are as follows

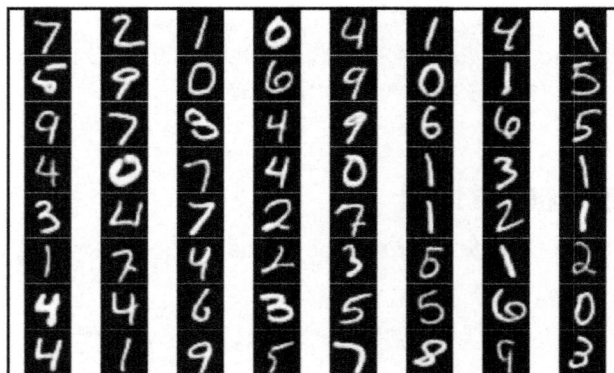

Here, we can observe that the denoising autoencoder does a decent job of removing noise from the images of 0 to 9 digits. To look more closely at the model's performance, we can plot the first image in the test data, the corresponding image with noise, and the reconstructed image after noise removal, like so:

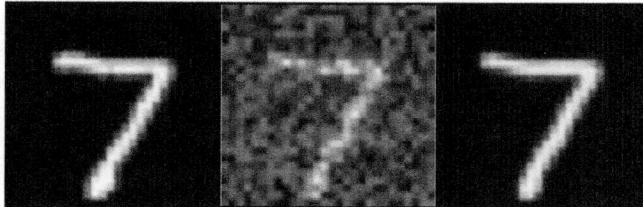

In the preceding screenshot, the first image is the original image, while the second image is the one that's obtained after adding noise. The autoencoder was provided the second image as input and the results that were obtained from the model (third image) were made to match the first image. Here, we can see that the denoising autoencoder network helps remove noise. Note that the third image is unable to retain some of the finer details of the original image that we can see in the first image. For example, in the original image, seven appears to be slightly thicker at the beginning and toward the lower part compared to the third image. However, it does successfully extract the overall pattern of seven from the image containing digit seven with noise.

Image correction

In this third application, we will go over an example where we'll develop an autoencoder model to remove certain artificially created marks on various pictures. We will use 25 images containing a black line across the picture. The code for reading the image files and carrying out the related processing is as follows:

```
# Reading images and image processing
setwd("~/Desktop/peoplex")
temp = list.files(pattern="*.jpeg")
mypic <- list()
for (i in 1:length(temp)) {mypic[[i]] <- readImage(temp[i])}
for (i in 1:length(temp)) {mypic[[i]] <- resize(mypic[[i]], 128, 128)}
for (i in 1:length(temp)) {dim(mypic[[i]]) <- c(128, 128,3)}
```

In the preceding code, we read images with .jpeg extensions from the peoplex folder and resize these images so that they have a height and width of 128 x 128. We also update the dimensions to 128 x 128 x 3 since all the images are color images.

Images that need correction

We will use the following code to combine the 25 images and then plot them:

```
# Combine and plot images
trainx <- combine(mypic)
str(trainx)
Formal class 'Image' [package "EBImage"] with 2 slots
  ..@ .Data    : num [1:128, 1:128, 1:3, 1:16] 0.04435 0 0.00357 0.05779
0.05815 ...
  ..@ colormode: int 2
trainx <- aperm(trainx, c(4,1,2,3)
par(mfrow = c(4,4), mar = rep(0, 4))
for (i in 1:16) plot(as.raster(trainx[i,,,]))
```

Here, we save the data involving all 25 images after combining them into trainx. Looking at the structure of tranix, we can see that, after combining the image data, the dimensions now become 128 x 128 x 3 x 16. In order to change this to the required format of 16 x 128 x 128 x 3, we use the aperm function. Then, we plot all 25 images. Note that if the images are plotted with rotation, they can be adjusted to the correct orientation very easily on any computer. The following are the 25 pictures, with a black line across all the images:

The autoencoder model in this application will use these images with a black line as input and will be trained so that the black lines are removed.

Clean images

We will also read the same 25 images without the black line and save them in `trainy`, as shown in the following code:

```
# Read image files without black line
setwd("~/Desktop/people")
temp = list.files(pattern="*.jpg")
mypic <- list()
for (i in 1:length(temp)) {mypic[[i]] <- readImage(temp[i])}
for (i in 1:length(temp)) {mypic[[i]] <- resize(mypic[[i]], 128, 128)}
for (i in 1:length(temp)) {dim(mypic[[i]]) <- c(128, 128,3)}
trainy <- combine(mypic)
trainy <- aperm(trainy, c(4,1,2,3))
par(mfrow = c(4,4), mar = rep(0, 4))
for (i in 1:16) plot(as.raster(trainy[i,,,]))
par(mfrow = c(1,1))
```

Here, after resizing and changing dimensions, we are combining the images, just like we did previously. We also need to make some adjustments to the dimensions to obtain the required format. Next, we will plot all 25 clean images, as follows:

At the time of training the autoencoder network, we will use these clean images as output. Next, we will specify the encoder model architecture.

Encoder model

For the encoder model, we will use three convolutional layers with 512, 512, and 256 filters, as shown in the following code:

```
# Encoder network
input_layer <- layer_input(shape = c(128,128,3))
encoder <-  input_layer %>%
        layer_conv_2d(filters = 512, kernel_size = c(3,3), activation =
'relu', padding = 'same') %>%
        layer_max_pooling_2d(pool_size = c(2,2),padding = 'same') %>%
        layer_conv_2d(filters = 512, kernel_size = c(3,3), activation =
'relu', padding = 'same') %>%
        layer_max_pooling_2d(pool_size = c(2,2),padding = 'same') %>%
        layer_conv_2d(filters = 256, kernel_size = c(3,3), activation =
'relu', padding = 'same') %>%
        layer_max_pooling_2d(pool_size = c(2,2), padding = 'same')
summary(encoder)
Output
Tensor("max_pooling2d_22/MaxPool:0", shape=(?, 16, 16, 256), dtype=float32)
```

Here, the encoder network is 16 x 16 x 256 in size. We will keep the other features similar to the encoder models that we used in the previous two examples. Now, we will specify the decoder architecture of the autoencoder network.

Decoder model

For the decoder model, the first three convolutional layers have 256, 512, and 512, filters, as shown in the following code:

```
# Decoder network
decoder <- encoder %>%
        layer_conv_2d(filters = 256, kernel_size = c(3,3), activation =
'relu',padding = 'same') %>%
        layer_upsampling_2d(c(2,2)) %>%
        layer_conv_2d(filters = 512, kernel_size = c(3,3), activation =
'relu',padding = 'same') %>%
        layer_upsampling_2d(c(2,2)) %>%
        layer_conv_2d(filters = 512, kernel_size = c(3,3), activation =
'relu',padding = 'same') %>%
        layer_upsampling_2d(c(2,2)) %>%
```

```
        layer_conv_2d(filters = 3, kernel_size = c(3,3), activation =
'sigmoid',padding = 'same')
summary(decoder)
Output
Tensor("conv2d_46/Sigmoid:0", shape=(?, 128, 128, 3), dtype=float32)
```

Here, we used upsampling layers. In the last convolutional layer, we made use of a sigmoid activation function. In the last convolutional layer, we used three filters since we are making use of color images. Finally, the output of the decoder model has 128 x 128 x 3 dimensions.

Compiling and fitting the model

Now, we can compile and fit the model using the following code:

```
# Compile and fit model
ae_model <- keras_model(inputs = input_layer, outputs = decoder)
ae_model %>% compile( loss='mse',
        optimizer='adam')
model_three <- ae_model %>% fit(trainx,
                    trainy,
                    epochs = 100,
                    batch_size = 128,
                    validation_split = 0.2)
plot(model_three)
```

In the preceding code, we compile the autoencoder model using mean squared error as the loss function and specify adam as the optimizer. We use trainx, which contains images with a black line across them, as input to the model and trainy, which contains clean images, as output that the model tries to match. We specify the number of epochs as 100 and use a batch size of 128. Using a validation split of 0.2 or 20%, we will use 20 images out of 25 for training and 5 images out of 25 for computing validation errors.

The following graph shows the mean square error for 100 epochs for the training and validation images for `model_three`:

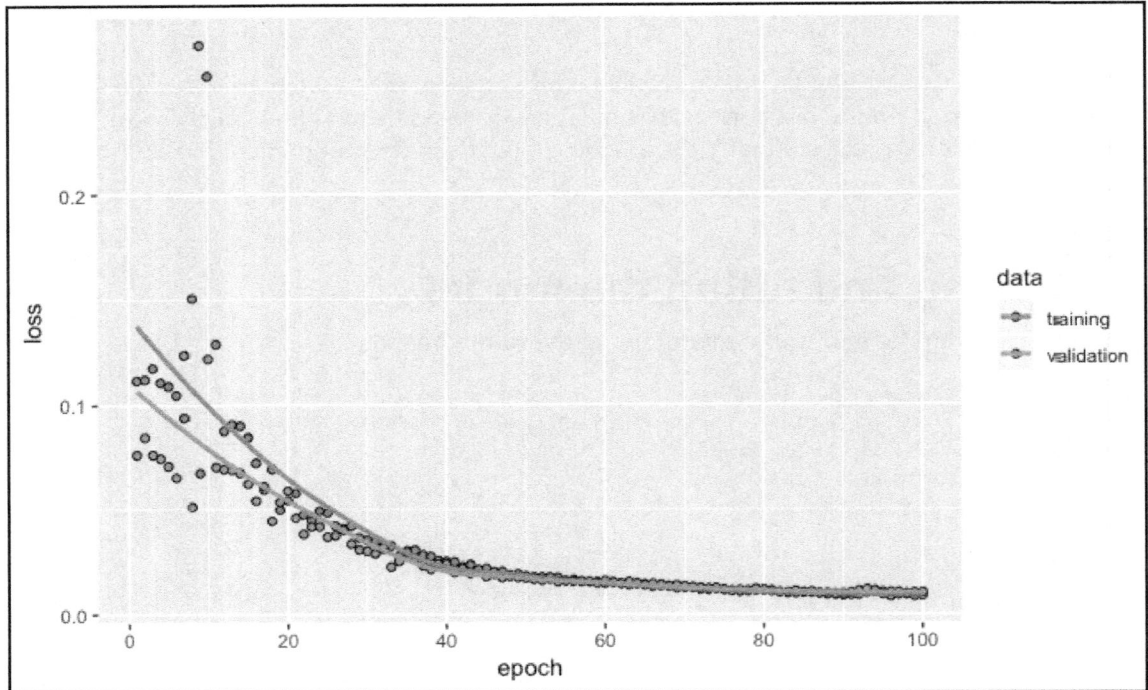

The plot for the mean square error shows that there is an improvement in model performance based on the training and validation data as the model training proceeds. We can also see that, between about 80 and 100 epochs, the model's performance becomes approximately flat. In addition to this, it's suggested that increasing the number of epochs isn't likely to improve model performance any further.

Reconstructing images from training data

Now, we can reconstruct images from the training data using the model that we have obtained. To do this, we can use the following code:

```
# Reconstructing images - training
rc <- ae_model %>% keras::predict_on_batch(x = trainx)
par(mfrow = c(5,5), mar = rep(0, 4))
for (i in 1:25) plot(as.raster(rc[i,,,]))
```

In the preceding code, we're using `predict_on_batch` to reconstruct the images after feeding `trainx`, which contains images with black lines across them. All 25 reconstructed images can be seen here:

From the preceding plot, it can be seen that the autoencoder model has learned to remove the black lines from the input images. The pictures are somewhat blurred since the autoencoder model tries to output only the main features from the images and misses certain details.

Reconstructing images from new data

To test the autoencoder model with new and unseen data, we will make use of 25 new images that have black lines across them. To do this, we will use the following code:

```
# 25 new images
setwd("~/Desktop/newx")
temp = list.files(pattern="*.jpg")
mypic <- list()
for (i in 1:length(temp)) {mypic[[i]] <- readImage(temp[i])}
```

```
for (i in 1:length(temp)) {mypic[[i]] <- resize(mypic[[i]], 128, 128)}
for (i in 1:length(temp)) {dim(mypic[[i]]) <- c(128, 128,3)}
newx <- combine(mypic)
newx <- aperm(newx, c(4,1,2,3))
par(mfrow = c(4,4), mar = rep(0, 4))
for (i in 1:16) plot(as.raster(newx[i,,,]))
```

As shown in the preceding code, we read the new image data and then formatted all images, like we did previously. All 25 new pictures with a black line across them are shown in the following plot:

Here, all 25 images have a black line across them. We will use the data from these new images and reconstruct the images using the autoencoder model that we've developed to remove the black lines. The code that's used for reconstructing and plotting the images is as follows:

```
# Reconstructing images - new images
rc <- ae_model %>% keras::predict_on_batch(x = newx)
par(mfrow = c(5,5), mar = rep(0, 4))
for (i in 1:25) plot(as.raster(rc[i,,,]))
```

The following screenshot shows the reconstructed images after using the autoencoder model based on the 25 new images that had a black line across them:

The preceding screenshot once again shows that the autoencoder model successfully removes the black lines from all the images. However, as we observed earlier, the image quality is low. This example provides promising results. If the results that were obtained also had a higher quality output for the images, then we could use this in several different situations. For example, we could reconstruct an image with glasses as an image without glasses or vice versa, or we may be able to reconstruct an image of a person without a smile to an image of them with a smile. There are several variants of such approaches that have the potential to have significant business value.

Summary

In this chapter, we went over three application examples of autoencoder networks. The first type of autoencoder involved a dimension reduction application. Here, we used an autoencoder network architecture that only allowed us to learn about the key features of the input image. The second type of autoencoder was illustrated using MNIST data containing images of numbers. We artificially added noise to the images of numbers and trained the network in such a way that it learned to remove noise from the input image. The third type of autoencoder network involved image correction application. The autoencoder network in this application was trained to remove a black line from input images.

In the next chapter, we will go over another class of deep networks, called **transfer learning**, and use them for image classification.

7
Image Classification for Small Data Using Transfer Learning

In the previous chapters, we developed deep learning networks and explored various application examples related to image data. One major difference compared to what we will be discussing in this chapter is that, in the previous chapters, we developed models from scratch.

Transfer learning can be defined as an approach where we reuse what a trained deep network has learned to solve a new but related problem. For example, we may be able to reuse a deep learning network that's been developed to classify thousands of different fashion items to develop a deep network to classify three different types of dresses. This approach is similar to what we can observe in real life, where a teacher transfers knowledge or learning gained over the years to students or a coach passes on learning or experience to new players. Another example is where learning to ride a bicycle is transferred to learning to ride a motorbike and this, in turn, becomes useful for learning how to drive a car.

In this chapter, we will make use of pretrained deep networks while developing models for image classification. Pretrained models allow us to transfer useful features that we've learned from a much larger dataset to models we are interested in developing with a somewhat similar, but new and relatively smaller dataset. The use of pretrained models not only allows us to overcome issues as a result of the dataset being small, but also helps reduce the time and cost of developing models.

To illustrate the use of pretrained image classification models, in this chapter, we will cover the following topics:

- Using a pretrained model to identify an image
- Working with the CIFAR10 dataset
- Image classification with CNN
- Classifying images using the pretrained RESNET50 model
- Model evaluation and prediction
- Performance optimization tips and best practices

Using a pretrained model to identify an image

Before we proceed, let's load three packages that we'll need in this section:

```
# Libraries used
library(keras)
library(EBImage)
library(tensorflow)
```

The Keras and TensorFlow libraries will be used for developing the pretrained image classification model, while the EBImage library will be used for processing and visualizing image data.

In Keras, the following pretrained image classification models are available:

- Xception
- VGG16
- VGG19
- ResNet50
- InceptionV3
- InceptionResNetV2
- MobileNet
- MobileNetV2
- DenseNet
- NASNet

These pretrained models are trained on images from ImageNet (http://www.image-net.org/). ImageNet is a huge image database that contains several million images.

We will start by using a pretrained model known as resnet50 to identify an image. The following is the code we can use to utilize this pretrained model:

```
# Pretrained model
pretrained <- application_resnet50(weights = "imagenet")
summary(pretrained)
```

Here, we have specified weights as "imagenet". This allows us to reuse the pretrained weights of the RESNET50 network. RESNET50 is a deep residual network that has a depth of 50 layers and includes convolutional neural network layers. Note that in case we only want to use the model architecture without the pretrained weights and we would like to train from scratch, then we can specify weights as null. By using summary, we can obtain the architecture of the RESNET50 network. However, to conserve space, we do not provide any output from the summary. The total number of parameters in this network is 25,636,712. The RESNET50 network is trained in using over a million images from ImageNet and has the capability to classify images into 1,000 different categories.

Reading an image

Let's start by reading an image of a dog in RStudio. The following code loads an image file and then obtains the respective output:

> When using the RESNET50 network, the maximum target size that's allowed is 224 x 224 and the minimum target size that's allowed is 32 x 32.

```
# Read image data
setwd("~/Desktop")
img <- image_load("dog.jpg", target_size = c(224,224))
x <- image_to_array(img)
str(x)
OUTPUT
num [1:224, 1:224, 1:3] 70 69 68 73 88 79 18 22 21 20 ...

# Image plot
plot(as.raster(x, max = 255))

# Summary and histogram
summary(x)
OUTPUT
```

```
Min. 1st Qu. Median Mean 3rd Qu. Max.
0.0 89.0 150.0 137.7 190.0 255.0
hist(x)
```

In the preceding code, we can observe the following:

- A picture of a Norwich terrier dog is loaded from the computer desktop that's 224 x 224 in size using the `image_load()` function from Keras.
- Note that the original image may not be 224 x 224 in size. However, specifying this dimension at the time of loading the image allows us to easily resize the original image so that it has new dimensions.
- This image is converted into an array of numbers using the `image_to_array()` function. The structure of this array shows a dimension of 224 x 224 x 3.
- The summary of the array shows that it contains numbers between zero and 255.

The following is the 224 x 224 color picture of a Norwich terrier dog. This can be obtained using a plot command:

The preceding image is a picture of a Norwich terrier dog sitting and looking forward. We will make use of this picture and check whether the RESNET50 model can accurately predict the type of dog in the picture.

A histogram that was developed from the values in the array is as follows:

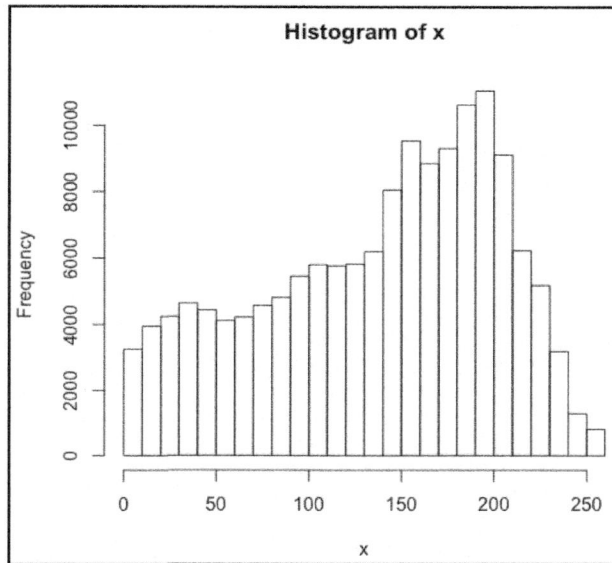

The preceding histogram of values in the array shows that the intensity values range from zero to 255, with most of the values concentrated around 200. Next, we will preprocess the image data. This histogram can be used to compare the resulting changes to the image data.

Preprocessing the input

We can now preprocess the input to prepare it so that it can be used with the pretrained RESNET50 model. The codes to preprocess the data are as follows:

```
# Preprocessing of input data
x <- array_reshape(x, c(1, dim(x)))
x <- imagenet_preprocess_input(x)
hist(x)
```

In the preceding code, we can observe the following:

- After applying the array_reshape() function, the dimensions of the array will change to 1 x 224 x 224 x 3.
- We used the imagnet_preprocess_input() function to prepare the data in the required format using the pretrained model.

A plot of the data in the form of a histogram after preprocessing is as follows:

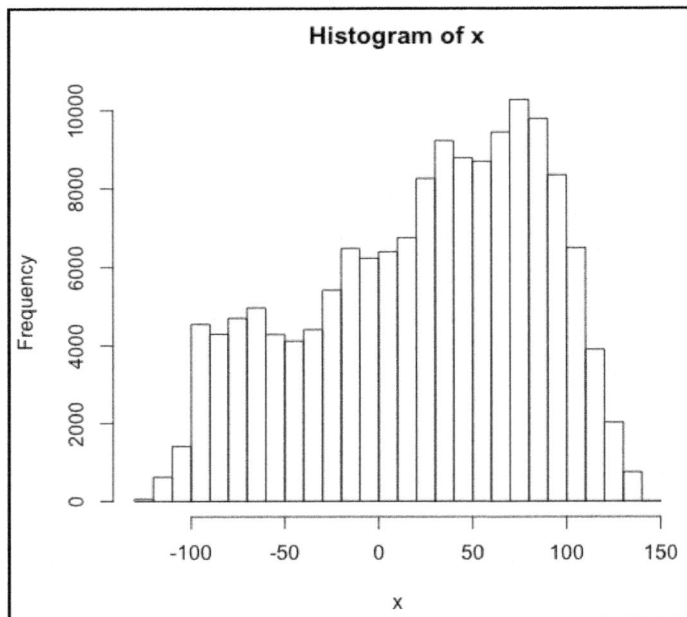

The histogram of values after preprocessing shows a shift in location. Most of the values are now concentrated between 50 and 100. However, there is no major change in the overall pattern of the histogram.

Top five categories

Now, we can use the pretrained model to make predictions by providing preprocessed image data as input. The code to achieve this is as follows:

```
# Predictions for top 5 categories
preds <- pretrained %>% predict(x)
imagenet_decode_predictions(preds, top = 5)[[1]]
Output
  class_name  class_description         score
1  n02094258      Norwich_terrier  0.769952953
2  n02094114      Norfolk_terrier  0.126662806
3  n02096294  Australian_terrier  0.046003290
4  n02096177                 cairn  0.040896162
5  n02093991        Irish_terrier  0.005021056
```

In the preceding code, we can observe the following:

- The predictions are made using the `predict` function and contain probabilities for 1,000 different categories, out of which the top five categories with the highest probabilities are obtained using the `imagenet_decode_predictions()` function.
- The highest score of about 0.7699 correctly identifies that the picture is of a Norwich terrier dog.
- The second highest score is for the Norfolk terrier dog, which looks very similar to the Norwich terrier dog.
- The predictions also suggest that the picture could be of another type of terrier dog; however, those probabilities are relatively small or negligible.

In the next section, we will look at a larger image dataset instead of a single image and use a pretrained network to develop an image classification model.

Working with the CIFAR10 dataset

For illustrating the use of pretrained models with new data, we will make use of the CIFAR10 dataset. CIFAR stands for *Canadian Institute For Advanced Research*, and 10 refers to the 10 categories of images that are contained in the data. The CIFAR10 dataset is part of the Keras library and the code for obtaining it is as follows:

```
# CIFAR10 data
data <- dataset_cifar10()
str(data)
OUTPUT
List of 2
 $ train:List of 2
  ..$ x: int [1:50000, 1:32, 1:32, 1:3] 59 154 255 28 170 159 164 28 134
125 ...
  ..$ y: int [1:50000, 1] 6 9 9 4 1 1 2 7 8 3 ...
 $ test :List of 2
  ..$ x: int [1:10000, 1:32, 1:32, 1:3] 158 235 158 155 65 179 160 83 23
217 ...
  ..$ y: num [1:10000, 1] 3 8 8 0 6 6 1 6 3 1 ...
```

In the preceding code, we can observe the following:

- We can read the dataset using the `dataset_cifar10()` function.
- The structure of the data shows that there are 50,000 training images available with labels.
- It also contains 10,000 test images with labels.

Next, we will extract the train and test data from CIFAR10 using the following code:

```
# Partitioning the data into train and test
trainx <- data$train$x
testx <- data$test$x
trainy <- to_categorical(data$train$y, num_classes = 10)
testy <- to_categorical(data$test$y, num_classes = 10)

table(data$train$y)
OUTPUT
   0    1    2    3    4    5    6    7    8    9
5000 5000 5000 5000 5000 5000 5000 5000 5000 5000

table(data$test$y)
OUTPUT
   0    1    2    3    4    5    6    7    8    9
1000 1000 1000 1000 1000 1000 1000 1000 1000 1000
```

From the preceding code, we can observe the following:

- We saved the training image data in `trainx` and the test image data in `testx`.
- We also carry out one-hot encoding of the train and test data labels using the `to_categorical()` function and save the results in `trainy` and `testy`, respectively.
- The table for the training data indicates that the images are classified in 10 different categories, with each category containing exactly 5,000 images.
- Similarly, the test data contains exactly 1,000 images for each of the 10 categories.

As an example, the labels for the first 64 images in the training data can be obtained using the following code:

```
# Category Labels
data$train$y[1:64,]
 [1] 6 9 9 4 1 1 2 7 8 3 4 7 7 2 9 9 9 3 2 6 4 3 6 6 2 6 3 5 4 0 0 9 1
[34] 3 4 0 3 7 3 3 5 2 2 7 1 1 1 2 2 0 9 5 7 9 2 2 5 2 4 3 1 1 8 2
```

As we can see, each picture is labeled using a number between 0 and 9. A description of the 10 different categories of images can be seen in the following table:

Label	Description
0	Airplane
1	Automobile
2	Bird
3	Cat
4	Deer
5	Dog
6	Frog
7	Horse
8	Ship
9	Truck

Note that there is no overlap between these 10 categories. For example, the automobile category refers to cars and SUVs, whereas the truck category only refers to large trucks.

Sample images

The first 64 images from the training data of CIFAR10 can be plotted using the following code. Doing this, we can get a glimpse of the type of images contained in the dataset:

```
# Plot of first 64 pictures
par(mfrow = c(8,8), mar = rep(0, 4))
for (i in 1:64) plot(as.raster(trainx[i,,], max = 255))
par(mfrow = c(1,1))
```

The images from CIFAR10 are all 32 x 32 color images. The following plot shows 64 images in an 8 x 8 grid:

From the preceding images, we can see that these images come with various backgrounds and are of low resolution. In addition, sometimes, these images aren't completely visible, which makes image classification a challenging task.

Preprocessing and prediction

We can use the pretrained RESNET50 model to identify the second image in the training data. Note that, since this second image in the training data is 32 x 32 in size, whereas RESNET50 is trained on images that are 224 x 224 in size, we need to resize the image before applying the code that we have used earlier. The following code is used for identifying the image:

```
# Pre-processing and prediction
x <- resize(trainx[2,,,], w = 224, h = 224)
x <- array_reshape(x, c(1, dim(x)))
x <- imagenet_preprocess_input(x)
preds <- pretrained %>% predict(x)
imagenet_decode_predictions(preds, top = 5)[[1]]
OUTPUT
  class_name class_description        score
1  n03796401        moving_van 9.988740e-01
2  n04467665     trailer_truck 7.548324e-04
3  n03895866     passenger_car 2.044246e-04
4  n04612504              yawl 2.441246e-05
5  n04483307          trimaran 1.862814e-05
```

From the preceding code, we can observe that the top category with a score of 0.9988 is for a moving van. The scores for the other four categories are comparatively negligible.

Image classification with CNN

In this section, we will use a subset of the CIFAR10 dataset to develop a convolutional neural network-based image classification model and assess its classification performance.

Data preparation

We will keep the data size smaller by using only the first 2,000 images in the training and test data from CIFAR10. This will allow the image classification model to be run on a regular computer or laptop. We will also resize the training and test images from 32 x 32 dimensions to 224 x 224 dimensions to be able to compare classification performance with the pretrained model. The following code includes the necessary preprocessing that we went over earlier in this chapter:

```
# Selecting first 2000 images
trainx <- data$train$x[1:2000,,,]
testx <- data$test$x[1:2000,,,]
```

```
# One-hot encoding
trainy <- to_categorical(data$train$y[1:2000,], num_classes = 10)
testy <- to_categorical(data$test$y[1:2000,] , num_classes = 10)

# Resizing train images to 224x224
x <- array(rep(0, 2000 * 224 * 224 * 3), dim = c(2000, 224, 224, 3))
for (i in 1:2000) { x[i,,,] <- resize(trainx[i,,,], 224, 224)  }

# Plot of before/after resized image
par(mfrow = c(1,2), mar = rep(0, 4))
plot(as.raster(trainx[2,,,], max = 255))
plot(as.raster(x[2,,,], max = 255))
par(mfrow = c(1,1))

trainx <- imagenet_preprocess_input(x)

# Resizing test images to 224x224
x <- array(rep(0, 2000 * 224 * 224 * 3), dim = c(2000, 224, 224, 3))
for (i in 1:2000) { x[i,,,] <- resize(testx[i,,,], 224, 224)  }
testx <- imagenet_preprocess_input(x)
```

In the preceding code, while resizing dimensions from 32 x 32 to 224 x 224, we use bilinear interpolation, which is included as part of the EBImage package. Bilinear interpolation extends linear interpolation to two variables, which in this case is the height and width of an image. The effect of bilinear interpolation can be observed from the before and after images of the truck shown in the following image:

Here, we can see that the after image (second image) looks smoother as it contains more pixels compared to the original image (first image).

CNN model

We will start by using a not-so-deep convolutional neural network to develop an image classification model. We will use the following code for this:

```
# Model architecture
model <- keras_model_sequential()
model %>%
  layer_conv_2d(filters = 32, kernel_size = c(3,3), activation = 'relu',
              input_shape = c(224,224,3)) %>%
  layer_conv_2d(filters = 32, kernel_size = c(3,3), activation = 'relu')
%>%
  layer_max_pooling_2d(pool_size = c(2,2)) %>%
  layer_dropout(rate = 0.25) %>%
  layer_flatten() %>%
  layer_dense(units = 256, activation = 'relu') %>%
  layer_dropout(rate = 0.25) %>%
  layer_dense(units = 10, activation = 'softmax')
summary(model)
```

Layer (type)	Output Shape	Param #
conv2d_6 (Conv2D)	(None, 222, 222, 32)	896
conv2d_7 (Conv2D)	(None, 220, 220, 32)	9248
max_pooling2d_22 (MaxPooling2D)	(None, 110, 110, 32)	0
dropout_6 (Dropout)	(None, 110, 110, 32)	0
flatten_18 (Flatten)	(None, 387200)	0
dense_35 (Dense)	(None, 256)	99123456
dropout_7 (Dropout)	(None, 256)	0
dense_36 (Dense)	(None, 10)	2570

```
Total params: 99,136,170
Trainable params: 99,136,170
Non-trainable params: 0
```

```
# Compile
model %>% compile(loss = 'categorical_crossentropy',
  optimizer = 'rmsprop',
  metrics = 'accuracy')
```

```
# Fit
model_one <- model %>% fit(trainx,
                           trainy,
                           epochs = 10,
                           batch_size = 10,
                           validation_split = 0.2)
```

From the preceding code, we can observe the following:

- The total number of parameters in this network is 99,136,170.
- When compiling the model, we use `categorical_crossentropy` as the loss function since the response has 10 categories.
- For the optimizer, we specify `rmsprop`, which is a gradient-based optimization method and is a popular choice that provides reasonably good performance.
- We train the model with 10 epochs and with a batch size of 10.
- Out of 2,000 images in the training data, 20% (or 400 images) is used for assessing validation errors and the remaining 80% (or 1,600 images) is used for training.

A plot of the accuracy and loss values after training the model is as follows for `model_one`:

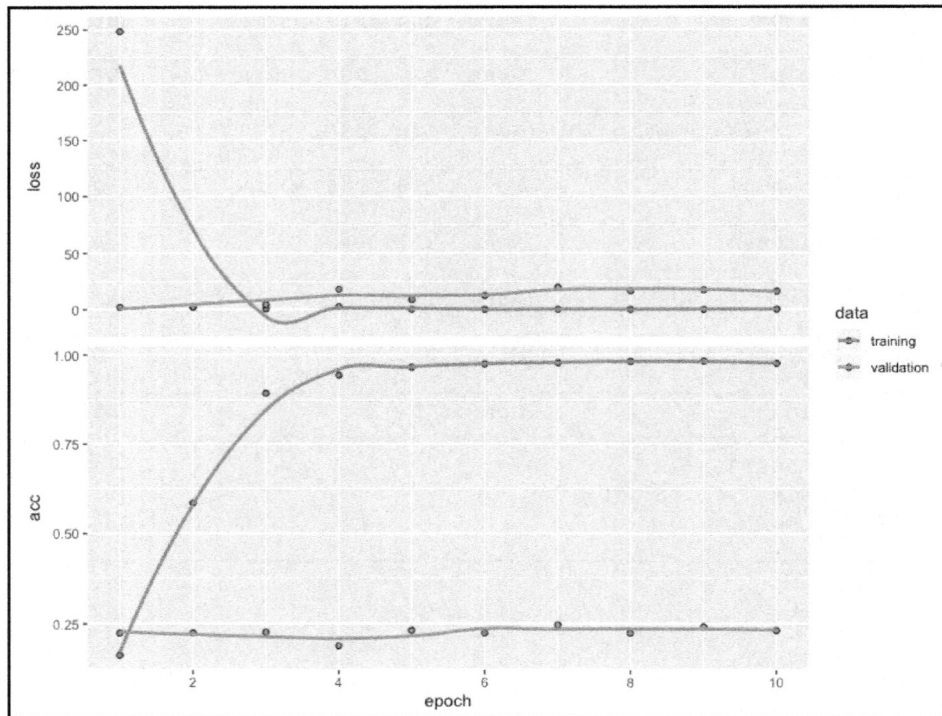

From the preceding plot, the following observations can be made:

- The plot of the accuracy and loss values shows that, after about 4 epochs, the loss and accuracy values for both training and validation data remain more or less constant.
- Although the accuracy for the training data reaches high values closer to 100%, there seems to be no impact on the accuracy based on the images in the validation data.
- In addition, the gap between the accuracy of the training and validation data seems to be high, suggesting the presence of overfitting. When assessing the model's performance, we expect to see low accuracy in terms of image classification by the model.

Note that developing a decent image classification model using CNN requires a large number of images for training, and therefore more time and resources. Later in this chapter, we will learn how to use pretrained networks to help us overcome this problem. For now, though, let's proceed by assessing the image classification model's performance.

Model performance

For assessing the model's performance, we will carry out calculations for the loss, accuracy, and confusion matrix for the training and test data.

Performance assessment with training data

The code for obtaining the loss, accuracy, and confusion matrix based on the training data is as follows:

```
# Loss and accuracy
model %>% evaluate(trainx, trainy)
$loss
[1] 3.335224
$acc
[1] 0.8455

# Confusion matrix
pred <- model %>%   predict_classes(trainx)
table(Predicted=pred, Actual=data$train$y[1:2000,])
         Actual
Predicted  0    1   2   3   4   5   6   7   8   9
        0 182   2   8   2   9   4   1   2  10   5
        1   1 176   3   5   6   5   2   3   4   7
```

```
2    1    0  167    4    3    4    3    2    0    1
3    0    0    0  157    2    1    1    2    1    0
4    2    1    5    6  167    4    2    1    0    0
5    2    0    4    4    3  149    3    4    4    3
6    1    1    3    6    5    2  173    5    0    0
7    3    2    4    2    4    3    9  166    0    1
8   10    1    7    1    6    4    2    2  173    5
9    0    8    2    8    9    7   11   12   11  181
```

Here, we can see that the loss and accuracy values for the training data are 3.335 and 0.846, respectively. The confusion matrix shows decent results based on the training data. However, for some types of images, misclassifications are high. For example, 12 images from category 7 (horse) are misclassified as category-9 (truck). Similarly, 11 images, each belonging to category-6 (frog) and category-8 (ship), are also misclassified as category-9 (truck).

Performance assessment with test data

The code for obtaining the loss, accuracy, and confusion matrix based on the test data is as follows:

```
# Loss and accuracy
model %>% evaluate(testx, testy)
$loss
[1] 16.4552
$acc
[1] 0.2325

# Confusion matrix
pred <- model %>% predict_classes(testx)
table(Predicted = pred, Actual = data$test$y[1:2000,])
         Actual
Predicted  0  1  2  3  4  5  6  7  8  9
        0 82 24 29 17 16 10 17 19 67 19
        1 16 65 20 26 18 21 26 26 33 53
        2 10  0 26 20 20 18 14  5  1  2
        3  6  5  8 21 12 22  9 12  9  3
        4  4  8 22 11 22 16 25  9  6  4
        5  5  7 12 29 17 29  9 19  4  9
        6  6  6 20 17 23 15 51 25  6 13
        7  3 10 10 15 21 16 11 37  3  5
        8 34 22 20 12 22  2  7  7 61 24
        9 30 51 28 31 27 36 47 34 27 71
```

From the preceding output, the following observations can be made:

- The loss and accuracy values for the test data are 16.456 and 0.232, respectively.
- These results are not as impressive as what we observed for the training data due to the overfitting problem.

Although we can try and develop a deeper network in an effort to improve image classification results or to try and increase training data to provide more samples to learn from, here, we will make use of pretrained networks to obtain better results.

Classifying images using the pretrained RESNET50 model

In this section, we will make use of the pretrained RESNET50 model to develop an image classification model. We will use the same training and test data that we used in the previous section to make comparing classification performance easier.

Model architecture

We will upload the RESNET50 model without including the top layer. This will help us customize the pretrained model for use with CIFAR10 data. Since the RESNET50 model is trained with the help of over 1 million images, it captures useful features and representations of images that can be reused with new but similar and smaller data. This reusability aspect of pretrained models not only helps to reduce the time and cost of developing an image classification model from scratch, but is especially useful when the training data is relatively small.

The code that's used for developing the model is as follows:

```
# RESNET50 network without the top layer
pretrained <- application_resnet50(weights = "imagenet",
                                    include_top = FALSE,
                                    input_shape = c(224, 224, 3))

model <- keras_model_sequential() %>%
        pretrained %>%
        layer_flatten() %>%
        layer_dense(units = 256, activation = "relu") %>%
        layer_dense(units = 10, activation = "softmax")
summary(model)
```

Layer (type)	Output Shape	Param #
resnet50 (Model)	(None, 7, 7, 2048)	23587712
flatten_6 (Flatten)	(None, 100352)	0
dense_12 (Dense)	(None, 256)	25690368
dense_13 (Dense)	(None, 10)	2570

Total params: 49,280,650
Trainable params: 49,227,530
Non-trainable params: 53,120

When uploading the RESNET50 model, the input dimensions for the data based on color images are specified as 224 x 224 x 3. Although smaller dimensions will work too, image dimensions cannot be less than 32 x 32 x 3. Images in the CIFAR10 dataset have dimensions of 32 x 32 x 3, but we have resized them to 224 x 224 x 3 as it gives us better image classification accuracy.

From the preceding summary, we can observe the following:

- The output dimensions from the RESNET50 network are 7 x 7 x 2,048.
- We use a flattened layer to change the output shape to a single column with 7 x 7 x 2,048 = 100,352 elements.
- A dense layer with 256 units and a `relu` activation function is added.
- This dense layer leads to (100,353 x 256) + 256 = 25,690,368 parameters.
- The last dense layer has 10 units for images with 10 categories and a `softmax` activation function. This network has a total of 49,280,650 parameters.
- Out of the total parameters in the network, 49,227,530 are trainable parameters.

Although we can train the network with all of these parameters, this is not advisable. Training and updating parameters related to the RESNET50 network will cause us to lose the benefits that we would get as a result of the features that have been learned from over 1 million images. We are only using data from 2,000 images for training and have 10 different categories. So, for each category, we only have approximately 200 images. Therefore, it is important to freeze the weights in the RESNET50 network, which will allow us to obtain the benefits of using a pretrained network.

Freezing pretrained network weights

The code for freezing the weights of the RESNET50 network and then compiling the model is as follows:

```
# Freeze weights of resnet50 network
freeze_weights(pretrained)

# Compile
model %>% compile(loss = 'categorical_crossentropy',
 optimizer = 'rmsprop',
 metrics = 'accuracy')

summary(model)
```

```
Layer (type) Output Shape Param #
=====================================================
resnet50 (Model) (None, 7, 7, 2048) 23587712

flatten_6 (Flatten) (None, 100352) 0

dense_12 (Dense) (None, 256) 25690368

dense_13 (Dense) (None, 10) 2570
=====================================================
Total params: 49,280,650
Trainable params: 25,692,938
Non-trainable params: 23,587,712
```

In the preceding code, we can observe the following:

- To freeze the weights in the RESNET50 network, we use the `freeze_weights()` function.
- Note that after freezing the pretrained network weights, the model needs to be compiled.
- After freezing the weights of the RESNET50 network, we observe that the number of trainable parameters goes down from 49,227,530 to a lower value of 25,692,938.
- These parameters belong to the two dense layers that we added and will help us customize the results from the RESNET50 network so that we can apply them to the images from the CIFAR10 data that we are using.

Fitting the model

The code for fitting the model is as follows:

```
# Fit model
model_two <- model %>% fit(trainx,
                          trainy,
                          epochs = 10,
                          batch_size = 10,
                          validation_split = 0.2)
```

From the preceding code, we can observe the following:

- We train the network with 10 epochs and with a batch size of 10.
- We specify 20% (or 400 images) to be used for assessing the validation loss and validation accuracy, and the remaining 80% (or 1,600 images) for training.

The plot of the accuracy and loss values after training the model is as follows:

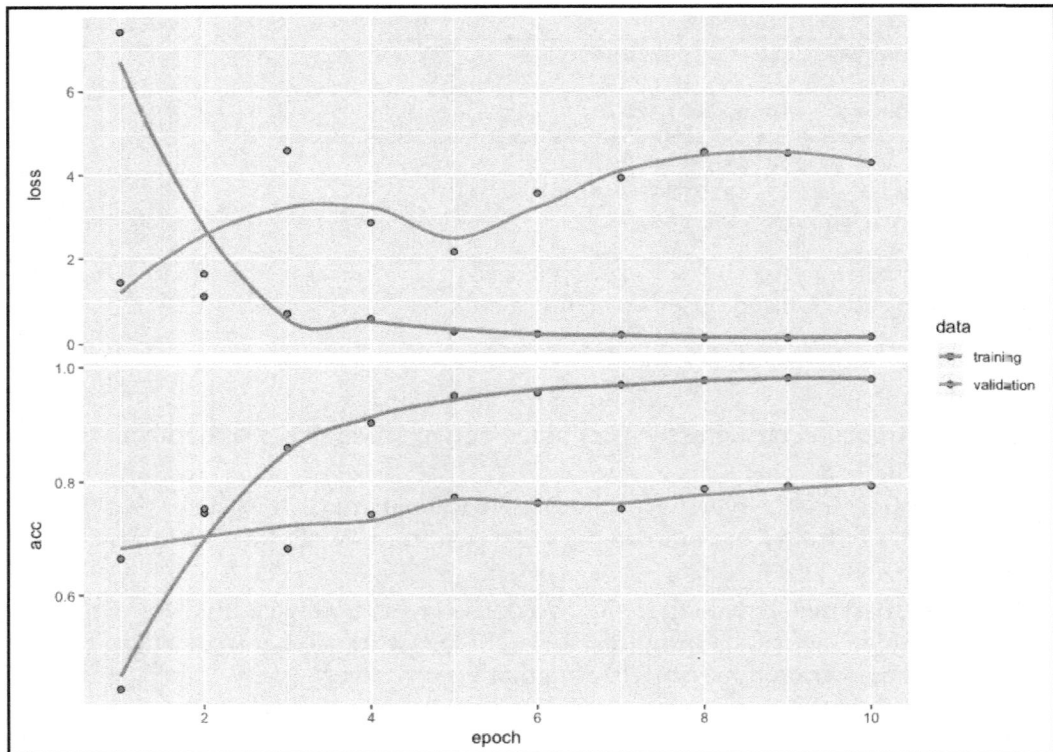

From the plot for the loss and accuracy values, we can make the following observations:

- There is an important difference compared to the previous plot, where the pretrained model wasn't used. This plot shows us that the model reaches an accuracy of over 60% by the second epoch itself compared to the previous plot, where it remained below 25%. Thus, we can see that the use of a pretrained model has an immediate impact on image classification.
- The improvements based on validation data are slow compared to those for the training data.
- Although the accuracy values based on the validation data show gradual improvement, the loss values for the validation data show more variability.

In the next section, we will evaluate the model and assess its prediction performance.

Model evaluation and prediction

Now, we will evaluate the performance of this model for the training and test data. Calculations relating to the loss, accuracy, and confusion matrix will be carried out so that we can evaluate the model image's classification performance. We will also obtain the accuracy for each of the 10 categories.

Loss, accuracy, and confusion matrix with the training data

The code for obtaining the loss, accuracy, and confusion matrix for the training data is as follows:

```
# Loss and accuracy
model %>% evaluate(trainx, trainy)
$loss
[1] 1.954347
$acc
[1] 0.8785

# Confusion matrix
pred <- model %>%   predict_classes(trainx)
table(Predicted=pred, Actual=data$train$y[1:2000,])
        Actual
Predicted   0   1   2   3   4   5   6   7   8   9
        0 182   0   5   2   3   0   2   0  10   1
        1   1 156   1   1   1   0   2   0   4   0
```

```
          2   2   0 172   3   4   0   4   0   1   0
          3   0   0   1 133   2  12   2   1   0   0
          4   1   0   8   4 188   3   4   2   0   0
          5   1   0   4  22   3 162   1   3   0   0
          6   0   0   3   9   3   0 192   1   1   0
          7   3   0   5  10  10   5   0 188   0   0
          8   5   0   3   3   0   1   0   1 182   0
          9   7  35   1   8   0   0   0   3   5 202
```

```
# Accuracy for each category
100*diag(tab)/colSums(tab)
       0        1        2        3        4
90.09901 81.67539 84.72906 68.20513 87.85047
       5        6        7        8        9
88.52459 92.75362 94.47236 89.65517 99.50739
```

From the preceding output, we can make the following observations:

- The loss and accuracy based on the training data are 1.954 and 0.879, respectively.
- Both of these numbers are an improvement over the corresponding results based on the previous model.
- The confusion matrix shows a decent image classification performance.
- The best image classification performance is seen for category 9 (truck), where only one image is misclassified as category-0 (airplane) and provides an accuracy of 99.5%.
- This model is the most confused regarding category-3 (cat), which is mostly classified as category-5 (dog) or category-7 (horse) and provides an accuracy of only 68.2% for this category.
- Among the misclassifications, the highest case (35 images) is when category-1 (automobile) is misclassified as category-9 (truck).

Next, we will assess the model's performance using the test data.

Loss, accuracy, and confusion matrix with the test data

The code for obtaining the loss, accuracy, and confusion matrix for the test data is as follows:

```
# Loss and accuracy
model %>% evaluate(testx, testy)
$loss
[1] 4.437256
$acc
[1] 0.768

# Confusion matrix
pred <- model %>% predict_classes(testx)
table(Predicted = pred, Actual = data$test$y[1:2000,])
         Actual
Predicted   0   1   2   3   4   5   6   7   8   9
        0 158   1  12   0   5   1   6   2  15   0
        1   3 142   0   2   0   2   3   1   9   2
        2   2   0 139   8   6   3   6   0   0   0
        3   0   0   3  86   5  13   6   1   0   0
        4   4   0  14   6 138   5  10   4   1   0
        5   0   0  15  47   6 148   2  12   0   0
        6   0   0   4  12   9   3 178   0   0   0
        7   2   0   4  23  27   9   3 169   0   0
        8  13   1   1   5   1   0   0   0 179   2
        9  14  54   3  10   1   1   2   4  13 199

# Accuracy for each category
100*diag(tab)/colSums(tab)
       0        1        2        3        4
80.61224 71.71717 71.28205 43.21608 69.69697
       5        6        7        8        9
80.00000 82.40741 87.56477 82.48848 98.02956
```

From the preceding output, we can make the following observations:

- The loss and accuracy based on the test data are 4.437 and 0.768, respectively.
- Although this performance based on the test data is inferior to the results based on the training data, it is a significant improvement over the results from the first model.

- The confusion matrix provides further insights into the model's performance. The best performance is for category 9 (truck), with 199 correct classifications and an accuracy of 98%.
- For the test data, the model seems to be the most confused regarding category-3 (cat), which has the most misclassifications. The accuracy of this category can be as low as 43.2%.
- The highest misclassification for a single category (54 images) is for category-1 (automobile), which is misclassified as category-9 (truck).

With 76.8% accuracy, we can say that this image classification performance is decent. The use of a pretrained model has allowed us to transfer our learning of a model trained on data involving over 1 million images to new data containing 2,000 images from the CIFAR10 dataset. This is a huge advantage compared to building an image classification model totally from scratch, which would involve more time and computing costs. Now that we've achieved a decent performance from the model, we can explore how to improve this even further.

Performance optimization tips and best practices

To explore further image classification improvement, in this section, we will try three experiments. In the first experiment, we will mainly use the `adam` optimizer when compiling the model. In the second experiment, we will carry out hyperparameter tuning by varying the number of units in the dense layer, the dropout percentage in the dropout layer, and the batch size when fitting the model. Finally, in the third experiment, we will work with another pretrained network called VGG16.

Experimenting with the adam optimizer

In this first experiment, we will use the `adam` optimizer when compiling the model. At the time of training the model, we will also increase the number of epochs to 20.

The plot of the accuracy and loss values after training the model is as follows:

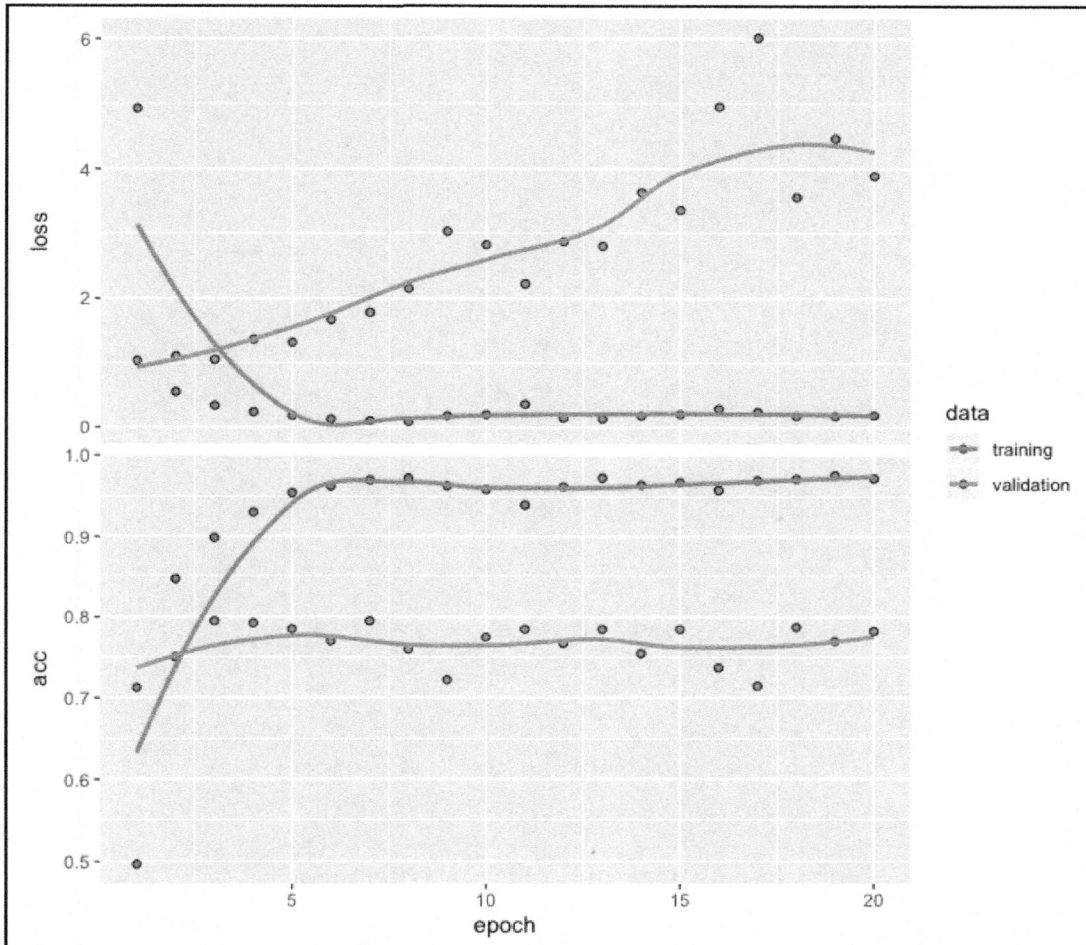

The preceding loss and accuracy plot for this model shows that the values related to the training data are flat after about six epochs. For the validation data, the loss values show a gradual increase, whereas the accuracy values are flat after the third epoch.

The code for obtaining the loss, accuracy, and confusion matrix for the test data is as follows:

```
# Loss and accuracy
model %>% evaluate(testx, testy)
$loss
[1] 4.005393
$acc
[1] 0.7715

# Confusion matrix
pred <- model %>% predict_classes(testx)
table(Predicted = pred, Actual = data$test$y[1:2000,])
          Actual
Predicted   0   1   2   3   4   5   6   7   8   9
        0 136   0  20   4   2   0   1   5   2   4
        1   3 177   1   1   0   0   0   0   2  26
        2   7   0 124   2   3   1   3   0   1   0
        3   2   0   4  80   7   6   7   2   1   0
        4   3   1  18   9 151   4   8   9   0   0
        5   2   0   3  58   3 152   4   5   0   3
        6   3   2   8  22   8   8 190   0   6   2
        7   1   0  14  18  22  14   2 172   0   0
        8  36  11   3   5   2   0   1   0 205  12
        9   3   7   0   0   0   0   0   0   0 156

# Accuracy for each category
100*diag(tab)/colSums(tab)
       0        1        2        3        4
69.38776 89.39394 63.58974 40.20101 76.26263
       5        6        7        8        9
82.16216 87.96296 89.11917 94.47005 76.84729
```

From the preceding output, we can make the following observations:

- The loss and accuracy of the test data are 4.005 and 0.772, respectively.
- These results are marginally better than they are for model_two.

- The confusion matrix shows a somewhat different image classification pattern compared to the previous model.
- The best classification results are obtained for category 8 (ship), with 205 correct image classifications out of 217 (94.5% accuracy).
- The lowest classification performance is for category 3 (cat), with 80 correct predictions out of 199 (40.2% accuracy).
- The worst misclassification is of 58 images from category 3 (cat) when they are misclassified as category-5 (dog).

Next, we will carry out an experiment with hyperparameter tuning.

Hyperparameter tuning

In this experiment, we will vary the units in the dense layer, the dropout rate, and the batch size to obtain values that help us improve classification performance. This also illustrates an efficient way of obtaining suitable parameter values through experimentation. We will start by creating a `TransferLearning.R` file using the following code:

```
# Model with RESNET50
pretrained <- application_resnet50(weights = 'imagenet',
                                   include_top = FALSE,
                                   input_shape = c(224, 224, 3))
# Flags for hyperparameter tuning
FLAGS <- flags(flag_integer("dense_units", 256),
               flag_numeric("dropout", 0.1),
               flag_integer("batch_size", 10))

# Model architecture
model <- keras_model_sequential() %>%
        pretrained %>%
        layer_flatten() %>%
        layer_dense(units = FLAGS$dense_units, activation = 'relu') %>%
        layer_dropout(rate = FLAGS$dropout) %>%
        layer_dense(units = 10, activation = 'softmax')
freeze_weights(pretrained)

# Compile
model %>% compile(loss = "categorical_crossentropy",
                  optimizer = 'adam',
                  metrics = 'accuracy')

# Fit model
history <- model %>% fit(trainx,
                         trainy,
```

```
                                    epochs = 5,
                                    batch_size = FLAGS$batch_size,
                                    validation_split = 0.2)
```

In the preceding code, after reading the pretrained model, we declare three flags for the parameters that we want to experiment with. Now, we can use these flags in the model architecture (dense units and dropout rate) and in the code for fitting the model (batch size). We have reduced the number of epochs to five and for the optimizer, while compiling the model, we retain `adam`. We will save this R file, which we'll call `TransferLearning.R`, on the desktop of our computer.

The code for running this experiment is as follows:

```
# Set working directory
setwd('~/Desktop')

# Hyperparameter tuning
library(tfruns)
runs <- tuning_run("TransferLearning.R",
                   flags = list(dense_units = c(256, 512),
                                dropout = c(0.1,0.3),
                                batch_size = c(10, 30)))
```

In the preceding code, we can see that the working directory is set at the location of the `TransferLearning.R` file. Note that the output from this experiment will be saved in this directory too. For running the hyperparameter tuning experiment, we will use the `tfruns` library. For the number of units in the dense layer, we will try 256 and 512 as the values. For the dropout rate, we will experiment with 0.1 and 0.3. Finally, for the batch size, we will try 10 and 30. With three parameters, each being tried at two values, the total number of experimental runs will be $2^3 = 8$.

An extract from the results that were obtained from this experiment is as follows:

```
# Results
runs[,c(6:10)]
Data frame: 8 x 5

  metric_val_loss metric_val_acc flag_dense_units flag_dropout
flag_batch_size
1          1.1935         0.7525              512          0.3
30
2          0.9521         0.7725              256          0.3
30
3          1.1260         0.8200              512          0.1
30
4          1.3276         0.7950              256          0.1
```

30				
5	1.1435	0.7700	512	0.3
10				
6	1.3096	0.7275	256	0.3
10				
7	1.3458	0.7850	512	0.1
10				
8	1.0248	0.7950	256	0.1
10				

The preceding output shows the loss and accuracy values based on the validation data for all eight experimental runs. For easy reference, it also includes parameter values. We can make the following observations from the preceding output:

- The highest accuracy value (row 3) is obtained when the number of dense units is 512, the dropout rate is 0.1, and the batch size is 30.
- On the other hand, the lowest accuracy value (row 6) is obtained when the number of dense units is 256, the dropout rate is 0.3, and the batch size is 10.

The code for obtaining the loss, accuracy, and confusion matrix using the test data for row 3 of the experiment is as follows:

```
# Loss and accuracy
model %>% evaluate(testx, testy)
$loss
[1] 1.095251
$acc
[1] 0.7975

# Confusion matrix
pred <- model %>% predict_classes(testx)
(tab <- table(Predicted = pred, Actual = data$test$y[1:2000,]))
          Actual
Predicted   0   1   2   3   4   5   6   7   8   9
        0 167   5  20   4   5   4   4  15  10   8
        1   1 176   0   3   0   0   1   1   2  15
        2   3   0 139   9   2   4   8   1   1   0
        3   0   0   3  92   6   6   5   0   0   0
        4   4   0  20  16 177  12  17  23   0   1
        5   0   0   7  50   1 149   1   9   0   0
        6   1   0   2  11   2   5 177   1   0   1
        7   0   0   0   5   3   4   1 143   0   0
        8  16   3   3   5   2   0   1   0 203   6
        9   4  14   1   4   0   1   1   0   1 172

# Accuracy for each category
100*diag(tab)/colSums(tab)
```

```
         0         1         2         3         4         5         6         7
 85.20408 88.88889 71.28205 46.23116 89.39394 80.54054 81.94444 74.09326
         8         9
 93.54839 84.72906
```

From the preceding results, we can make the following observations:

- Both the loss and accuracy values for the test data are better than the results we've obtained so far.
- The best classification results are obtained for category 8 (ship), with 203 correct image classifications out of 217 (93.5% accuracy).
- The lowest classification performance is for category 3 (cat), with 92 correct predictions out of 199 (46.2% accuracy).
- The worst misclassification is of 50 images from category 3 (cat) when they are misclassified as category-5 (dog).

In the next experiment, we will use another pretrained network: VGG16.

Experimenting with VGG16 as a pretrained network

In this experiment, we will use a pretrained network called VGG16. VGG16 is a convolutional neural network that is 16 layers deep and can classify images into thousands of categories. This network is also trained using over 1 million images from the ImageNet database. The code for the model's architecture and compiling and then fitting the model is as follows:

```
# Pretrained model
pretrained <- application_vgg16(weights = 'imagenet',
                        include_top = FALSE,
                        input_shape = c(224, 224, 3))

# Model architecture
model <- keras_model_sequential() %>%
  pretrained %>%
  layer_flatten() %>%
  layer_dense(units = 256, activation = "relu") %>%
  layer_dense(units = 10, activation = "softmax")
summary(model)

freeze_weights(pretrained)
summary(model)
```

Layer (type)	Output Shape	Param #
vgg16 (Model)	(None, 7, 7, 512)	14714688
flatten (Flatten)	(None, 25088)	0
dense (Dense)	(None, 256)	6422784
dense_1 (Dense)	(None, 10)	2570

```
Total params: 21,140,042
Trainable params: 6,425,354
Non-trainable params: 14,714,688
```

```
# Compile model
model %>% compile(loss = 'categorical_crossentropy',
                  optimizer = 'adam',
                  metrics = 'accuracy')

# Fit model
model_four <- model %>% fit(trainx,
                            trainy,
                            epochs = 10,
                            batch_size = 10,
                            validation_split = 0.2)
```

From the preceding summary, we can observe the following:

- This model has 21,140,042 parameters, which, after freezing the weights of VGG16, goes down to a total of 6,425,354 trainable parameters.
- When compiling the model, we retain the use of the adam optimizer.
- In addition, we run 10 epochs to train the model. All the other settings are the same ones that we used for the previous models.

A plot of the accuracy and loss values after training the model is as follows:

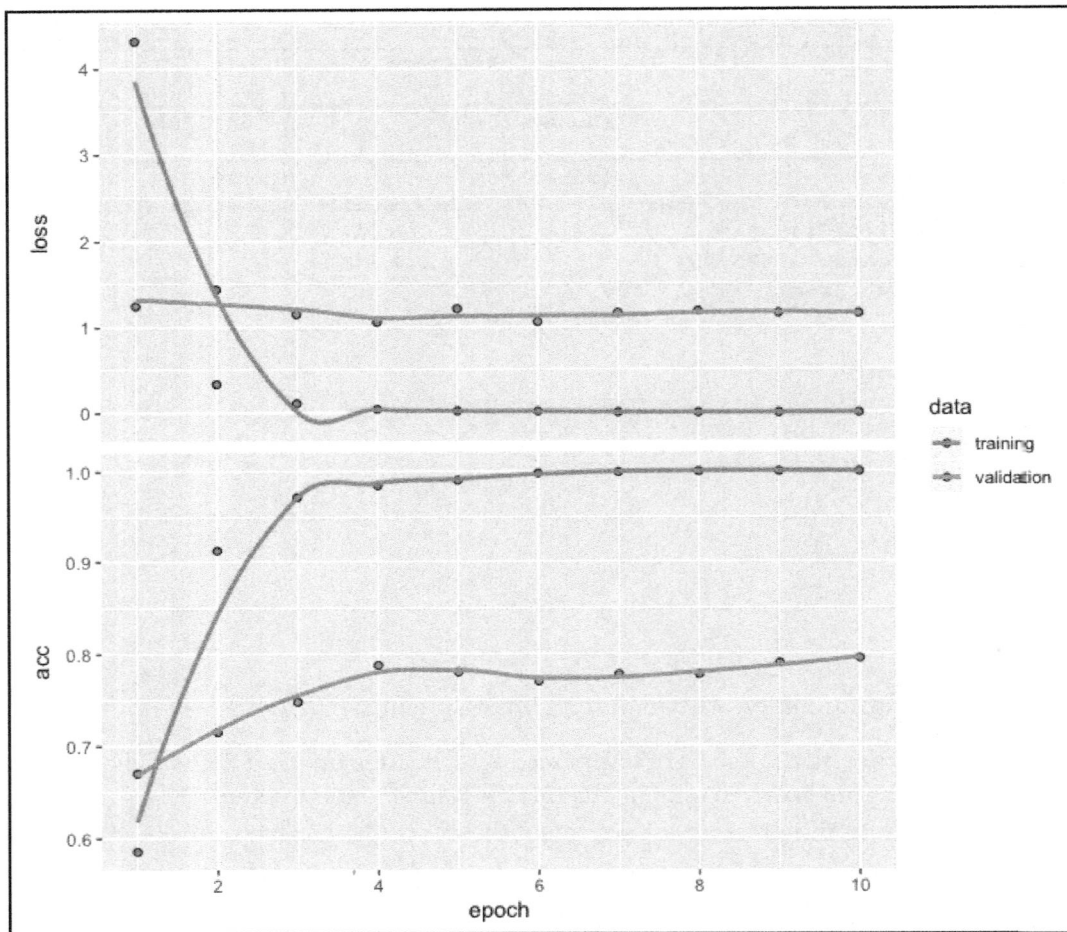

The preceding loss and accuracy plot for the training and validation data indicates that, after about four epochs, the model performance remains flat. This is in contrast to the previous model, where the loss values for the validation data showed a gradual increase.

The code for obtaining the loss, accuracy, and confusion matrix for the test data is as follows:

```
# Loss and accuracy
model %>% evaluate(testx, testy)
$loss
 [1] 1.673867
```

```
$acc
 [1] 0.7565

# Confusion matrix
pred <- model %>% predict_classes(testx)
(tab <- table(Predicted = pred, Actual = data$test$y[1:2000,]))
         Actual
Predicted   0   1   2   3   4   5   6   7   8   9
        0 137   2  12   0   6   0   0   1  11   6
        1   9 172   1   0   0   0   0   1   9  21
        2   7   0 123  11  11   3   3   5   3   0
        3   3   0  11 130  10  35   7   7   0   0
        4   7   0  13   5 118   7  10   5   1   0
        5   1   0  11  27   3 125   2   7   0   0
        6   2   5  20  18  21   8 192   3   4   1
        7   6   0   4   6  25   7   2 163   2   1
        8  18   6   0   2   4   0   0   1 182   3
        9   6  13   0   0   0   0   0   0   5 171

# Accuracy for each category
100*diag(tab)/colSums(tab)
        0        1        2        3        4
69.39796 86.86869 63.07692 65.32663 59.59596
        5        6        7        8        9
67.56757 88.88889 84.45596 83.87097 84.23645
```

From the preceding output, we can make the following observations:

- The loss and accuracy of the test data are 1.674 and 0.757, respectively.
- The confusion matrix provides further insights. This model has the best classification accuracy of 88.9% when classifying category 6 (frog).
- On the other hand, the accuracy when classifying category 4 (deer) images is only about 59.6%.

In this section, we experimented with three situations:

- The use of the adam optimizer improved the results a little bit and provided test data accuracy of about 77.2%.
- In the second experiment, hyperparameter tuning provided the best results for the number of dense units at 512, a dropout rate at 0.1, and a batch size at 30. This combination of parameters helped us obtain a test data accuracy of about 79.8%.
- The third experiment, where we used the VGG16 pretrained network, also provided decent results. However, it provided test data accuracy of slightly lower than 75.7%.

Another approach when working with smaller datasets is to use data augmentation. In this approach, the existing images are modified (by flipping, rotation, shifting, and so on) to create new samples. Since images in image datasets aren't always centered, such artificially created new samples help us to learn about useful features that, in turn, improve image classification performance.

Summary

In this chapter, we illustrated the use of pretrained deep neural networks for developing image classification models. Such pretrained networks, which are trained using over 1 million images, capture reusable features that can be applied to similar but new data This aspect becomes valuable when developing image classification models with relatively smaller datasets. In addition, they provide savings in terms of the use of computational resources and time. We started by making use of the RESNET50 pretrained network to identify an image of a Norwich terrier dog. Subsequently, we made use of 2,000 images from the CIFAR10 dataset to illustrate the usefulness of applying pretrained networks to a relatively smaller dataset. The initial convolutional neural networks model that we built from scratch suffered from overfitting and did not yield useful results.

Next, we used the pretrained RESNET50 network and customized it to suit our needs by adding two dense layers on top of the pretrained network. We obtained decent results, with a test data accuracy of about 76.8%. Although pretrained models can provide faster results that require fewer epochs, we need to explore improvements that we can make to the model's performance with the help of some experimentation. In an effort to explore better results, we experimented with the `adam` optimizer, which yielded test data accuracy of about 77.2%. We also carried out hyperparameter tuning, which yielded the best levels in terms of the number of units in the dense layer, which was 512, the dropout rate in the dropout layer, which was 0.1, and the batch size at the time of fitting the model, which was 30. The image classification accuracy with this combination yielded a test data accuracy of about 79.8%. Finally, we experimented with the pretrained VGG16 network, where we obtained test data accuracy of about 75.6%. These experiments illustrated how we can explore and improve model performance.

In the next chapter, we will explore another interesting and popular class of deep networks, called **generative adversarial networks (GANs)**. We will make use of GANs to create new images.

8
Creating New Images Using Generative Adversarial Networks

This chapter illustrates the application of **generative adversarial networks** (**GANs**) for generating new images using a practical example. So far in this book, using image data, we have illustrated the use of deep networks for image classification tasks. However, in this chapter, we will explore an interesting and popular approach that helps create new images. Generative adversarial networks have been applied for generating new images, improving image quality, and generating new text and new music. Another interesting application of GANs is in the area of anomaly detection. Here, a GAN is trained to generate data that is considered normal. When this network is used for reconstructing data that is considered not normal or anomalous, the differences in results can help us detect the presence of an anomaly. We will look at an example of generating new images in this chapter.

More specifically, in this chapter, we will cover the following topics:

- Generative adversarial network overview
- Processing MNIST image data
- Developing the generator network
- Developing the discriminator network
- Training the network
- Reviewing results
- Performance optimization tips and best practices

Generative adversarial network overview

GANs make use of two networks:

- Generator network
- Discriminator network

For the generator network, noisy data, which is usually random numbers that have been generated from a standard normal distribution are provided as input. A flow chart showing an overview of a generative adversarial network is as follows:

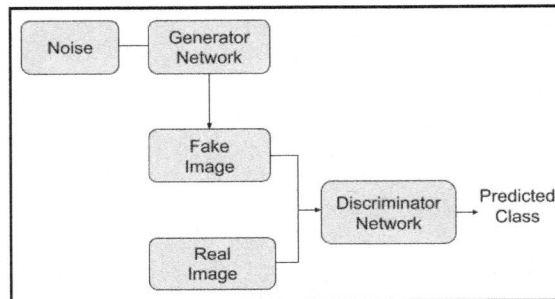

As indicated in the preceding flowchart, the generator network uses noisy data as input and tries to create an image that we can label as fake. These fake images, along with the labels representing them as fake, are provided as input to the discriminator network. Along with the labeled fake images, we can also provide real images with labels as input to the discriminator network.

During the training process, the discriminator network tries to differentiate between a fake image created by the generator network and a real image. While developing a generative adversarial network, this process continues so that a generator network tries its best to generate an image that a discriminator network cannot classify as fake. At the same time, the discriminator network gets better and better at correctly discriminating between a fake and a real image.

Success is achieved when the generator network learns to consistently produce images that are not available in the training data and the discriminator network is unable to classify them as fake. For the real images in this chapter, we will make use of MNIST train data that contains images of handwritten digits.

In the upcoming sections, we will illustrate the steps we need to follow in order to develop a generative adversarial network for the handwritten digit five, which is available in the MNIST data.

Processing MNIST image data

In this section, will use the Keras library, which also includes MNIST data. We will also make use of the EBImage library, which is useful for processing image data. MNIST data contains handwritten images from 0 to 9. Let's take a look at the following code to understand this data:

```
# Libraries and MNIST data
library(keras)
library(EBImage)
mnist <- dataset_mnist()
str(mnist)
List of 2
 $ train:List of 2
 ..$ x: int [1:60000, 1:28, 1:28] 0 0 0 0 0 0 0 0 0 0 ...
 ..$ y: int [1:60000(1d)] 5 0 4 1 9 2 1 3 1 4 ...
 $ test :List of 2
 ..$ x: int [1:10000, 1:28, 1:28] 0 0 0 0 0 0 0 0 0 0 ...
 ..$ y: int [1:10000(1d)] 7 2 1 0 4 1 4 9 5 9 ...
```

From the preceding code, we can make the following observations:

- Looking at the structure of this data, we can see that there are 60,000 images in the training data and 10,000 images in the test data.
- These handwritten images are 28 x 28 in size and are black and white in color. This means that there's one channel.

In this chapter, we will only make use of digit five from the training data for training the generative adversarial network and for generating new images of digit five.

Digit five from the training data

Although a generative adversarial network can be developed to generate all 10 digits, for someone just getting started, it is advisable to get started with just one digit. Let's take a look at the following code:

```
# Data on digit five
c(c(trainx, trainy), c(testx, testy)) %<-% mnist
trainx <- trainx[trainy==5,,]
str(trainx)
 int [1:5421, 1:28, 1:28] 0 0 0 0 0 0 0 0 0 0 ...
summary(trainx)
   Min. 1st Qu.  Median    Mean 3rd Qu.    Max.
   0.00    0.00    0.00   33.32    0.00  255.00
```

```
par(mfrow = c(8,8), mar = rep(0, 4))
for (i in 1:64) plot(as.raster(trainx[i,,], max = 255))
par(mfrow = c(1,1))
```

As seen in the preceding code, we are selecting images that contain digit five and are saving them in `trainx`. The structure of `trainx` shows us that there are 5,421 such images and they all have dimensions of 28 x 28. The summary function shows that the values in `trainx` range from 0 to 255. The first 64 images of the handwritten digit five from the train data can be seen in the following image:

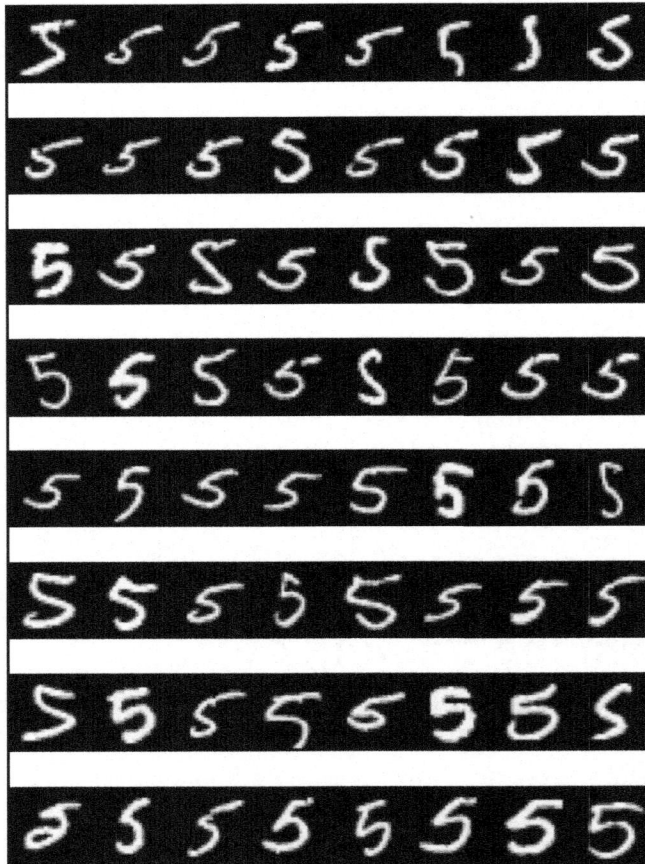

These handwritten images show a high amount of variability. Such variability is expected since different people have different handwriting styles. Although most of these digits are clearly written and easy to recognize, there are some that are somewhat less clear.

Data processing

To prepare our data for the steps that follow, we'll reshape `trainx` so that its dimensions are 5,421 x 28 x 28 x 1, as shown in the following code:

```
# Reshaping data
trainx <- array_reshape(trainx, c(nrow(trainx), 28, 28, 1))
trainx <- trainx / 255
```

Here, we also divide the values in `trainx` by 255 to obtain a range of values between 0 and 1. With the data processed in the required format, we can move on and develop the architecture for the generator network.

Developing the generator network

The generator network will be used for generating fake images from data that's provided in the form of noise. In this section, we will develop the architecture of the generator network and look at the parameters that are involved by summarizing the network.

Network architecture

Let's take a look at the code for developing the generator network architecture:

```
# Generator network
h <- 28; w <- 28; c <- 1; l <- 28
gi <- layer_input(shape = l)
go <- gi %>% layer_dense(units = 32 * 14 * 14) %>%
        layer_activation_leaky_relu() %>%
        layer_reshape(target_shape = c(14, 14, 32)) %>%
        layer_conv_2d(filters = 32,
                    kernel_size = 5,
                    padding = "same") %>%
        layer_activation_leaky_relu() %>%
        layer_conv_2d_transpose(filters = 32,
                            kernel_size = 4,
                            strides = 2,
                            padding = "same") %>%
        layer_activation_leaky_relu() %>%
        layer_conv_2d(filters = 1,
                    kernel_size = 5,
                    activation = "tanh",
                    padding = "same")
g <- keras_model(gi, go)
```

In the preceding code, we can observe the following:

- We have specified height (h), width (w), number of channels (c), and the latent dimension (l) as 28, 28, 1, and 28, respectively.
- We have specified the input shape for the generator input (gi) as 28. At the time of training, the generator network will be provided an input of 28 random numbers that have been obtained from a standard normal distribution which is simply noise.
- Next, we have specified the architecture for the generator network's output (go).
- The last layer is a convolutional 2D layer with a `tanh` activation function. In the last layer, we have set the filter as 1 since we will not be using color images.
- Note that `layer_conv_2d_transpose` is required to be 28 x 28 in size.
- The output dimensions from the generator output will be 28 x 28 x 1.
- The other values that were used, such as the number of filters, `kernel_size`, or strides can be experimented with later if you wish to explore improving the results.
- `gi` and `go` are used for the generator network (g).

Now, let's look at the summary of this network.

Summary of the generator network

A summary of the generator network is as follows:

```
# Summary of generator network model
summary(g)
```

Layer (type)	Output Shape	Param #
input_7 (InputLayer)	[(None, 28)]	0
dense_4 (Dense)	(None, 6272)	181888
leaky_re_lu_8 (LeakyReLU)	(None, 6272)	0
reshape_2 (Reshape)	(None, 14, 14, 32)	0

conv2d_6 (Conv2D)	(None, 14, 14, 32)	25632
leaky_re_lu_9 (LeakyReLU)	(None, 14, 14, 32)	0
conv2d_transpose_2 (Conv2DTranspose)	(None, 28, 28, 32)	16416
leaky_re_lu_10 (LeakyReLU)	(None, 28, 28, 32)	0
conv2d_7 (Conv2D)	(None, 28, 28, 1)	801

```
=================================================================
=
Total params: 224,737
Trainable params: 224,737
Non-trainable params: 0
```

The summary of the generator network shows the output's shape and the number of parameters for each layer. Note that the final output shape is 28 x 28 x 1. The fake images that will be generated will have these dimensions. Overall, for this network, we have 224,737 parameters.

Now that we've specified the structure of the generator network, we can develop the architecture for the discriminator network.

Developing the discriminator network

The discriminator network will be used for classifying fake and real images. The architecture and summary of the network will be discussed in this section.

Architecture

The code that's used for developing the discriminator network architecture is as follows:

```
# Discriminator network
di <- layer_input(shape = c(h, w, c))
do <- di %>%
        layer_conv_2d(filters = 64, kernel_size = 4) %>%
```

```
            layer_activation_leaky_relu() %>%
            layer_flatten() %>%
            layer_dropout(rate = 0.3) %>%
            layer_dense(units = 1, activation = "sigmoid")
    d <- keras_model(di, do)
```

From the preceding code, we can observe the following:

- We provided an input shape (di) with h = 28, w = 28, and c = 1. This is the dimension of fake and real images that will be used at the time of training the network.
- In the last layer of the discriminator output (do), we have specified the activation function as `sigmoid` and the units as 1, since an image is differentiated as either real or fake.
- `di` and `do` are used for the discriminator network model (d).

Summary of the discriminator network

The summary of the discriminator network shows the output shape and number of parameters for each layer:

```
# Summary of discriminator network model
summary(d)
```

Layer (type)	Output Shape	Param #
input_10 (InputLayer)	[(None, 28, 28, 1)]	0
conv2d_12 (Conv2D)	(None, 25, 25, 64)	1088
leaky_re_lu_17 (LeakyReLU)	(None, 25, 25, 64)	0
flatten_2 (Flatten)	(None, 40000)	0
dropout_2 (Dropout)	(None, 40000)	0
dense_7 (Dense)	(None, 1)	40001

```
Total params: 41,089
Trainable params: 41,089
Non-trainable params: 0
```

Here, the output of the first layer is 28 x 28 x 1 in size, which matches the dimensions of the fake and real images. The total number of parameters is 41,089.

Now, we can compile the discriminator network model using the following code:

```
# Compile discriminator network
d %>% compile(optimizer = 'rmsprop',
        loss = "binary_crossentropy")
```

Here, we have compiled the discriminator network using the `rmsprop` optimizer. For the loss, we have specified `binary_crossentropy`.

Next, we freeze the weight of the discriminator network. Note that we freeze these weights after compiling the discriminator network so that it applies them to the `gan` model only:

```
# Freeze weights and compile
freeze_weights(d)
gani <- layer_input(shape = 1)
gano <- gani %>% g %>% d
gan <- keras_model(gani, gano)
gan %>% compile(optimizer = 'rmsprop',
            loss = "binary_crossentropy")
```

Here, the generative adversarial network's output (gano) uses the generator network and the discriminator network with frozen weights. The generative adversarial network (gan) is based on gani and gano. The network is then compiled with the `rmsprop` optimizer and with the loss specified as `binary_crossentropy`.

Now, we are ready to train the network.

Training the network

In this section, we will out training of the network. While training the network, we will save fake images and store loss values to review the training progress. They will help us assess the effectiveness of the network when creating realistic fake images.

Initial setup for saving fake images and loss values

We will start by specifying a few things that we will need for the training process. Let's take a look at the following code:

```
# Initial settings
b <- 50
setwd("~/Desktop/")
```

```
dir <- "FakeImages"
dir.create(dir)
start <- 1; dloss <- NULL; gloss <- NULL
```

From the preceding code, we can observe the following:

- We will use a batch size (b) of 50.
- We will save fake images in the `FakeImages` directory, which is created on the desktop of our computer.
- We will also make use of discriminator loss values (dloss) and GAN loss values (gloss), which are initialized with `NULL`.

Training process

Next, we will train the model. Here, we will be using 100 iterations. Let's go over the code for this, which has been summarized into five points:

```
# 1. Generate 50 fake images from noise
for (i in 1:100) {noise <- matrix(rnorm(b*l), nrow = b, ncol= l)}
fake <- g %>% predict(noise)

# 2. Combine real & fake images
stop <- start + b - 1
real <- trainx[start:stop,,,]
real <- array_reshape(real, c(nrow(real), 28, 28, 1))
rows <- nrow(real)
both <- array(0, dim = c(rows * 2, dim(real)[-1]))
both[1:rows,,,] <- fake
both[(rows+1):(rows*2),,,] <- real
labels <- rbind(matrix(runif(b, 0.9,1), nrow = b, ncol = 1),
 matrix(runif(b, 0, 0.1), nrow = b, ncol = 1))
start <- start + b

# 3. Train discriminator
dloss[i] <- d %>% train_on_batch(both, labels)

# 4. Train generator using gan
fakeAsReal <- array(runif(b, 0, 0.1), dim = c(b, 1))
gloss[i] <- gan %>% train_on_batch(noise, fakeAsReal)

# 5. Save fake image
f <- fake[1,,,]
dim(f) <- c(28,28,1)
image_array_save(f, path = file.path(dir, paste0("f", i, ".png")))}
```

In the preceding code, we can observe the following:

1. We start by simulating random data points from the standard normal distribution and the save results as noise. Then, we use the generator network `g` to create fake images from this data containing random noise. Note that `noise` is 50 x 28 in size and that `fake` is 50 x 28 x 28 x 1 in size and contains 50 fake images in each iteration.

2. We update the values of start and stop based on the batch size. For the first iteration, start and stop have values of 1 and 50, respectively. For the second iteration, start and stop have values of 51 and 100, respectively. Similarly, for the 100th iteration, start and stop have values of 4,951 and 5,000, respectively. Since `trainx`, which contains the handwritten digit five, has more than 5,000 images, none of the images are repeated during these 100 iterations. Thus, in each iteration, 50 real images are selected and stored in `real`, which is 50 x 28 x 28 in size. We use reshape to change the dimensions to 50 x 28 x 28 x 1, so that they match the dimensions of the fake images.

3. Then, we create an empty array called `both` that's 100 x 28 x 28 x 1 in size to store real and fake image data. The first 50 images in `both` contain fake data while the next 50 images contain real images. We also generate 50 random numbers between 0.9 and 1 using uniform distribution to use as labels for fake images and similar random numbers between 0 and 0.1 to use as labels for real images. Note that we do not use 0 to represent real and 1 to represent fake images and instead introduce some randomness or noise. Artificially introducing some noise in the values of labels helps at the time of training the network.

4. We train the discriminator network using image data contained in `both` and the correct category information contained in `labels`. We also store the discriminator loss values in `dloss` for all 100 iterations. If the discriminator network learns to do well in classifying fake and real images, then this loss value will be low.

5. We try to fool the network by labeling the noise containing random values between 0 and 0.1, which we had used for real images. The resulting loss values are stored in `gloss` for all 100 iterations. If the network learns to do well in presenting fake images and makes the network classify them as real, then this loss value will be low.

6. We save the first fake image from each of the 100 iterations so that we can review it and observe the impact of the training process.

Note that, usually, the training process for generative adversarial networks requires a significant amount of computational resources. However, the example we are using here is meant to quickly illustrate how this process works and complete the training process in a reasonable amount of time. For 100 iterations and a computer with 8 GB of RAM, it should take less than a minute to run all the code.

Reviewing results

In this section, we will review the network losses that were obtained from 100 iterations. We will also take a look at the progress of using fake images from iteration 1 to 100.

Discriminator and GAN losses

The discriminator and GAN loss values that were obtained from our 100 iterations can be plotted as follows. The discriminator loss is based on the loss values for the fake and real images:

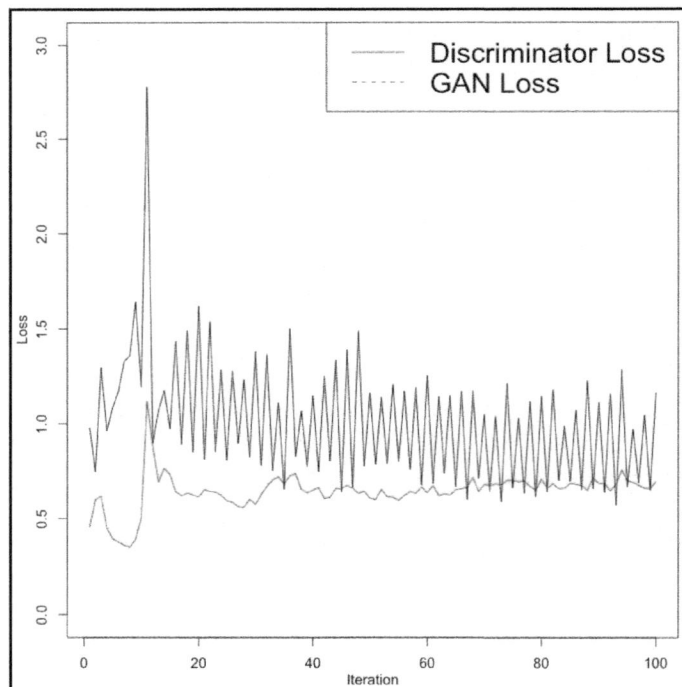

From the preceding plot, we can make the following observations:

- The loss values for the discriminator network and the GAN show high variability during the first 20 iterations. This variability is an outcome of the learning process.
- The discriminator and generator networks are competing against each other and trying to do better than one another. When one network performs better, it is at the cost of the other network. This is the reason why, if dloss and gloss were plotted on a scatter plot, we would expect to see some amount of negative correlation between them. The correlation is not expected to be perfectly negative, but the overall pattern is expected to indicate a negative relationship. In the long run, both loss values are expected to converge.
- The loss values that were obtained from the GAN show higher fluctuations compared to the loss values that are obtained from the discriminator network.
- After about 50 iterations, we notice that the discriminator loss values show a small but gradual increase. This suggests that the discriminator network is finding it increasingly difficult to differentiate between the real and fake images that are being generated by the generator network.
- Note that an increase in loss values is not necessarily a negative outcome. In this case, this is positive feedback and it indicates that pitting the generator network against the discriminator network is yielding results. This means that the generator network is able to create fake images that increasingly look like real images and helps us achieve our main objective.

Fake images

We will use the following code to read fake images and then plot them:

```
# Fake image data
library(EBImage)
setwd("~/Desktop/FakeImages")
temp = list.files(pattern = "*.png")
mypic <- list()
for (i in 1:length(temp)) {mypic[[i]] <- readImage(temp[[i]])}
par(mfrow = c(10,10))
for (i in 1:length(temp)) plot(mypic[[i]])
```

In the preceding code, we have made use of the EBImage library to process fake image data. We have read all 100 images that are saved in the `FakeImages` directory. Now, we can plot all the images in a 10 x 10 grid, as shown in the following image:

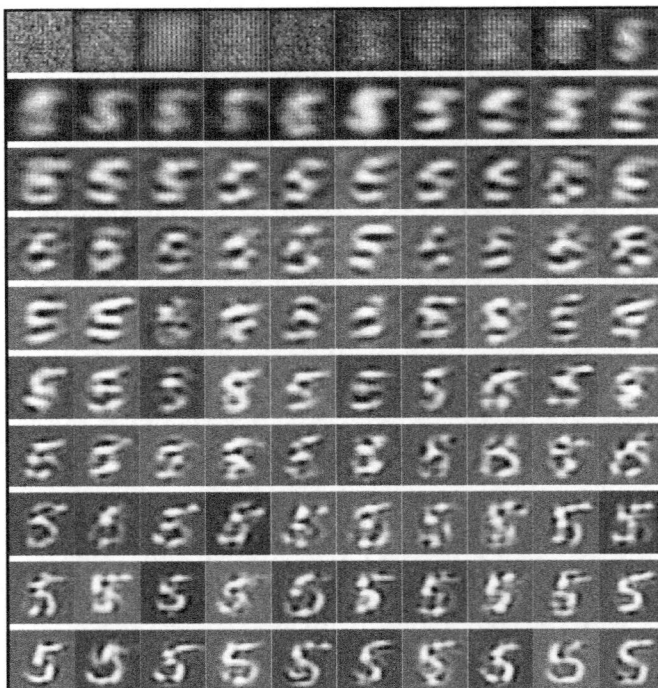

In the preceding image, the first fake image from each of the 100 iterations is shown. From this, we can make the following observations:

- The first ten images in the first row represent the first 10 iterations.
- The first image simply reflects random noise. As we reach 10 iterations, the image begins to capture the essence of the handwritten digit five.
- By the time the network training goes through iterations 91 to 100, digit five becomes visually more clear.

In the next section, we will carry out an experiment by making some changes in the network and observing its impact on the network's training process.

Performance optimization tips and best practices

In this section, we will carry out an experiment by inserting an additional convolutional layer into the generator network, as well as in the discriminator network. Through this experiment, we will convey performance optimization tips and best practices.

Changes in the generator and discriminator network

The changes in the generator network are shown in the following code:

```
# Generator network
gi <- layer_input(shape = 1)
go <- gi %>% layer_dense(units = 32 * 14 * 14) %>%
        layer_activation_leaky_relu() %>%
        layer_reshape(target_shape = c(14, 14, 32)) %>%
        layer_conv_2d(filters = 32,
                    kernel_size = 5,
                    padding = "same") %>%
        layer_activation_leaky_relu() %>%
        layer_conv_2d_transpose(filters = 32,
                            kernel_size = 4,
                            strides = 2,
                            padding = "same") %>%
        layer_activation_leaky_relu() %>%
        layer_conv_2d(filters = 64,
                    kernel_size = 5,
                    padding = "same") %>%
        layer_activation_leaky_relu() %>%
        layer_conv_2d(filters = 1,
                    kernel_size = 5,
                    activation = "tanh",
                    padding = "same")
  g <- keras_model(gi, go)
```

Here, we can see that, in the generator network, we are adding the `layer_conv_2d` and `layer_activation_leaky_relu` layers just before the last layer. The total number of parameters for the generator network has increased to 276,801.

The changes in the discriminator network are shown in the following code:

```
# Discriminator network
di <- layer_input(shape = c(h, w, c))
do <- di %>%
        layer_conv_2d(filters = 64, kernel_size = 4) %>%
        layer_activation_leaky_relu() %>%
        layer_conv_2d(filters = 64, kernel_size = 4, strides = 2) %>%
        layer_activation_leaky_relu() %>%
        layer_flatten() %>%
        layer_dropout(rate = 0.3) %>%
        layer_dense(units = 1, activation = "sigmoid")
d <- keras_model(di, do)
```

Here, we have added the `layer_conv_2d` and `layer_activation_leaky_relu` layers before the flattening layer in the discriminator network. The number of parameters in the discriminator network has increased to 148,866. We have kept everything else the same and then trained the network again for 100 iterations.

Now, we can assess the impact of these changes.

Impact of these changes on the results

The discriminator and GAN loss values for 100 iterations can be plotted as follows:

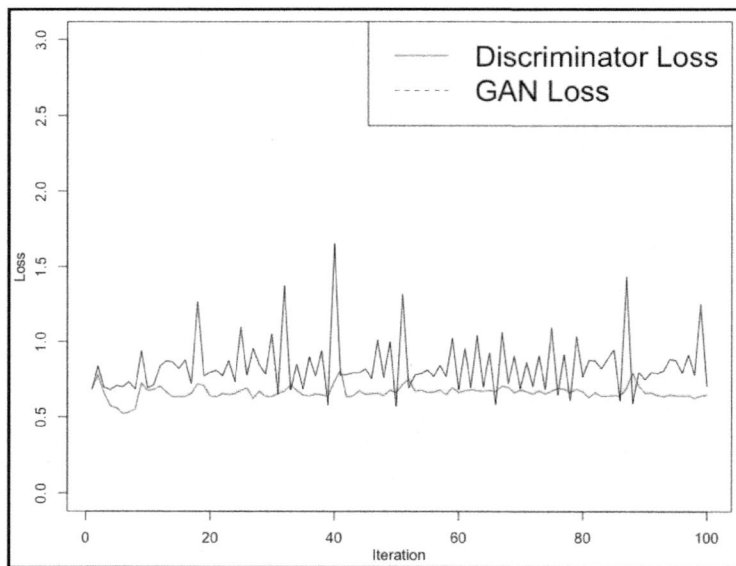

From the preceding plot, we can observe the following:

- By increasing the number of layers, the fluctuation in the loss values for the discriminator and GAN network has reduced compared to the results we obtained earlier.
- The spikes or high loss values that have been observed for some of the iterations indicate the corresponding network struggling, while competing against the other network.
- The variability in the GAN loss values continues to be higher compared to those for discriminator network-related loss.

The following plot is of the first fake image in each of the 100 iterations:

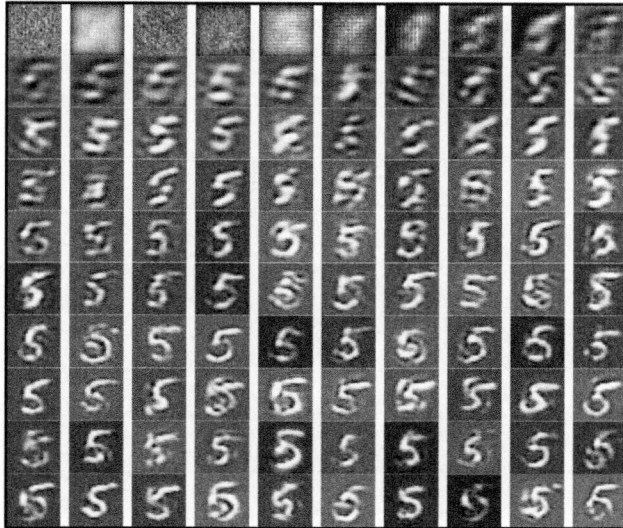

From the preceding images, we can observe the following:

- With additional convolutional layers in the generator and discriminator networks, the network begins to generate images replicating the handwritten digit five much earlier.
- In the previous network, fake images that consistently looked like handwritten digit five did not appear until about 70-80 iterations.
- Due to the use of additional layers, we can see the digit five being formed more or less consistently after about 20-30 iterations, which suggests an improvement.

Next, we will try to use this network to generate another handwritten digit.

Generating a handwritten image of digit eight

In this experiment, we will make use of the same network architecture as the previous one. However, we will use it for generating a handwritten image of digit eight. The discriminator and GAN loss values for 100 iterations for this experiment can be plotted as follows:

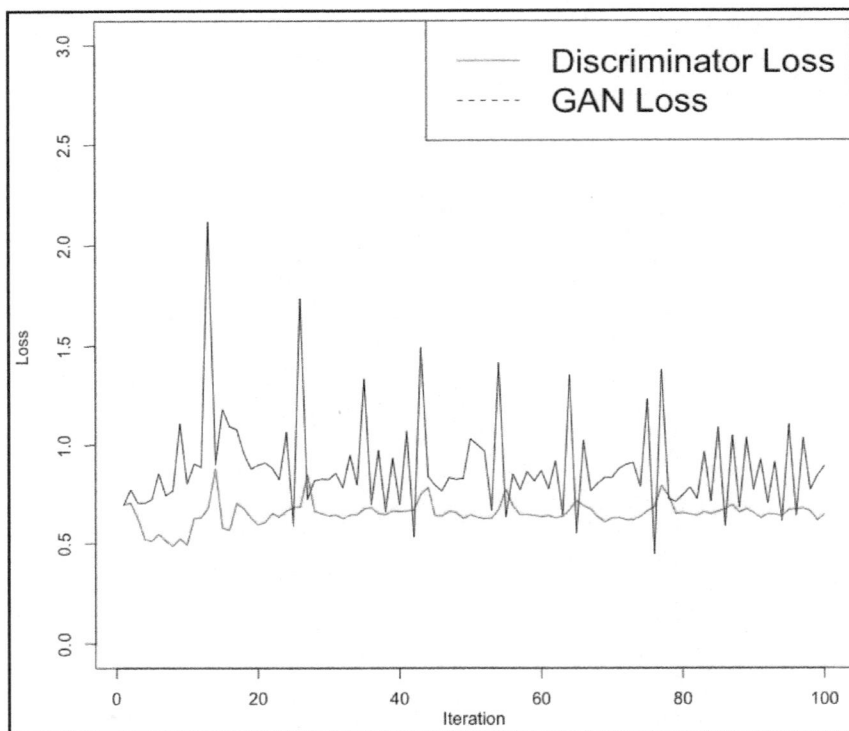

From the preceding plot, we can make the following observations:

- The discriminator and GAN loss values show variability that tends to reduce as the number of iterations goes from 1 to 100.
- High spikes at certain intervals for the GAN loss are diminishing as the network's training proceeds.

A plot of the first fake image from each iteration is as follows:

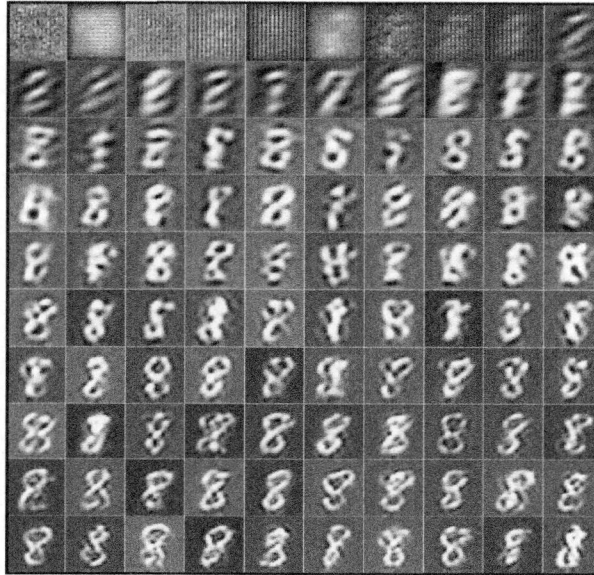

Compared to digit five, digit eight takes more iterations before it starts to form a recognizable pattern.

In this section, we experimented with additional convolutional layers in the generator and the discriminator networks. Due to this, we can make the following observations:

- Additional convolutional layers seem to have a positive impact on the generation of fake images that began to look like handwritten images of digit five much quicker.
- Although the results for the data that we referred to in this chapter were decent, for other data, we may have to make other changes to the model architecture.
- We also used the network with the same architecture to generate realistic-looking fake images of handwritten digit eight. It was observed that, for digit eight, it took more iterations of training the network before a recognizable pattern started to emerge.
- Note that a network for generating all 10 handwritten digits at the same time can be more complex and is likely to require many more iterations.
- Similarly, if we have color images that have significantly larger dimensions than 28 x 28, which is what we used for this chapter, we will need more computational resources and the task will be even more challenging.

Summary

In this chapter, we used a generative adversarial network to illustrate how to generate images of a single handwritten digit. Generative adversarial networks make use of two networks: generator and discriminator networks. Generator networks create fake images from data containing random noise, while discriminator networks are trained to differentiate between fake images and real images. These two networks compete against each other so that realistic-looking fake images can be created. Although in this chapter we provided an example of using a generative adversarial network to generate new images, these networks are also known to have applications in generating new text or new music, as well as in anomaly detection.

In this section, we went over various deep learning networks that are useful for dealing with image data. In the next section, we will go over deep learning networks for natural language processing.

Section 4: Deep Learning for Natural Language Processing

This section discusses how to apply deep neural networks for working on real-world problems involving natural language processing. It consists of four chapters that illustrate the use of popular deep learning networks such as **Recurrent Neural Networks (RNNs)**, **Long Short-Term Memory (LSTM)**, and **Convolutional Recurrent Neural Networks (CRNNs)**.

This section contains the following chapters:

- Chapter 9, *Deep Network for Text Classification*
- Chapter 10, *Text Classification Using Recurrent Neural Networks*
- Chapter 11, *Text Classification Using Long Short-Term Memory Networks*
- Chapter 12, *Text Classification Using Convolutional Recurrent Networks*

Deep Networks for Text Classification

9

Text data belongs to the unstructured category of data. When developing deep network models, we need to complete additional preprocessing steps due to the unique nature of such data. In this chapter, you will learn about the steps you'll need to follow to develop text classification models using deep neural networks. This process will be illustrated with easy– to– follow examples. Text data, such as customer comments, product reviews, and movie reviews, plays an important role in businesses, and text classification is an important deep learning problem.

In this chapter, we will discuss two text datasets, learn how to prepare text data when developing deep network classification models, look at IMDb movie review data, develop a deep network architecture, fit and evaluate the model, and discuss some tips and best practices. More specifically, in this chapter, we will cover the following topics:

- Text datasets
- Preparing the data for model building
- Developing deep neural networks
- Model evaluation and prediction
- Performance optimization tips and best practices

Text datasets

Text data can be used when we want to practice developing deep network models. Such data can be obtained from several publicly available sources. We will go over two such resources in this section:

- The UCI machine learning repository
- Text data within Keras

The UCI machine learning repository

The following link provides a variety of datasets that contain text sentences that have been extracted from reviews of products (from `amazon.com`), reviews of movies (from `IMDE.com`), and reviews of restaurants (from `yelp.com`): `https://archive.ics.uci.edu/ml/datasets/Sentiment+Labelled+Sentences`.

Each sentence is labeled in terms of the sentiment that was expressed in the reviews. This sentiment is either positive or negative. For each website, there are 500 positive and 500 negative sentences, which means there are 3,000 labeled sentences in total. This data can be used to develop a sentiment classification deep networking model that can help us automatically classify a customer review as either positive or negative.

The following are some examples of negative reviews from IMDb that have been labeled as 0:

- A very, very, very slow-moving, aimless movie about a distressed, drifting young man
- Not sure who was more lost—the flat characters or the audience, nearly half of whom walked out
- Attempting artiness with black and white and clever camera angles, the movie disappointed—became even more ridiculous—as the acting was poor and the plot and lines almost non-existent
- Very little music or anything to speak of

The following are some examples of positive reviews from IMDb that have been labeled as 1:

- The best scene in the movie was when Gerardo was trying to find a song that kept running through his head
- Saw the movie today and thought it was a good effort, good messages for kids
- Loved the casting of Jimmy Buffet as the science teacher
- And those baby owls were adorable
- The movie showed a lot of Florida at its best, made it look very appealing

The following are some examples of negative reviews from Amazon that are labeled as 0:

- So there is no way for me to plug it in here in the US unless I go by a converter
- Tied to charger for conversations lasting more than 45 minutes. MAJOR PROBLEMS!!
- I have to jiggle the plug to get it to line up right to get decent volume
- If you have several dozen or several hundred contacts, then imagine the fun of sending each of them one by one
- I advise EVERYONE DO NOT BE FOOLED!

The following are some examples of positive reviews from Amazon that are labeled as 1:

- Good case, Excellent value
- Great for the jawbone
- The mic is great
- If you are Razr owner...you must have this!
- And the sound quality is great

Text data within Keras

There are two text datasets available within Keras, as follows:

- The **Internet Movie Database (IMDb)**, which contains movie review sentiment classification
- Reuters Newswire's topics classification data

The IMDb review data contains 25,000 reviews that have been classified as containing positive or negative sentiments. This data has already been preprocessed, with each review encoded as a sequence of integers. Reuters Newswire's topics classification data contains 11,228 newswires, and these have also been preprocessed, with each encoded as a sequence of integers. The newswires have been classified into 46 groups or topics, such as livestock, gold, and housing, jobs.

The following is an example of a positive movie review from the IMDb data from Keras:

"lavish production values and solid performances in this straightforward adaption of jane ? satirical classic about the marriage game within and between the classes in ? 18th century england northam and paltrow are a ? mixture as friends who must pass through ? and lies to discover that they love each other good humor is a ? virtue which goes a long way towards explaining the ? of the aged source material which has been toned down a bit in its harsh ? i liked the look of the film and how shots were set up and i thought it didn't rely too much on ? of head shots like most other films of the 80s and 90s do very good results."

The following is an example of a negative movie review from the IMDb data from Keras:

"worst mistake of my life br br i picked this movie up at target for 5 because i figured hey it's sandler i can get some cheap laughs i was wrong completely wrong mid way through the film all three of my friends were asleep and i was still suffering worst plot worst script worst movie i have ever seen i wanted to hit my head up against a wall for an hour then i'd stop and you know why because it felt damn good upon bashing my head in i stuck that damn movie in the ? and watched it burn and that felt better than anything else i've ever done it took american psycho army of darkness and kill bill just to get over that crap i hate you sandler for actually going through with this and ruining a whole day of my life."

Preparing the data for model building

The steps we need to follow in order to prepare the data for model building are as follows:

1. Tokenization
2. Converting text into integers
3. Padding and truncation

To illustrate the steps involved in data preparation, we will make use of a very small text dataset involving five tweets related to when the Apple iPhone X released in September 2017. We will use this small dataset to understand the steps that are involved in data preparation and then we will switch to a larger IMDb dataset in order to build a deep network classification model. The following are the five tweets that we are going to store in t1 to t5:

```
t1 <- "I'm not a huge $AAPL fan but $160 stock closes down $0.60 for the
day on huge volume isn't really bearish"
t2 <- "$AAPL $BAC not sure what more dissapointing: the new iphones or the
presentation for the new iphones?"
t3 <- "IMO, $AAPL animated emojis will be the death of $SNAP."
t4 <- "$AAPL get on board. It's going to 175. I think wall st will have
issues as aapl pushes 1 trillion dollar valuation but 175 is in the cards"
t5 <- "In the AR vs. VR battle, $AAPL just put its chips behind AR in a big
way."
```

The preceding tweets include text that's in both lowercase and uppercase, punctuation, numbers, and special characters.

Tokenization

Each word or number in the tweet is a token, and the process of splitting tweets into tokens is called **tokenization**. The code that's used to carry out tokenization is as follows:

```
tweets <- c(t1, t2, t3, t4, t5)
token <- text_tokenizer(num_words = 10) %>%
        fit_text_tokenizer(tweets)
token$index_word[1:3]
$`1`
[1] "the"

$`2`
[1] "aapl"

$`3`
[1] "in"
```

From the preceding code, we can see the following:

- We started by saving five tweets in tweets.
- For the tokenization process, we specified num_words as 10 to indicate we want to use 10 of the most frequent words and ignore any others.

- Although we specified that we will have `10` frequent words, the maximum value of integers that will be used is actually going to be 10 - 1 = 9.
- We used `fit_text_tokenizer`, which automatically converts text into lowercase and removes any punctuation from the tweets.
- We observed that the top three most frequent words in these five tweets are `the`, `aapl`, and `in`.

> Note that words that have a high frequency may or may not be important for text classification.

Converting text into sequences of integers

The following code is used to convert text into sequences of integers. The output is also provided:

```
seq <- texts_to_sequences(token, tweets)
seq
[[1]]
[1] 4 5 6 2 7 8 1 9 6

[[2]]
[1] 2 4 1 1 8 1

[[3]]
[1] 2 1

[[4]]
[1] 2 9 2 7 3 1

[[5]]
[1] 3 1 2 3 5
```

From the preceding code, we can see the following:

- We have used `texts_to_sequences` to convert tweets into sequences of integers.
- Since we've chosen the most frequent words for tokens to be `10`, the integers within each sequence of integers have a maximum value of 9.
- For each tweet, the number of integers in the sequence is less than how many words there are due to only the most frequent words being used.

- The sequences of integers have different lengths, ranging from 2 to 9.
- For the purpose of developing a classification model, all of the sequences need to be the same length. This is achieved by performing padding or truncation.

Padding and truncation

The code for making all the sequences of integers equal is as follows:

```
pad_seq <- pad_sequences(seq, maxlen = 5)
pad_seq
       [,1]  [,2]  [,3]  [,4]  [,5]
[1,]      7     8     1     9     6
[2,]      4     1     1     8     1
[3,]      0     0     0     2     1
[4,]      9     2     7     3     1
[5,]      3     1     2     3     5
```

From the preceding code, we can see the following:

- We have used `pad_sequences` so that all of the sequences of integers are equal in length.
- When we specify the maximum length of all the sequences (using `maxlen`) to be 5, this will truncate sequences that are longer than 5 and add zeros to sequences that are shorter than 5.
- Note that the default setting for padding here is "pre". This means that when a sequence is longer than 5, truncation will effect integers at the beginning of the sequence. We can observe this for the first sequence in the preceding output, where 4, 5, 6, and 2 have been removed.
- Similarly, for the third sequence, which has a length of two, three zeros have been added to the beginning of the sequence.

There may be situations where you may prefer to truncate or add zeroes to the end of the sequences of integers. The code to achieve this is as follows:

```
pad_seq <- pad_sequences(seq, maxlen = 5, padding = 'post')
pad_seq
       [,1]  [,2]  [,3]  [,4]  [,5]
[1,]      7     8     1     9     6
[2,]      4     1     1     8     1
[3,]      2     1     0     0     0
[4,]      9     2     7     3     1
[5,]      3     1     2     3     5
```

In the preceding code, we have specified the padding as `post`. The impact of this type of padding can be seen in the output, where zeros have been added to the end of sequence 3, which adds up to less than 5.

Developing a tweet sentiment classification model

To develop a tweet sentiment classification model, we need labels for each tweet. However, getting labels that accurately reflect tweet sentiment is challenging. Let's take a look at some existing lexicons for sentiment classification and see why it isn't easy to get appropriate labels. With just five tweets, it isn't possible to develop a sentiment classification model. However, the idea here is to look at the process of arriving at an appropriate label for each tweet. This will help us appreciate the challenges involved in obtaining accurate labels. To automatically extract sentiment scores for each tweet, we will make use of the `syuzhet` package. We will also make use of commonly used lexicons for this purpose. The **National Research Council (NRC)** lexicon helps capture various emotions based on certain words. We will use the following code to obtain a sentiment score for the five tweets:

```
library(syuzhet)
get_nrc_sentiment(tweets)
  anger anticipation disgust fear joy sadness surprise trust negative
positive
```

	anger	anticipation	disgust	fear	joy	sadness	surprise	trust	negative	positive
1	1	0	0	1	0	0	0	0	0	0
2	0	0	0	0	0	0	0	0	0	0
3	1	1	1	1	1	1	1	0	1	1
4	0	1	0	0	0	0	0	0	0	0
5	1	0	0	0	0	0	0	0	1	0

The first tweet results in a score of 1 for both anger and fear. Although it contains the word `'bearish'`, if we were to read this tweet, we would determine that it's actually positive.

Let's look at the following code, which contains sentiment scores for the words `'bearish'`, `'death'`, and `'animated'`:

```
get_nrc_sentiment('bearish')
  anger anticipation disgust fear joy sadness surprise trust negative
positive
1      1            0       0    1   0       0        0     0        0
0

get_nrc_sentiment('death')
  anger anticipation disgust fear joy sadness surprise trust negative
positive
1      1            1       1    1   0       1        1     0        1
0

get_nrc_sentiment('animated')
  anger anticipation disgust fear joy sadness surprise trust negative
positive
1      0            0       0    0   1       0        0     0        0
1
```

From the preceding code, we can determine the following:

- The overall score for the first tweet is based on the word italics, and nothing else.
- The third tweet has a score of 1 for each category except trust.
- From reading the tweet, it is obvious to us that the person writing this tweet actually feels that animated emojis will be positive for Apple and will be negative for Snapchat.
- The sentiment scores are based on two words in this tweet: death and animated. They fail to capture the real sentiment that's expressed in the third tweet, which is very positive for Apple.

When we manually label each of the five tweets with a negative sentiment, which is represented by 0, and a positive sentiment, which is represented by 1, we are likely to arrive at 1, 0, 1, 1, and 1 for our scores. Let's use the following code to arrive at these sentiment scores by using the syuzhet, bing, and afinn lexicons:

```
get_sentiment(tweets, method="syuzhet")
[1]  0.00  0.80 -0.35  0.00 -0.25

get_sentiment(tweets, method="bing")
[1] -1  0 -1 -1  0

get_sentiment(tweets, method="afinn")
[1]  4  0 -2  0  0
```

Looking at results from the `syuzhet`, `bing`, and `afinn` lexicons, we can observe the following:

- The results vary significantly from the actual sentiments contained in the tweets. Thus, trying to automatically label a tweet with an appropriate sentiment score is difficult.
- We saw that automatically labeling text sequences is a challenging problem. However, one solution is to label a very large number of text sequences, such as tweets, manually and then use that to develop a sentiment classification model.
- In addition, it is important to note that such a sentiment classification model will only be helpful for the specific types of text data that were used to develop the model.
- It isn't possible to use the same model for different text sentiment classification applications.

Developing deep neural networks

Although we won't be developing a classification model based on just five tweets, let's look at the code for our model's architecture:

```
model <- keras_model_sequential()
model %>% layer_embedding(input_dim = 10,
                          output_dim = 8,
                          input_length = 5)
summary(model)
```

OUTPUT

Layer (type)	Output Shape	Param #
embedding_1 (Embedding)	(None, 5, 8)	30

Total params: 80
Trainable params: 80
Non-trainable params: 0

```
print(model$get_weights(), digits = 2)
```

```
[[1]]
          [,1]      [,2]      [,3]      [,4]      [,5]      [,6]      [,7]      [,8]
[1,]    0.0055  -0.0364  -0.0475   0.049  -0.0139  -0.0114  -0.0452  -0.0298
[2,]    0.0398  -0.0143  -0.0406   0.023  -0.0496  -0.0124   0.0087  -0.0104
[3,]    0.0370  -0.0321  -0.0491  -0.021  -0.0214   0.0391   0.0428  -0.0398
[4,]   -0.0257   0.0294   0.0433   0.048   0.0259  -0.0323  -0.0308   0.0224
[5,]   -0.0079  -0.0255   0.0164   0.023  -0.0486   0.0273   0.0245  -0.0020
[6,]    0.0372   0.0464   0.0454  -0.020   0.0086  -0.0375  -0.0188   0.0395
[7,]    0.0293   0.0305   0.0130   0.037  -0.0324  -0.0069  -0.0248   0.0178
[8,]   -0.0116  -0.0087  -0.0344   0.027   0.0132   0.0430  -0.0196  -0.0356
[9,]    0.0314  -0.0315   0.0074  -0.044  -0.0198  -0.0135  -0.0353   0.0081
[10,]   0.0426   0.0199  -0.0306  -0.049   0.0259  -0.0341  -0.0155   0.0147
```

From the preceding code, we can observe the following:

- We initialized the model using `keras_model_sequential()`.
- We specified the input dimension as 10, which is the number of most frequent words.
- The output dimension of 8 leads to the number of parameters being 10 x 8 = 80.
- The input length is the length of the sequence of integers.
- We can get the weights for these 80 parameters using `model$get_weights()`.

Note that these weights will change every time the model is initialized.

Obtaining IMDb movie review data

Now, we will make use of IMDb movie review data, where the sentiment for each review has already been labeled as positive or negative. The code for accessing the IMDb movie review data from Keras is as follows:

```
imdb <- dataset_imdb(num_words = 500)
c(c(train_x, train_y), c(test_x, test_y)) %<-% imdb
z <- NULL
for (i in 1:25000) {z[i] <- print(length(train_x[[i]]))}
summary(z)
   Min. 1st Qu.  Median    Mean 3rd Qu.    Max.
   11.0   130.0   178.0   238.7   291.0  2494.0
```

From the preceding code, we can observe the following:

- We have used `train_x` and `train_y` to store the data in sequences of integers and labels representing positive or negative sentiment, respectively.
- We used a similar convention for the test data, too.
- Both the training and test data consist of 25,000 reviews each.
- The summary of the sequence length shows that the minimum length for the movie reviews based on the most frequent words is 11 and that the maximum sequence length is `2494`.
- The median sequence length is `178`.
- The median value is less than the mean, which suggests that this data will be skewed to the right and will have a longer tail on the right-hand side.

The histogram for the sequence length of the training data can be plotted as follows:

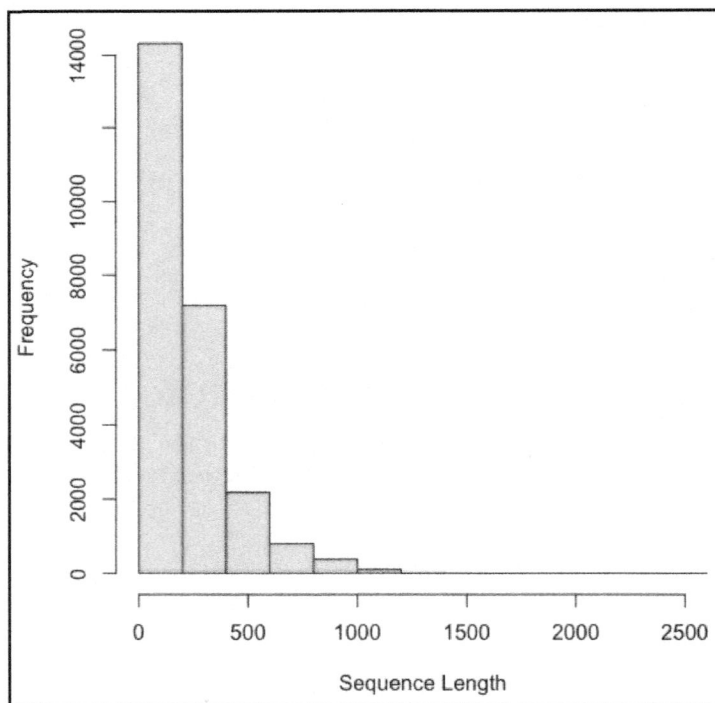

The preceding histogram for the length of the sequence of integers shows a right-skewed pattern. Most of the sequences have less than 500 integers.

Next, we will make the length of the sequence of integers equal using the following code:

```
train_x <- pad_sequences(train_x, maxlen = 100)
test_x <- pad_sequences(test_x, maxlen = 100)
```

From the preceding code, we can observe the following:

- We have used `maxlen` of 100 to standardize the length of each sequence to 100 integers.
- Sequences longer than 100 will have any additional integers truncated or removed, and sequences shorter than 100 will have zeros added to artificially increase the length of the sequence so that it reaches 100. We do this for both the train and test sequences.

Now, we are ready to build a classification model.

Building a classification model

For the model architecture and model summary, we will use the following code:

```
model <- keras_model_sequential()
model %>% layer_embedding(input_dim = 500,
                          output_dim = 16,
                          input_length = 100) %>%
        layer_flatten() %>%
        layer_dense(units = 16, activation = 'relu') %>%
        layer_dense(units = 1, activation = "sigmoid")
summary(model)
```

OUTPUT

Layer (type)	Output Shape	Param #
embedding_12 (Embedding)	(None, 100, 16)	8000
flatten_3 (Flatten)	(None, 1600)	0
dense_6 (Dense)	(None, 16)	25616
dense_7 (Dense)	(None, 1)	17

```
Total params: 33,633
Trainable params: 33,633
Non-trainable params: 0
```

From the preceding code, we can observe the following:

- Here, we've added `layer_flatten()` after `layer_embedding()`.
- This is followed by a dense layer with 16 nodes and a `relu` activation function.
- The summary of the model shows that there are 33,633 parameters in total.

Now, we can compile the model.

Compiling the model

We need to use the following code to compile the model:

```
model %>% compile(optimizer = "rmsprop",
        loss = "binary_crossentropy",
        metrics = c("acc"))
```

From the preceding code, we can observe the following:

- We have used the `rmsprop` optimizer to compile the model.
- For loss, we have used `binary_crossentropy` since the response has two values, that is, positive or negative. Metrics will make use of accuracy.

Now, let's start fitting the model.

Fitting the model

We need to use the following code to fit the model:

```
model_1 <- model %>% fit(train_x, train_y,
                    epochs = 10,
                    batch_size = 128,
                    validation_split = 0.2)
plot(model_1)
```

As shown in the preceding code, we're using `train_x` and `train_y` to fit the model as well as `10` epochs and a batch size of `128`. We are using 20% of the training data to assess the model's performance in terms of loss and accuracy values. After fitting the model, we obtain a plot for loss and accuracy, as shown in the following plot:

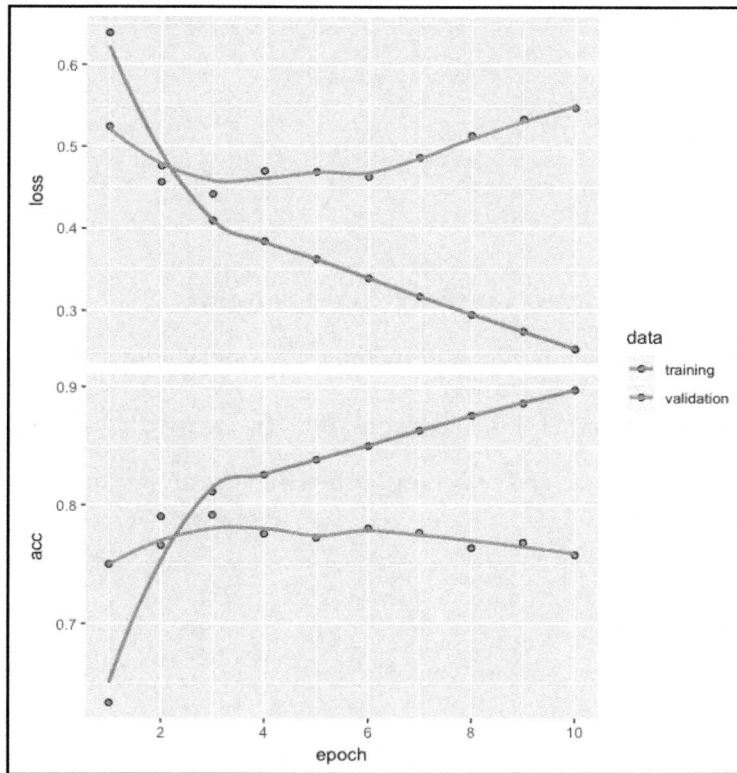

From the preceding plot, we can observe the following:

- The plot for loss and accuracy shows divergence between the training and validation data after about four epochs.
- Divergence between the training and validation data is observed for both the loss and accuracy values.
- We won't be using this model since there is clear evidence that there's an overfitting problem.

To overcome this overfitting problem, we need to modify the preceding code so that it appears as follows:

```
model <- keras_model_sequential()
model %>% layer_embedding(input_dim = 500,
                          output_dim = 16,
                          input_length = 100) %>%
        layer_flatten() %>%
        layer_dense(units = 16, activation = 'relu') %>%
```

```
            layer_dense(units = 1, activation = "sigmoid")
model %>% compile(optimizer = "rmsprop",
          loss = "binary_crossentropy",
          metrics = c("acc"))
model_2 <- model %>% fit(train_x, train_y,
                        epochs = 10,
                        batch_size = 512,
                        validation_split = 0.2)
plot(model_2)
```

Looking at the preceding code, we can observe the following:

- We're re-running the model and making only one change; that is, we're increasing the batch size to 512
- We keep everything else the same and then fit the model using the training data

After fitting the model, the loss and accuracy values that are stored in model_2 are plotted, as shown in the following plot:

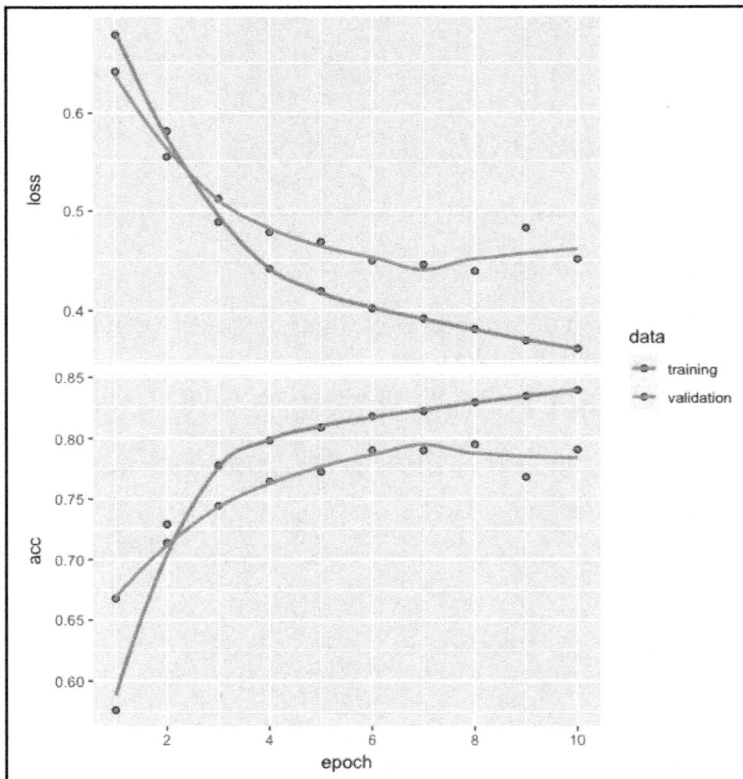

From the preceding plot, we can observe the following:

- The loss and accuracy values show better results this time.
- The curves for training and validation are closer to each other for both loss and accuracy.
- In addition, the loss and accuracy values that are based on validation data don't show the severe deterioration that we had observed for the previous model, where the values for the last three epochs are flat here.
- We were able to overcome the problem of overfitting by making minor changes to our code.

We will use this model for evaluation and prediction.

Model evaluation and prediction

Now, we will evaluate the model using training and test data to obtain the loss, accuracy, and confusion matrices. Our objective is to obtain a model that can classify sentiment contained in movie reviews as either positive or negative.

Evaluation using training data

The code to obtain the loss and accuracy values from the training data is as follows:

```
model %>% evaluate(train_x, train_y)
$loss
[1] 0.3745659
$acc
[1] 0.83428
```

As we can see, for training data, the loss and accuracy are 0.375 and 0.834, respectively. To look deeper into the model's sentiment classification performance, we need to develop a confusion matrix. To do so, use the following code:

```
pred <- model %>%  predict_classes(train_x)
table(Predicted=pred, Actual=imdb$train$y)
         Actual
Predicted    0     1
        0 11128  2771
        1  1372  9729
```

In the preceding code, we are predicting that the classes for the training data are using the model and comparing the results with the actual sentiment classes of the movie reviews. This is summarized in a confusion matrix. We can make the following observations about the confusion matrix:

- The model correctly predicts the negative sentiments contained in 11,128 movie reviews.
- The model correctly predicts the positive sentiments contained in 9,729 movie reviews.
- Misclassifying a positive review as a negative review is higher (2,771) than misclassifying movie reviews that have a negative sentiment and have been incorrectly classified as positive (1,372).

Next, we'll repeat this process with the test data.

Evaluation using test data

The code to obtain the loss and accuracy values from the test data is as follows:

```
model %>% evaluate(test_x, test_y)
$loss
[1] 0.4431483
$acc
[1] 0.79356
```

As we can see, in terms of the test data, the loss and accuracy are 0.443 and 0.794, respectively. These results are slightly inferior to the ones that were obtained for the training data. We can predict classes for the test data using the model and compare them with the actual classes of the movie reviews. This can be summarized in a confusion matrix, as follows:

```
pred1 <- model %>%   predict_classes(test_x)
table(Predicted=pred1, Actual=imdb$test$y)
         Actual
Predicted    0    1
        0 10586 3247
        1  1914 9253
```

From the preceding confusion matrix, we can observe the following:

- Overall, this model seems to be more accurate in correctly predicting negative movie reviews (10,586) compared to positive movie reviews (9,253).
- This pattern is consistent with the results that were obtained with the training data.
- In addition, although 79% accuracy for test data is decent, there is still scope for improving the model's sentiment classification performance.

In the next section, we will explore performance optimization tips and best practices.

Performance optimization tips and best practices

Now that we've obtained the test data's movie review classification accuracy, that is, 79%, we can work on improving this accuracy even further. Arriving at such an improvement may involve experimenting with the parameters in the model's architecture, the parameters that were used when we compiled the model, and/or the settings that were used while we were fitting a model. In this section, we will carry out an experiment by changing the maximum length of the sequence of words and, at the same time, use a different optimizer compared to what we used in the previous model.

Experimenting with the maximum sequence length and the optimizer

Let's start by creating `train` and `test` data for the sequence of integers representing movie reviews and their labels using the following code:

```
c(c(train_x, train_y), c(test_x, test_y)) %<-% imdb
z <- NULL
for (i in 1:25000) {z[i] <- print(length(train_x[[i]]))}
summary(z)
   Min. 1st Qu.  Median    Mean 3rd Qu.    Max.
   11.0   130.0   178.0   238.7   291.0  2494.0
```

In the preceding code, we're storing the length of the sequences based on the training data in z. By doing this, we get a summary of z. From here, we can obtain numeric summary values such as the minimum, first quartile, median, mean, third quartile, and maximum. The median value for the sequence of words is 178. In the previous sections, we used a maximum length of 100 at the time of padding the sequences so that they were of equal length. We will increase this to 200 in this experiment so that we have a number closer to the median value, as shown in the following code:

```
imdb <;- dataset_imdb(num_words = 500)
c(c(train_x, train_y), c(test_x, test_y)) %<-% imdb
train_x <- pad_sequences(train_x, maxlen = 200)
test_x <- pad_sequences(test_x, maxlen = 200)
model <- keras_model_sequential()
model %>% layer_embedding(input_dim = 500,
                          output_dim = 16,
                          input_length = 200) %>%
        layer_flatten() %>%
        layer_dense(units = 16, activation = 'relu') %>%
        layer_dense(units = 1, activation = "sigmoid")
model %>% compile(optimizer = "adamax",
                  loss = "binary_crossentropy",
                  metrics = c("acc"))
model_3 <- model %>% fit(train_x, train_y,
                         epochs = 10,
                         batch_size = 512,
                         validation_split = 0.2)
plot(model_3)
```

Another change we'll make is using the adamax optimizer when compiling the model. Note that this a variant of the popular adam optimizer. We keep everything else the same. After training the model, we plot the resulting loss and accuracy, as shown in the following plot:

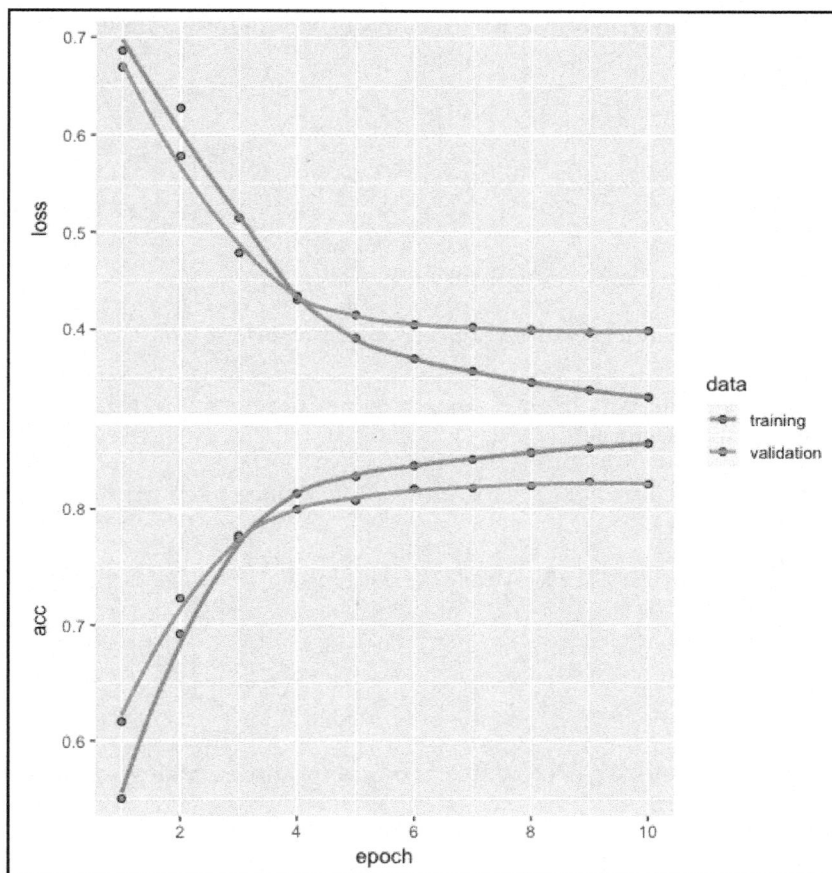

From the preceding plot for loss and accuracy, we can observe the following:

- The loss and accuracy values for the training and validation data show rapid improvements for about four epochs.
- After four epochs, these improvements slow down for the training data.
- For the validation data, the loss and accuracy values become flat for the last few epochs.
- The plot doesn't show any cause for concern regarding overfitting.

Next, we need to calculate the loss and accuracy based on the test data using the following code:

```
model %>% evaluate(test_x, test_y)
$loss
[1] 0.3906249
$acc
[1] 0.82468
```

Looking at the preceding code, we can observe the following:

- The model's loss and accuracy, based on the test data, are `0.391` and `0.825`, respectively.
- Both numbers indicate improvements compared to the performance we retrieved in the previous section.

To look into the model's sentiment classification performance even further, we can use the following code:

```
pred1 <- model %>%   predict_classes(test_x)
table(Predicted=pred1, Actual=imdb$test$y)
         Actual
Predicted    0     1
        0  9970  1853
        1  2530 10647
```

From the preceding confusion matrix, which is based on movie reviews of test data, we can observe the following:

- The correct classifications of negative (9,970) and positive movie reviews (10,647) are much closer now.
- The correct classification of positive movie reviews is slightly better compared to the correct classification of negative reviews.
- This model misclassifies a negative movie review as positive at a slightly higher rate (2,530) compared to a positive review being misclassified as a negative review (1,853).

Here, experimenting with the maximum sequence length and the type of optimizer that's used to compile the model resulted in improved sentiment classification performance. You are encouraged to continue experimenting and improve the model's sentiment classification performance.

Summary

In this chapter, we started by developing deep neural networks for text classification. Due to the unique characteristics of text data, several extra preprocessing steps are required before a deep neural network sentiment classification model can be developed. We used a small sample of five tweets to go over the preprocessing steps, including tokenization, converting text data into a sequence of integers, and padding/truncation to arrive at the same sequence length. We also highlighted that automatically labeling text sequences with the appropriate sentiment is a challenging problem and general lexicons may be unable to provide useful results.

To develop a deep network sentiment classification model, we switched to a larger and ready-to-use IMDb movie review dataset that's available as part of Keras. To optimize the model's performance, we also experimented with parameters such as the maximum sequence length at the time of data preparation, as well as the type of optimizer that's used for compiling the model. These experiments yielded decent results; however, we will continue to explore this data so that we can improve the model's sentiment classification performance on the deep network model even further.

In the next chapter, we will make use of the recurrent neural network classification model, which is better suited to working with data involving sequences.

Text Classification Using Recurrent Neural Networks **10**

Recurrent neural networks are useful for solving problems where data involves sequences. Some examples of applications involving sequences are seen in text classification, time series prediction, the sequence of frames in videos, DNA sequences, and speech recognition.

In this chapter, we will develop a sentiment (positive or negative) classification model using a recurrent neural network. We will begin by preparing the data for developing the text classification model, followed by developing a sequential model, compiling the model, fitting the model, evaluating the model, prediction, and model performance assessment using a confusion matrix. We will also review some tips for sentiment classification performance optimization.

More specifically, in this chapter, we will cover the following topics:

- Preparing data for model building
- Developing a recurrent neural network model
- Fitting the model
- Model evaluation and prediction
- Performance optimization tips and best practices

Preparing data for model building

In this chapter, we'll be using the **Internet Movie Database** (**IMDb**) movie reviews text data that's available in the Keras package. Note that there is no need to download this data from anywhere as it can be easily accessed from the Keras library using code that we will discuss soon. In addition, this dataset is preprocessed so that text data is converted into a sequence of integers. We cannot use text data directly for model building, and such preprocessing of text data into a sequence of integers is necessary before the data can be used as input for developing deep learning networks.

We will start by loading the `imdb` data using the `dataset_imdb` function, where we will also specify the number of most frequent words as 500 using `num_words`. Then, we'll split the `imdb` data into `train` and `test` datasets. Let's take a look at the following code to understand this data:

```
# IMDB data
imdb <- dataset_imdb(num_words = 500)
c(c(train_x, train_y), c(test_x, test_y)) %<-% imdb
length(train_x); length(test_x)
[1] 25000
[1] 25000

table(train_y)
train_y
    0     1
12500 12500

table(test_y)
test_y
    0     1
12500 12500
```

Let's take a look at the preceding code:

- `train_x` and `test_x` contain integers representing reviews in the train and test data, respectively.
- Similarly, `train_y` and `test_y` contain 0 and 1 labels, representing negative and positive sentiments, respectively.
- Using the `length` function, we can see that both `train_x` and `test_x` are based on 25,000 movie reviews each.
- The tables for `train_y` and `test_y` show that there is an equal number of positive (12,500) and negative (12,500) reviews in the train and test data.

Having such a balanced dataset is useful in avoiding any bias due to class imbalance issues.

The words in the movie review are represented by unique integers and each integer that is assigned to a word is based on its overall frequency in the dataset. For example, integer 1 represents the most frequent word, while integer 2 represents the second most frequent word, and so on. In addition, integer 0 is not used for any specific word but it indicates an unknown word.

Let's take a look at the third and sixth sequences in the `train_x` data using the following code:

```
# Sequence of integers
train_x[[3]]
  [1]    1   14   47    8   30   31    7    4  249  108    7    4    2   54   61  369
 [17]   13   71  149   14   22  112    4    2  311   12   16    2   33   75   43    2
 [33]  296    4   86  320   35    2   19  263    2    2    4    2   33   89   78   12
 [49]   66   16    4  360    7    4   58  316  334   11    4    2   43    2    2    8
 [65]  257   85    2   42    2    2   83   68    2   15   36  165    2  278   36   69
 [81]    2    2    8  106   14    2    2   18    6   22   12  215   28    2   40    6
 [97]   87  326   23    2   21   23   22   12  272   40   57   31   11    4   22   47
[113]    6    2   51    9  170   23    2  116    2    2   13  191   79    2   89    2
[129]   14    9    8  106    2    2   35    2    6  227    7  129  113

train_x[[6]]
  [1]    1    2  128   74   12    2  163   15    4    2    2    2    2   32   85  156   45
 [18]   40  148  139  121    2    2   10   10    2  173    4    2    2   16    2    8    4
 [35]  226   65   12   43  127   24    2   10   10

for (i in 1:6) print(length(train_x[[i]]))

Output

[1] 218
[1] 189
[1] 141
[1] 550
[1] 147
[1] 43
```

From the preceding code and output, we can observe the following:

- From the output of the third movie review-related sequence of integers, we can observe that the third review contains 141 integers between 1 (1st integer) and 369 (16th integer).
- Since we restricted the use of the most frequent words to 500, for the third review, there is no integer larger than 500.

- Similarly, from the output of the sixth review's related sequence of integers, we can observe that the sixth review contains 43 integers between 1 (1st integer) and 226 (35th integer).
- Looking at the length of the first six sequences in the train_x data, we can observe that the length of the movie review varies between 43 (6th review in train data) and 550 (4th review in train data). Such variation in the length of the movie reviews is normal and is as expected.

Before we can develop a movie review sentiment classification model, we need to find a way to make the length of a sequence of integers the same for all the movie reviews. We can achieve this by padding sequences.

Padding sequences

Padding the text sequences is carried out to ensure that all the sequences have the same length. Let's take a look at the following code:

```
# Padding and truncation
train_x <- pad_sequences(train_x, maxlen = 100)
test_x <- pad_sequences(test_x, maxlen = 100)
```

From the preceding code, we can observe the following:

- We can achieve equal length for all the sequences of integers with the help of the pad_sequences function and by specifying a value for maxlen.
- In this example, we have restricted the length of each movie review sequence in the train and test data to 100. Note that before padding of sequences, the structure of train_x and test_x is a list of 25,000 reviews.
- However, after padding the sequences, the structure for both changes to a matrix that's 25,000 x 100. This can be easily verified by running str(train_x) before and after padding.

To observe the impact of padding on a sequence of integers, let's take a look at the following code, along with its output:

```
# Sequence of integers
train_x[3,]
 [1]    2    4    2   33   89   78   12   66   16    4  360    7    4   58  316  334
[17]   11    4    2   43    2    2    8  257   85    2   42    2    2   83   68    2
[33]   15   36  165    2  278   36   69    2    2    8  106   14    2    2   18    6
[49]   22   12  215   28    2   40    6   87  326   23    2   21   23   22   12  272
[65]   40   57   31   11    4   22   47    6    2   51    9  170   23    2  116    2
[81]    2   13  191   79    2   89    2   14    9    8  106    2    2   35    2    6
```

```
[97]  227    7 129 113

train_x[6,]
  [1]    0    0    0    0    0    0    0    0    0    0    0    0    0    0    0    0
 [17]    0    0    0    0    0    0    0    0    0    0    0    0    0    0    0    0
 [33]    0    0    0    0    0    0    0    0    0    0    0    0    0    0    0    0
 [49]    0    0    0    0    0    0    0    0    0    1    2 128   74   12    2 163
 [65]   15    4    2    2    2    2   32   85  156   45   40 148 139 121    2    2
 [81]   10   10    2 173    4    2    2   16    2    8    4 226   65   12   43 127
 [97]   24    2   10   10
```

The output of the third sequence of integers after padding of the `train_x` can be seen in the preceding code. Here, we can observe the following:

- The third sequence now has a length of 100. The third sequence originally had 141 integers and we can observe that 41 integers that were located at the beginning of the sequence have been truncated.
- On the other hand, the output of the sixth sequence shows a different pattern.
- The sixth sequence originally had a length of 43, but now 57 zeros have been added to the beginning of the sequence to artificially extended the length to 100.
- All 25,000 sequences of integers related to movie reviews in each of the train and test data are impacted in a similar way.

In the next section, we will develop an architecture for a recurrent neural network that will be used for developing a movie review sentiment classification model.

Developing a recurrent neural network model

In this section, we will develop the architecture for the recurrent neural network and compile it. Let's look at the following code:

```
# Model architecture
model <- keras_model_sequential()
model %>%
        layer_embedding(input_dim = 500, output_dim = 32) %>%
        layer_simple_rnn(units = 8) %>%
        layer_dense(units = 1, activation = "sigmoid")
```

We start by initializing the model using the `keras_model_sequential` function. Then, we add embedding and simple **recurrent neural network (RNN)** layers. For the embedding layer, we specify `input_dim` to be 500, which is the same as the number of most frequent words that we had specified earlier. The next layer is a simple RNN layer, with the number of hidden units specified as 8.

> Note that the default activation function for the `layer_simple_rnn` layer is a hyperbolic tangent (tanh), which is an S-shaped curve where the output ranges from -1 to +1.

The last dense layer has one unit to capture movie review sentiment (positive or negative) with the activation function sigmoid. When an output lies between 0 and 1, as in this case, it is convenient for interpretation as it can be thought of as a probability.

> Note that the sigmoid activation function is an S-shaped curve where the output ranges between 0 and 1.

Now, let's look at the model summary and understand how we can calculate on the number of parameters that are required.

Calculation of parameters

The summary of the RNN model is as follows:

```
# Model summary
model

OUTPUT
```

Model

Layer (type)	Output Shape	Param #
embedding_21 (Embedding)	(None, None, 32)	16000
simple_rnn_23 (SimpleRNN)	(None, 8)	328
dense_24 (Dense)	(None, 1)	9

```
Total params: 16,337
Trainable params: 16,337
```

```
Nor-trainable params: 0
```

The number of parameters for the embedding layer is arrived at by multiplying 500 (number of most frequent words) and 32 (output dimension) to obtain 16,000. To arrive at the number of parameters for the simple RNN layer, we use *(h(h+i) + h)*, where *h* represents the number of hidden units and *i* represents the input dimension for this layer. In this case, this is 32.

Thus, we have (8(8 + 32)+8) = 328 parameters.

> Note that if we consider a fully connected dense layer here, we would have obtained (8 x 32 + 8) = 264. However, the additional 64 parameters are due to the fact that we use recurrent layers to capture sequences in the text data.

In recurrent layers, information from the previous input is also used, which leads to these extra parameters that we can see here. This is the reason why RNNs are better suited for handling sequence data compared to a regular densely connected neural network layer. For the last layer, which is a dense layer, we have (1 x 8 + 1) = 9 parameters. Overall, this architecture has 16,337 parameters.

> In recurrent layers, the use of information from the previous input helps to provide a better representation of a sequence that is present in text or similar data that contains some kind of sequence.

Compiling the model

The code for compiling the model is as follows:

```
# Compile model
model %>% compile(optimizer = "rmsprop",
        loss = "binary_crossentropy",
        metrics = c("acc"))
```

We compile the model with the `rmsprop` optimizer, which is recommended for recurrent neural networks. We make use of `binary_crossentropy` as the loss function due to a binary type of response since movie reviews are either positive or negative. Finally, for metrics, we have specified accuracy.

In the next section, we will use this architecture to develop a movie review sentiment classification model that uses recurrent neural networks.

Fitting the model

The code for fitting the model is as follows:

```
# Fit model
model_one <- model %>% fit(train_x, train_y,
        epochs = 10,
        batch_size = 128,
        validation_split = 0.2)
```

For fitting the model, we will make use of a 20% validation split, which uses 20,000 movie review data from training data for building the model. The remaining 5,000 movie review training data is used for assessing validation in the form of loss and accuracy. We run 10 epochs with a batch size of 128.

> **TIP**
>
> When using a validation split, it is important to note that, with 20%, it uses the first 80% of the training data for training and the last 20% of the training data for validation. Thus, if the first 50% of the review data was negative and the last 50% was positive, the 20% validation split will cause model validation to be based only on positive reviews. Therefore, before using a validation split, we must verify that this is not the case; otherwise, it will introduce significant bias.

Accuracy and loss

The accuracy and loss values after 10 epochs for training and validation data using `plot(model_one)` can be seen in the following graph:

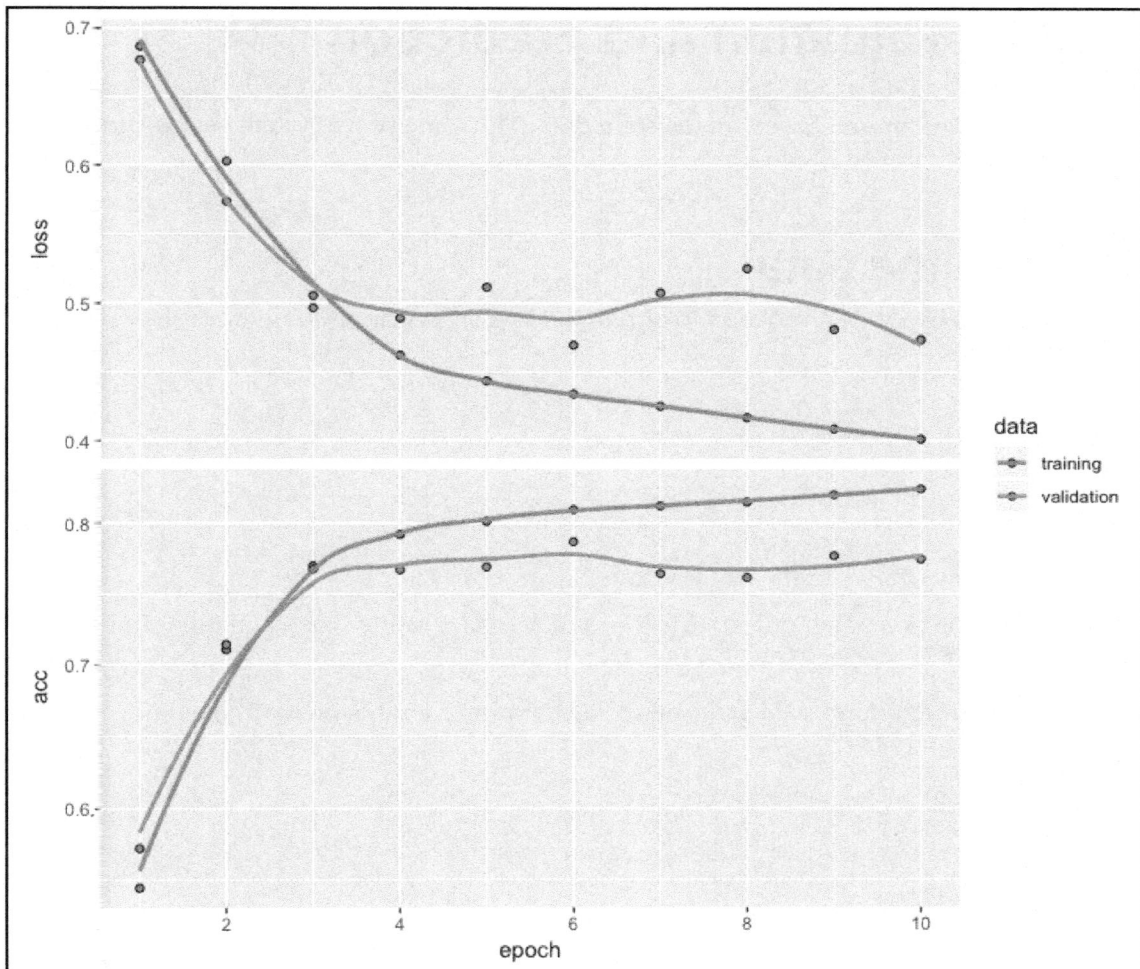

From the preceding graph, the following observations can be made:

- The training loss continues to decrease from epoch 1 to 10.
- Validation loss reduces initially, but it starts to look flat after 3 epochs.
- A similar pattern is also observed for accuracy in the opposite direction.

In the next section, we will evaluate the classification model and assess model prediction performance with the help of train and test data.

Model evaluation and prediction

First, we will evaluate the model based on the train data for loss and accuracy. We will also obtain a confusion matrix based on the train data. The same process shall be repeated with the test data.

Training the data

We will use the `evaluate` function to obtain the loss and accuracy values, as shown in the following code:

```
# Loss and accuracy
model %>% evaluate(train_x, train_y)
$loss
[1] 0.4057531

$acc
[1] 0.8205
```

As seen from the preceding output, the loss and accuracy values based on the training data are 0.406 and 0.821, respectively.

Predictions using training data are used for developing a confusion matrix, as shown in the following code:

```
# Prediction and confusion matrix
pred <- model %>% predict_classes(train_x)
table(Predicted=pred, Actual=imdb$train$y)
 Actual
Predicted 0 1
 0 9778 1762
 1 2722 10738
```

The following observations can be made by looking at the preceding confusion matrix:

- There are 9,778 movie reviews that are correctly classified as negative and there are 10,738 movie reviews that are correctly classified as positive. We can observe that the model does a decent job of classifying the reviews as positive or negative.
- Looking at the misclassifications, we can also observe that, on 2,722 occasions, negative movie reviews are misclassified as positive movie reviews. This is relatively higher compared to the misclassification of positive reviews as negative (1,762 times) by the classification model.

Next, let's do a similar assessment based on test data.

Testing the data

The code to obtain the loss and accuracy values is as follows:

```
# Loss and accuracy
mocel %>% evaluate(test_x, test_y)
$lcss
[1] 0.4669374

Sacc
[1] 0.77852
```

Here, we can see that the loss and accuracy based on the test data are 0.467 and 0.778, respectively. These results are slightly inferior to what we observed for the train data.

Next, we'll predict the classes for the test data and use the results to obtain a confusion matrix, as shown in the following code:

```
# Prediction and confusion matrix
pred1 <- model %>%   predict_classes(test_x)
table(Predicted=pred1, Actual=imdb$test$y)
         Actual
Predicted    0    1
        0  9134  2171
        1  3366 10329
```

Apart from the overall results being slightly inferior to the ones that we obtained from the train data, we can't see any major differences between the train and test data.

In the next section, we will explore a few strategies to improve model performance.

Performance optimization tips and best practices

When developing a recurrent neural network model, we come across situations where we need to make several decisions related to the network. These decisions could include trying a different activation function rather than the default one that we had used. Let's make such changes and see what impact they have on the movie review sentiment classification performance of the model.

In this section, we will experiment with the following four factors:

- Number of units in the simple RNN layer
- Using different activation functions in the simple RNN layer
- Adding more recurrent layers
- Changes in the maximum length for padding sequences

Number of units in the simple RNN layer

The code for incorporating this change and then compiling/fitting the model is as follows:

```
# Model architecture
model <- keras_model_sequential()
model %>%
        layer_embedding(input_dim = 500, output_dim = 32) %>%
        layer_simple_rnn(units = 32) %>%
        layer_dense(units = 1, activation = "sigmoid")

# Compile model
model %>% compile(optimizer = "rmsprop",
        loss = "binary_crossentropy",
        metrics = c("acc"))

# Fit model
model_two <- model %>% fit(train_x, train_y,
        epochs = 10,
        batch_size = 128,
        validation_split = 0.2)
```

Here, we change the architecture by increasing the number of units in the simple RNN layer from 8 to 32. Everything else is kept the same. Then, we compile and fit the model, as shown in the preceding code.

The accuracy and loss values after 10 epochs can be seen in the following graph:

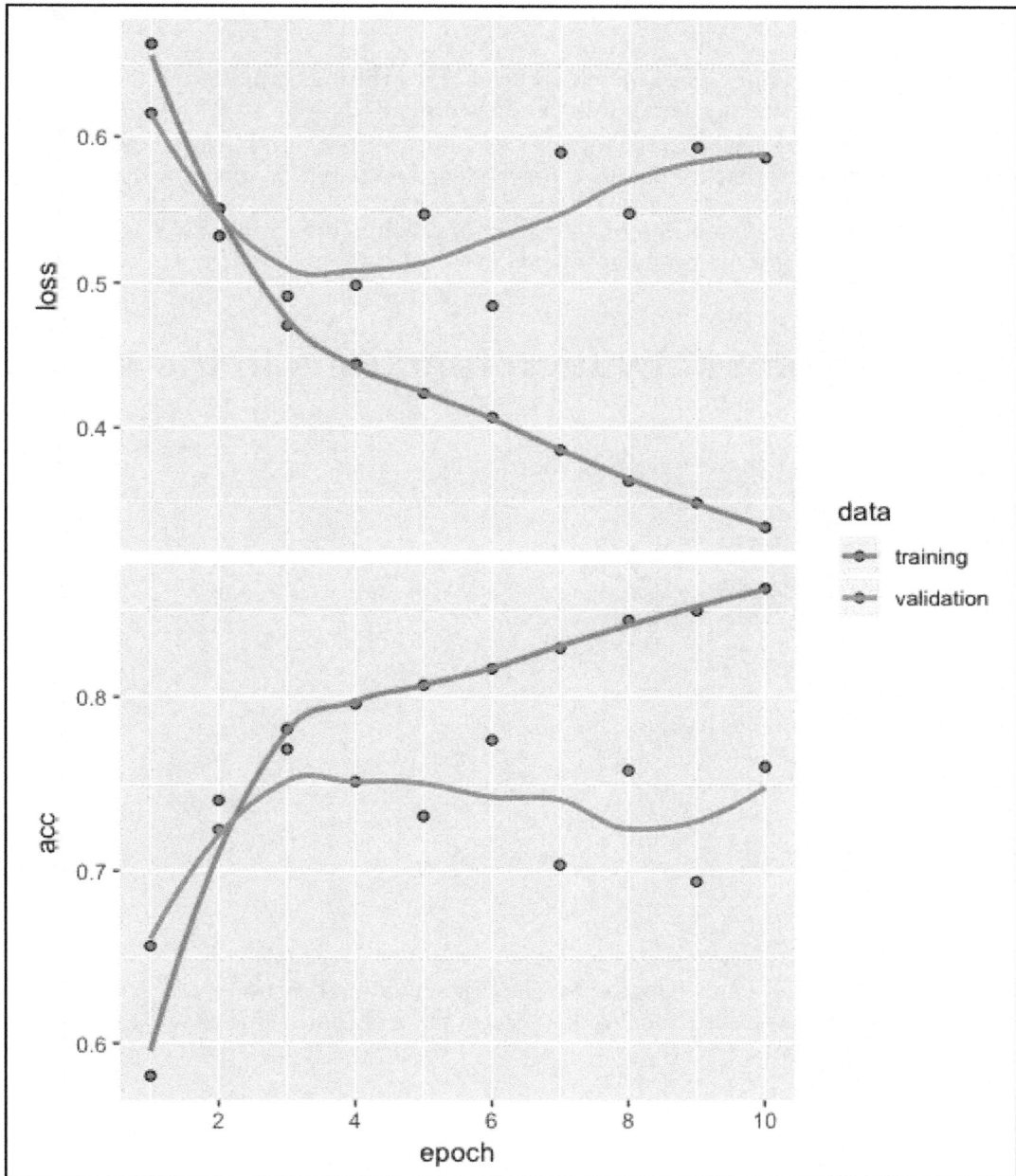

The preceding plot indicates the following:

- A significantly bigger gap between training and validation data on epoch 3 onward.
- This clearly suggests an increased level of overfitting compared to the preceding plot, where the number of units in the simple RNN was 8.
- This is also reflected in the higher loss value of 0.585 and the lower accuracy value of 0.757 that we obtained for the test data based on this new model.

Now, let's experiment with a different activation function in the simple RNN layer and see whether this overfitting issue can be resolved.

Using different activation functions in the simple RNN layer

This change can be seen in the following code:

```
# Model architecture
model <- keras_model_sequential()
model %>%
        layer_embedding(input_dim = 500, output_dim = 32) %>%
        layer_simple_rnn(units = 32, activation = "relu") %>%
 layer_dense(units = 1, activation = "sigmoid")

# Compile model
model %>% compile(optimizer = "rmsprop",
 loss = "binary_crossentropy",
 metrics = c("acc"))

# Fit model
model_three <- model %>% fit(train_x, train_y,
 epochs = 10,
 batch_size = 128,
 validation_split = 0.2)
```

In the preceding code, we are changing the default activation function in the simple RNN layer to a ReLU activation function. We keep everything else the same as what we had in the previous experiment.

The accuracy and loss values after 10 epochs can be seen in the following graph:

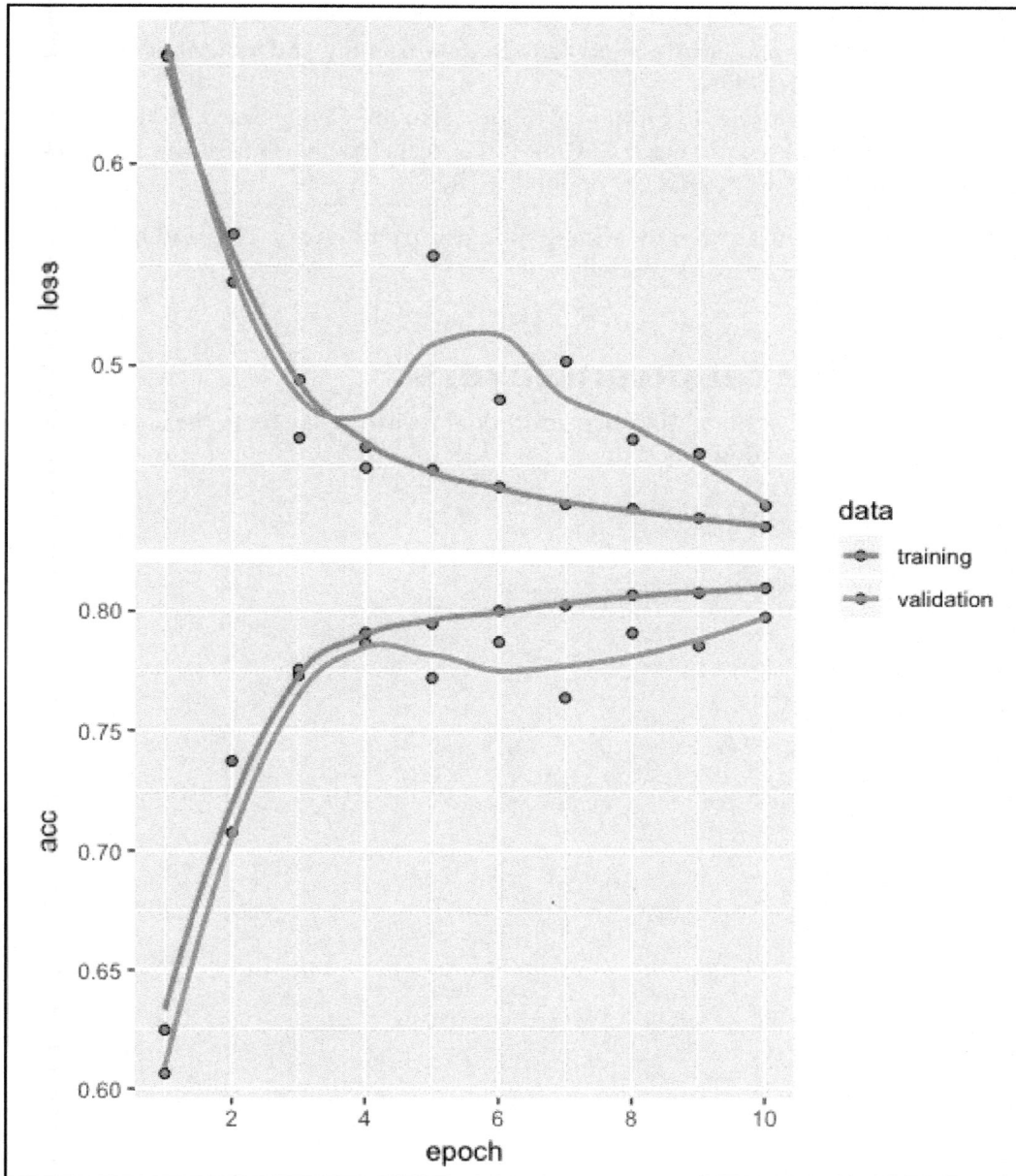

From the preceding plot, we can observe the following:

- The loss and accuracy values look much better now.
- Both the loss and accuracy curves based on training and validation are now closer to each other.
- We used the model to find the loss and accuracy values based on the test data that we obtained, that is, 0.423 and 0.803, respectively. This shows better results compared to the results we've obtained so far.

Next, we will experiment further by adding more recurrent layers. This will help us build a deeper recurrent neural network model.

Adding more recurrent layers

Now, we will experiment by adding two additional recurrent layers to the current network. The code that's incorporating this change is as follows:

```
# Model architecture
model <- keras_model_sequential() %>%
        layer_embedding(input_dim = 500, output_dim = 32) %>%
        layer_simple_rnn(units = 32,
                         return_sequences = TRUE,
                         activation = 'relu') %>%
        layer_simple_rnn(units = 32,
                         return_sequences = TRUE,
                         activation = 'relu') %>%
        layer_simple_rnn(units = 32,
                         activation = 'relu') %>%
        layer_dense(units = 1, activation = "sigmoid")

# Compile model
model %>% compile(optimizer = "rmsprop",
 loss = "binary_crossentropy",
 metrics = c("acc"))

# Fit model
model_four <- model %>% fit(train_x, train_y,
0 epochs = 10,
 batch_size = 128,
 validation_split = 0.2)
```

When we add these additional recurrent layers, we also set `return_sequences` to `TRUE`. We keep everything else the same and compile/fit the model. The plot for the loss and accuracy values based on the training and validation data is as follows:

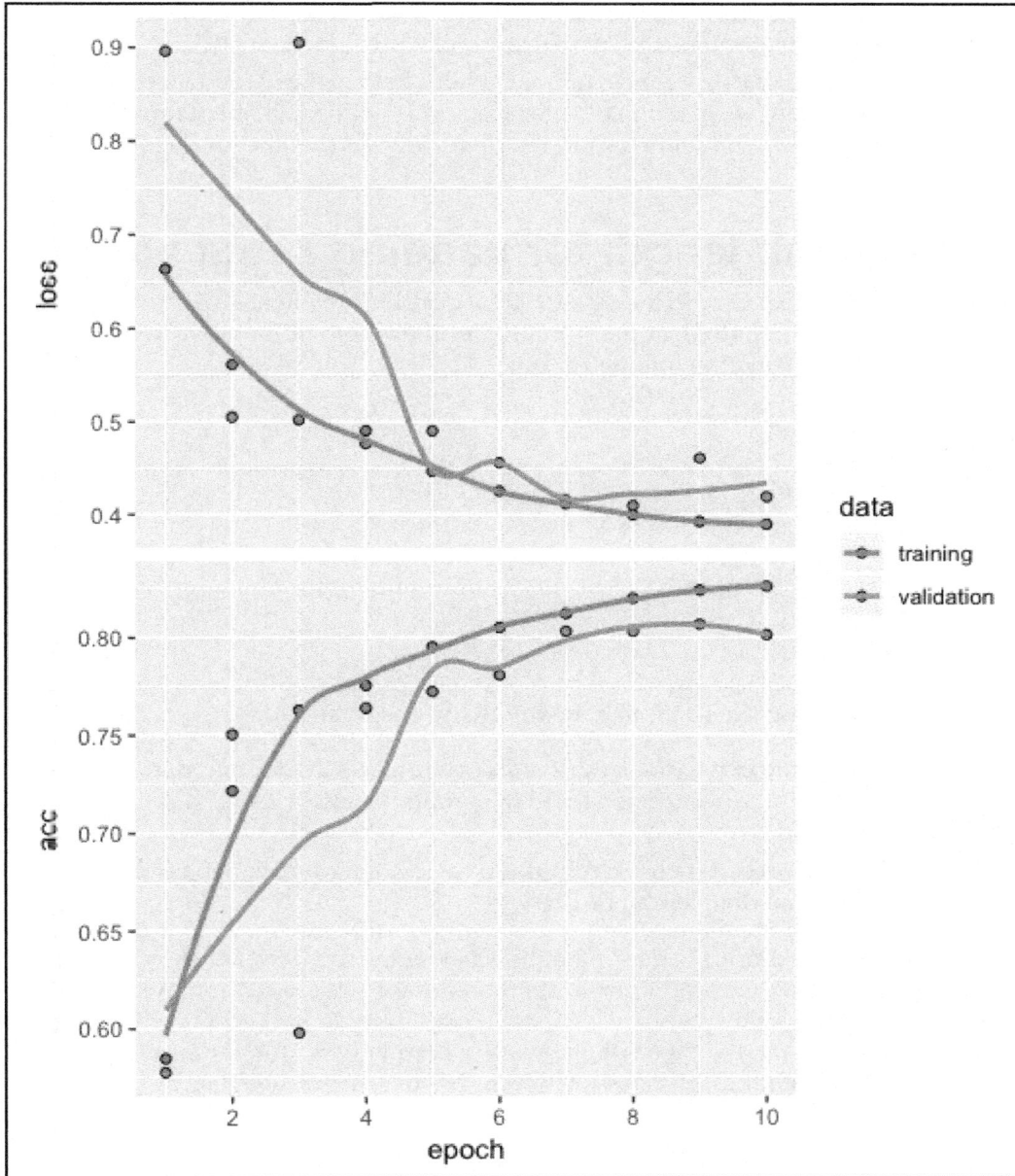

From the preceding plot, we can observe the following:

- After 10 epochs, the loss and accuracy values for training and validation show a reasonable level of closeness, indicating the absence of overfitting.
- The loss and accuracy based on the test data we calculated show a decent improvement in the results with 0.403 and 0.816, respectively.
- This shows that deeper recurrent layers did help capture sequences of words in the movie reviews in a much better way. This, in turn, enabled improved classification of the sentiment in movie reviews as positive or negative.

The maximum length for padding sequences

So far, we have used a maximum length of 100 for padding sequences of movie reviews in the train and test data. Let's look at the summary of the length of movie reviews in the train and test data using the following code:

```
# Summary of padding sequences
z <- NULL
for (i in 1:25000) {z[i] <- print(length(train_x[[i]]))}
   Min. 1st Qu.  Median   Mean 3rd Qu.   Max.
   11.0   130.0   178.0   238.7   291.0   2494.0

z <- NULL
for (i in 1:25000) {z[i] <- print(length(test_x[[i]]))}
   Min. 1st Qu.  Median   Mean 3rd Qu.   Max.
    7.0   128.0   174.0   230.8   280.0   2315.0
```

From the preceding code, we can make the following observations:

- From the summary of the length of movie reviews in the train data, we can see that the minimum length is 11, the maximum length is 2,494, and that the median length is 178.
- Similarly, the test data has a minimum review length of 7, a maximum length of 2,315, and a median length of 174.

Note that when the maximum padding length is below the median (which is the case with a maximum length of 100), we tend to truncate more movie reviews by removing words beyond 100. At the same time, when we choose a maximum length for padding to be significantly above the median, we will have a situation where a higher number of movie reviews will need to contain zeros and fewer number of reviews will be truncated.

In this section, we are going to explore the impact of keeping the maximum length of the sequence of words in the movie reviews near the median value. The code for incorporating this change is as follows:

```
# IMDB data
c(c(train_x, train_y), c(test_x, test_y)) %<-% imdb
train_x <- pad_sequences(train_x, maxlen = 200)
test_x <- pad_sequences(test_x, maxlen = 200)

# Model architecture
model <- keras_model_sequential() %>%
        layer_embedding(input_dim = 500, output_dim = 32) %>%
        layer_simple_rnn(units = 32,
                        return_sequences = TRUE,
                        activation = 'relu') %>%
        layer_simple_rnn(units = 32,
                        return_sequences = TRUE,
                        activation = 'relu') %>%
        layer_simple_rnn(units = 32,
                        return_sequences = TRUE,
                        activation = 'relu') %>%
        layer_simple_rnn(units = 32,
                        activation = 'relu') %>%
        layer_dense(units = 1, activation = "sigmoid")

# Compile model
model %>% compile(optimizer = "rmsprop",
        loss = "binary_crossentropy",
        metrics = c("acc"))

# Fit model
model_five <- model %>% fit(train_x, train_y,
        epochs = 10,
        batch_size = 128,
        validation_split = 0.2)
```

From the preceding code, we can see that we run the model after specifying `maxlen` as 200. We keep everything else the same as what we had for `model_four`.

The plot for the loss and accuracy for the training and validation data is as follows:

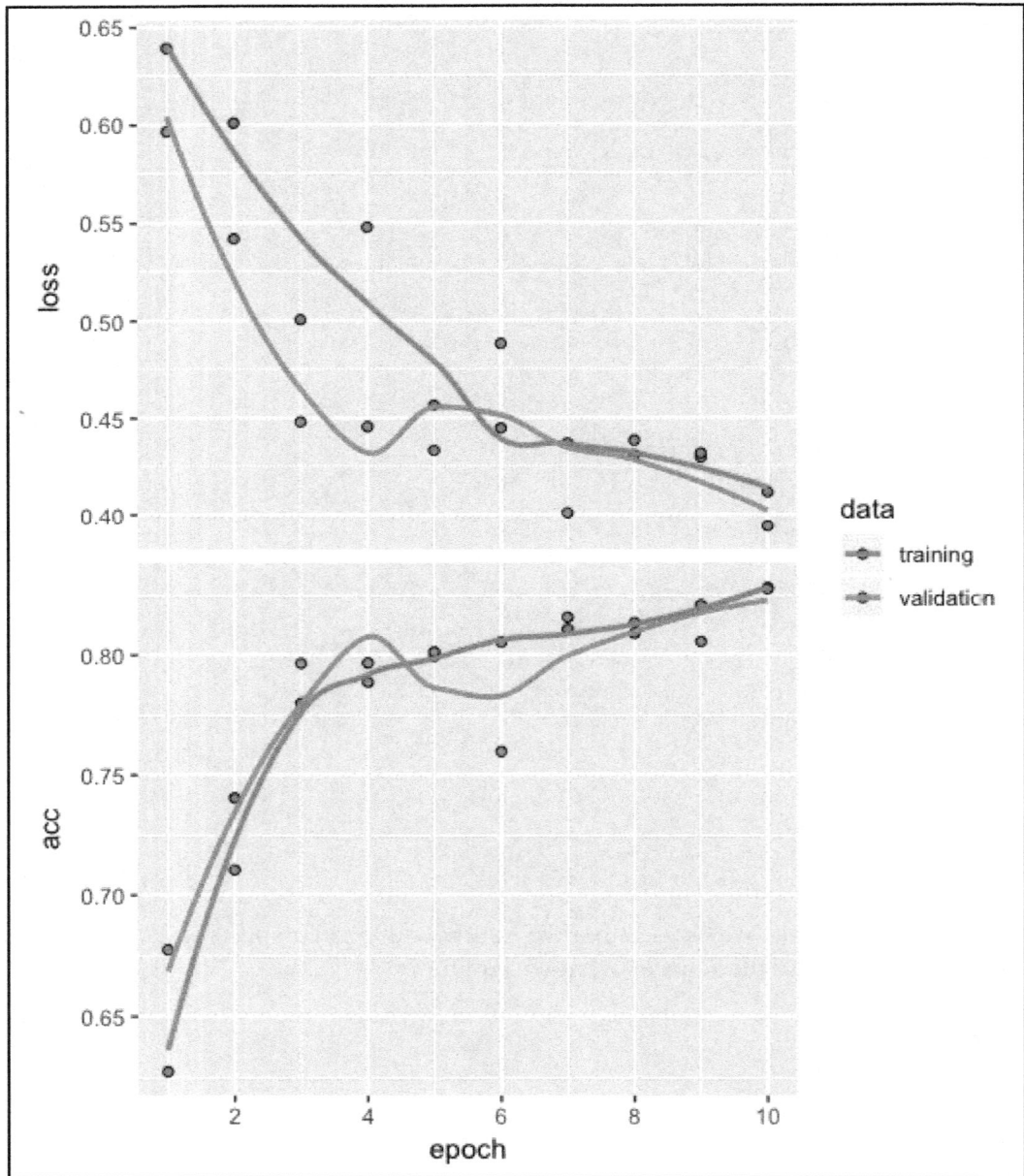

From the preceding plot, we can make the following observations:

- There's the absence of an overfitting issue since the training and validation data points are very close to each other.
- The loss and accuracy based on the test data were calculated as 0.383 and 0.830, respectively.
- The loss and accuracy values are at their best level at this stage.

The confusion matrix based on the test data is as follows:

```
# Prediction and confusion matrix
pred1 <- model %>%   predict_classes(test_x)
table(Predicted=pred1, Actual=imdb$test$y)
         Actual
Predicted     0      1
        0 10066   1819
        1  2434  10681
```

From the confusion matrix, we can make the following observations:

- This classification model seems to performs slightly better when correctly classifying the movie review as positive (10,681) compared to when classifying a negative (10,066) review correctly.
- As far as reviews that are classified incorrectly are concerned, the trend that we had observed earlier, where negative movie reviews were mistakenly classified by the model as positive being on the higher side, exists in this case too.

In this section, we experimented with a number of units, activation functions, the number of recurrent layers in the network, and the amount of padding in order to improve the movie review sentiment classification model. Some other factors that you could explore further include the number of most frequent words to include and changing the maximum length at the time of padding sequences.

Summary

In this chapter, we illustrated the use of the recurrent neural network model for text sentiment classification using IMDb movie review data. Compared to a regular densely connected network, recurrent neural networks are better suited to deal with data that has sequences in it. Text data is one such example that we worked with in this chapter.

In general, deep networks involve many factors or variables, and this calls for some amount of experimentation involving making changes to the levels for such factors before arriving at a useful model. In this chapter, we also developed five different movie review sentiment classification models.

A variant of recurrent neural networks that has become popular is **Long Short-Term Memory (LSTM)** networks. LSTM networks are capable of learning long-term dependencies and help recurrent networks remember inputs for a longer time.

In the next chapter, we will go over an application example of using an LSTM network, where we will continue to use IMDb movie review data and explore further improvements that can be made to the sentiment classification model's performance.

11
Text classification Using Long Short-Term Memory Network

In the previous chapter, we used a recurrent neural network to develop a movie review sentiment classification model for text data that are characterized by a sequence of words. **Long Short-Term Memory (LSTM)** neural networks are a special type of **Recurrent Neural Networks (RNNs)** that are useful with data involving sequences and provide advantages that we will discuss in the next section. This chapter illustrates the steps for using an LSTM neural network for sentiment classification. The steps involved in applying an LSTM network to a business problem may include text data preparation, creating the LSTM model, training the model, and assessing the model performance.

More specifically, in this chapter, we will cover the following topics:

- Why do we use LSTM networks?
- Preparing text data for model building
- Creating a long short-term memory network model
- Fitting the LSTM model
- Evaluating model performance
- Performance optimization tips and best practices

Why do we use LSTM networks?

We have seen, in the previous chapter, that recurrent neural networks provide decent performance when working with data involving sequences. One of the key advantages of using LSTM networks lies in the fact that they address the vanishing gradient problem that makes network training difficult for a long sequence of words or integers. Gradients are used for updating RNN parameters and for a long sequence of words or integers; these gradients become smaller and smaller to the extent that, effectively, no network training can take place. LSTM networks help to overcome this problem and make it possible to capture long-term dependencies between keywords or integers in sequences that are separated by a large distance. For example, consider the following two sentences, where the first sentence is short and the second sentence is relatively longer:

- **Sentence-1**: I like to eat chocolates.
- **Sentence-2**: I like, whenever there is a chance and usually there are many of them, to eat chocolates.

In these sentences, the two important words that capture the main essence of the sentence are **like** and **chocolates**. In the first sentence, the words **like** and **chocolates** are closer to each other and they are separated by just two words in between. On the other hand, in the second sentence, these two words are separated by as many as 14 words that lie between them. LSTM networks are designed to deal with such long-term dependencies that are observed in longer sentences or longer sequences of integers. In this chapter, we focus on applying LSTM networks for developing a movie review sentiment classification model.

Preparing text data for model building

We will continue to use IMDB movie review data that we used in the previous chapter on recurrent neural networks. This data is already available in a format where we can use it for developing deep network models with minimum need for data processing.

Let's take a look at the following code:

```
# IMDB data
library(keras)
imdb <- dataset_imdb(num_words = 500)
c(c(train_x, train_y), c(test_x, test_y)) %<-% imdb
train_x <- pad_sequences(train_x, maxlen = 200)
test_x <- pad_sequences(test_x, maxlen = 200)
```

The sequence of integers capturing train and test data is stored in `train_x` and `test_x` respectively. Similarly, `train_y` and `test_y` store labels capturing information about whether movie reviews are positive or negative. We have specified the number of most frequent words to be 500. For padding, we are using 200 as the maximum length of a sequence of integers for both train and test data.

When the actual length of integers is less than 200, then zeros get added at the beginning of the sequence to artificially increase the length of integers to 200. However, when the length of integers is more than 200, integers at the beginning are removed so that the total length of integers is maintained at 200.

As mentioned earlier, both train and test datasets are balanced and contain data involving 25,000 movie reviews each. For each movie review, positive or negative labels are also available.

> Note that the choice of value for `maxlen` can impact model performance. If the value chosen is too small, more words or integers in a sequence will get truncated. On the other hand, if the value chosen is too large, then more words or integers in a sequence will need padding, with zeroes getting added. One way to avoid too much padding or too much truncation is to choose a value closer to the median.

Creating a long short-term memory network model

In this section, we will start with a simple LSTM network architecture and look at calculations to arrive at the number of parameters. Subsequently, we will compile the model.

LSTM network architecture

We will start with a simple flow chart of the LSTM network architecture, as shown in the following screenshot:

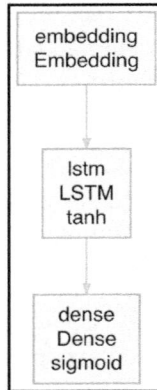

The preceding flow chart for the LSTM network highlights the layers in the architecture and activation functions used. In the LSTM layer, the `tanh` activation function is used which is the default activation function for the layer. In the dense layer, the `sigmoid` activation function is used.

Let's have a look at the following code and summary of the model:

```
# Model architecture
model <- keras_model_sequential() %>%
        layer_embedding(input_dim = 500, output_dim = 32) %>%
        layer_lstm(units = 32) %>%
        layer_dense(units = 1, activation = "sigmoid")
model
```

Layer (type)	Output Shape	Param #
embedding (Embedding)	(None, None, 32)	16000
lstm (LSTM)	(None, 32)	8320
dense (Dense)	(None, 1)	33

```
Total params: 24,353
Trainable params: 24,353
Non-trainable params: 0
```

Apart from what we used for the RNN model in the last chapter, we are replacing `layer_simple_rnn` with `layer_lstm` for the LSTM network in this example. For the embedding layer, we have a total of 16,000 (500 x 32) parameters. The calculation shown as follows calculates the number of parameters for the LSTM layer:

=4 x [units in LSTM layer x (units in LSTM layer + output dimension) + units in LSTM layer]

= 4 x [32(32+32) + 32]

= 8320

For a similar architecture involving the RNN layer, we will have 2,080 parameters. The four-fold increase in the number of parameters for the LSTM layer also leads to more training time and hence requires relatively higher processing costs. The number of parameters for the dense layer is *[(32x1) + 1]*, which comes to 33. Hence, overall there are 24,353 parameters in this network.

Compiling the LSTM network model

For compiling the LSTM network model, we will use the following code:

```
# Compile
model %>% compile(optimizer = "rmsprop",
        loss = "binary_crossentropy",
        metrics = c("acc"))
```

We are using `rmsprop` as optimizer and `binary_crossentropy` for loss, since movie reviews have a binary response or, in other words, they are either positive or negative. For metrics, we are making use of classification accuracy. After compiling the model, we are ready to go to the next step of fitting the LSTM model.

Fitting the LSTM model

For training the LSTM model, we will use the following code:

```
# Fit model
model_one <- model %>% fit(train_x, train_y,
        epochs = 10,
        batch_size = 128,
        validation_split = 0.2)
plot(model_one)
```

We will use train data to fit the LSTM model with ten epochs and use a batch size of ⎺28. We will also reserve 20% of train data as validation data for assessing loss and accuracy values during model training.

Loss and accuracy plot

The following screenshot shows the loss and accuracy plot for `model_one`:

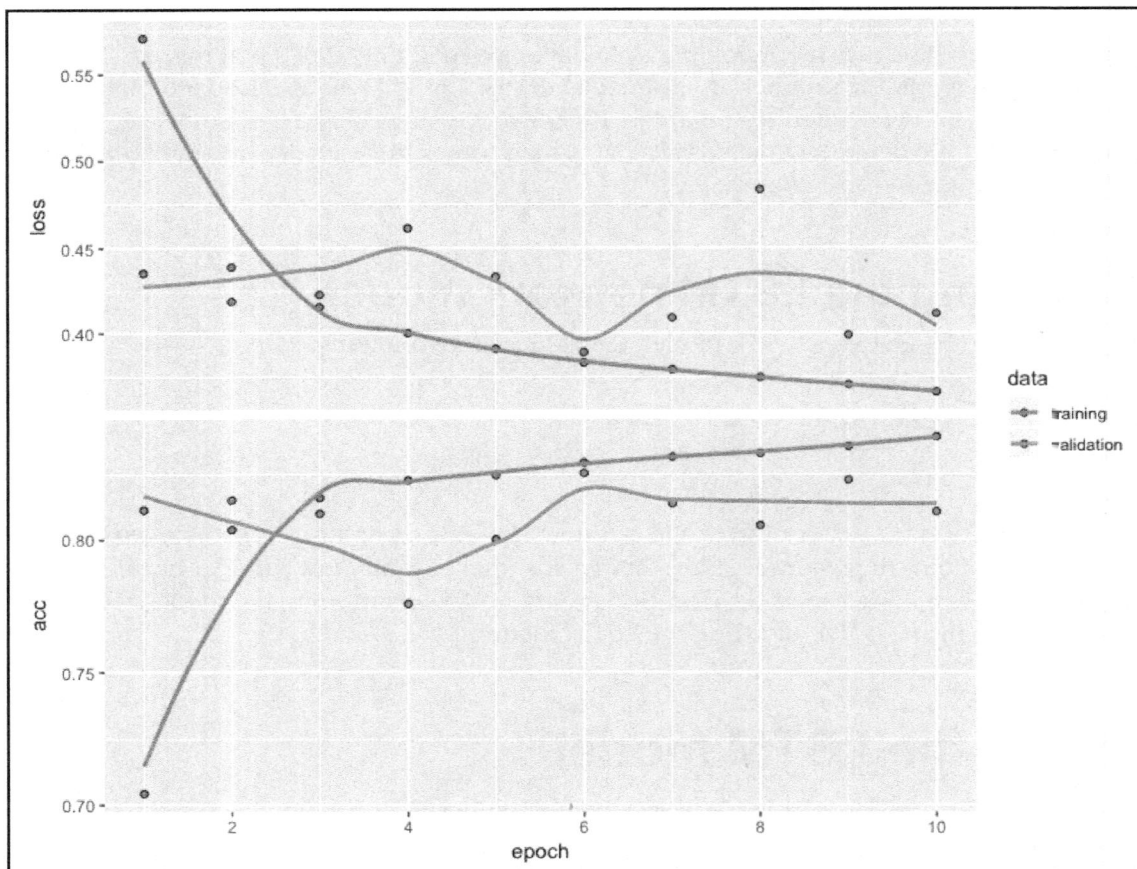

The plot for loss and accuracy based on training and validation data shows overall closeness between the curves. The observations from the plot are as follows:

- There is no major divergence between the two lines, which indicates the lack of an over-fitting problem.
- An increase in the number of epochs may not provide any significant improvement in model performance.
- However, the loss and accuracy values based on the validation data show some amount of unevenness or oscillation where they deviate from the training loss and accuracy by a relatively high amount.
- Epochs 4 and 8 especially stand out in this regard showing significant deviation from the loss and accuracy based on training data.

Next, we will move toward evaluating `model_one` and use it for prediction of the movie review sentiment.

Evaluating model performance

In this section, we will evaluate the model based on both training and test data. We will also create a confusion matrix for both train and test data to gain further insights into the movie review sentiment classification performance of the model.

Model evaluation with train data

We will first evaluate the model performance with train data using the following code:

```
# Evaluate
model %>% evaluate(train_x, train_y)
$loss
 [1]  0.3749587
$acc
 [1]  0.82752
```

As seen from the preceding output, for the training data, we obtain a loss value of 0.375 and an accuracy of about 0.828. This is a decent performance considering a relatively simple LSTM architecture. We next use this model to make predictions for the movie review sentiment and summarize the results by developing a confusion matrix using the following code:

```
# Confusion Matrix
pred <- model %>% predict_classes(train_x)
table(Predicted=pred, Actual=imdb$train$y)
          Actual
 Predicted     0     1
         0  9258  1070
         1  3242 11430
```

We can make the following observations from the confusion matrix:

- It is observed that this model seems to be more accurate in predicting positive movie reviews (11,430 correct predictions) compared to negative movie reviews (9,258 correct predictions). In other words, this model correctly classifies positive reviews at the rate of about 91.4% (also called the sensitivity of the model) for the training data.
- Similarly, this model correctly classifies negative reviews at the rate of about 74.1% (also called specificity of the model) for the training data.
- It is also observed that the negative movie reviews are being misclassified as a positive review at the rate of about three times (3,242 reviews) more compared to a positive review being misclassified as negative (1,070 reviews).
- Hence, although overall, this model seems to perform well for the training data, looking deeper, we observe some bias toward correctly classifying positive movie reviews at the cost of lower accuracy in correctly classifying negative reviews.

It will be interesting to see whether the model performance observed, based on training data, results in similar behavior for the test data or not.

Model evaluation with test data

We will now use the test data to obtain loss and accuracy values for the model using the following code:

```
# Evaluate
model %>% evaluate(test_x, test_y)
$loss
 [1] 0.3997277
$acc
 [1] 0.81992
```

As seen from the preceding output, for the test data, we obtain a loss value of 0.399 and an accuracy of about 0.819. These values, as expected, are slightly inferior to those obtained for the train data. However, they are close enough to results based on the train data to consider this model behavior consistent.

The code to obtain a confusion matrix using test data is as follows:

```
# Confusion Matrix
pred1 <- model %>$ predict_classes(text_x)
table(Predicted=pred1, Actual=imdb$test$y)
         Actual
 Predicted    0     1
         0  9159  1161
         1  3341 11339
```

From the confusion matrix shown above, the following observations can be made:

- The confusion matrix based on predictions using the test data shows a similar pattern that we observed earlier for the training data.
- This model also seems to perform better when accurately classifying positive movie reviews (at a rate of about 90.7%), compared to correctly classifying negative reviews (at a rate of about 73.3%).
- Hence, the model continues to show bias in the performance when correctly classifying positive movie reviews.

In the next section, we will carry out some experimentation to explore possible improvements for the model's movie review sentiment classification performance.

Performance optimization tips and best practices

In this section, we will carry out three different experiments to search for an improved LSTM based movie review sentiment classification model. This will involve trying a different optimizer at the time of compiling the model, adding another LSTM layer when developing the model architecture, and using a bidirectional LSTM layer in the network.

Experimenting with the Adam optimizer

We will use the adam (Adaptive Moment Optimization) optimizer instead of the rmsprop (Root Mean Square Propagation) optimizer that we used earlier when compiling the model. To make a comparison of model performance easier, we will keep everything else the same as earlier, as shown in the following code:

```
# Model architecture
model <- keras_model_sequential() %>%
        layer_embedding(input_dim = 500, output_dim = 32) %>%
        layer_lstm(units = 32) %>%
        layer_dense(units = 1, activation = "sigmoid")

# Compile
model %>% compile(optimizer = "adam",
        loss = "binary_crossentropy",
        metrics = c("acc"))

# Fit model
model_two <- model %>% fit(train_x, train_y,
        epochs = 10,
        batch_size = 128,
        validation_split = 0.2)
plot(model_two)
```

After running the preceding codes and training the model, the accuracy and loss values for each epoch are stored in model_two. We use the loss and accuracy values in model_two to develop the following plot:

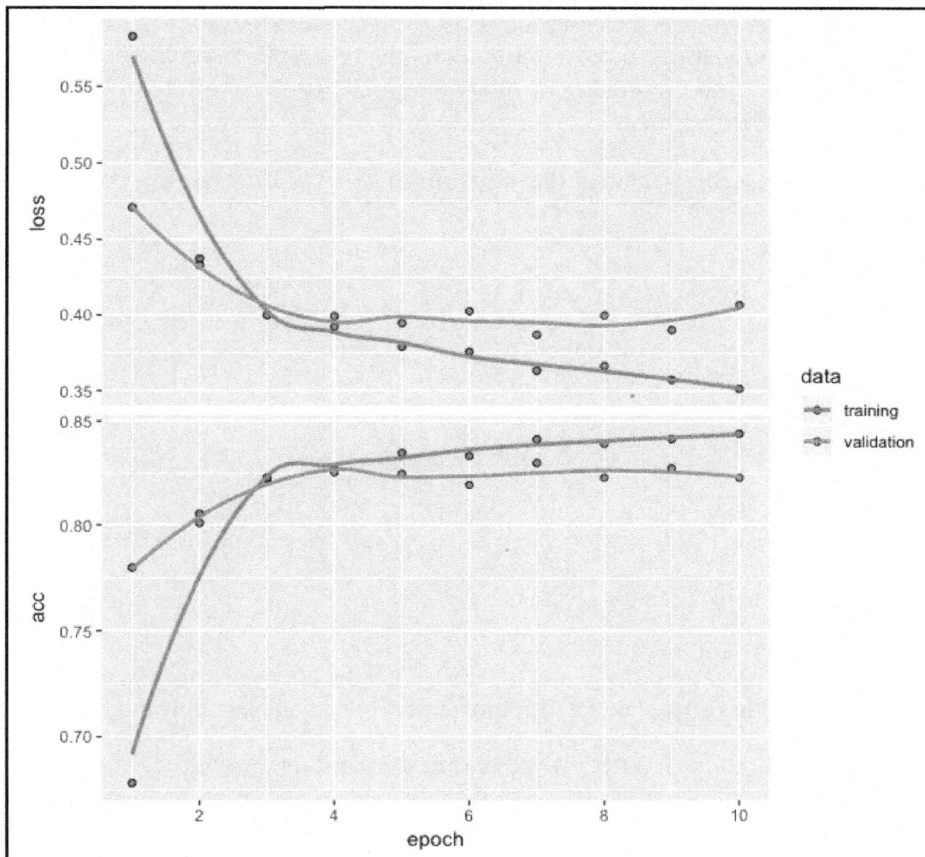

From the preceding loss and accuracy plot, we can make the following observations:

- The loss and accuracy plot based on the training and validation data shows a slightly improved pattern compared to the plot for the first model that we built with model_one.
- In the plot based on model_one, we observed that loss and accuracy values for validation data occasionally showed major deviations from the values based on the training data. In this plot, we do not see any such major deviation between the two lines.

- Also, the loss and accuracy values based on the last few values of validation data seem flat, suggesting that the ten epochs that we have used are sufficient to train the model and an increasing number of epochs is not likely to help in improving the model performance.

Next, let's obtain the loss, accuracy, and confusion matrix for the training data using the following code:

```
# Loss and accuracy
model %>% evaluate(train_x, train_y)
$loss
[1] 0.3601628
$acc
[1] 0.8434

pred <- model %>%    predict_classes(train_x)

# Confusion Matrix
table(Predicted=pred, Actual=imdb$train$y)
         Actual
Predicted     0     1
        0 11122  2537
        1  1378  9963
```

From the preceding code output, we can make the following observations:

- By using the adam optimizer, we obtain loss and accuracy for training data as 0.360 and 0.843 respectively. Both these numbers show an improvement compared to the earlier model where we had used the rmsprop optimizer
- Another difference can be observed from the confusion matrix. This model performs better when correctly classifying negative movie reviews (at a rate of about 88.9%) compared to the correct classification of positive reviews (at a rate of about 79.7%).
- This behavior is the opposite of what was observed in the previous model. This model seems to be biased toward correctly classifying negative movie review sentiment compared to correctly classifying positive reviews.

Having reviewed the performance of the model using the training data, we will now repeat the process with the test data, with the following code for obtaining the loss, accuracy, and confusion matrix:

```
# Loss and accuracy
model %>% evaluate(test_x, test_y)
$loss
[1] 0.3854687
```

```
$acc
[1] 0.82868

pred1 <- model %>%    predict_classes(test_x)

# Confusion Matrix
table(Predicted=pred1, Actual=imdb$test$y)
          Actual
Predicted      0      1
        0  10870   2653
        1   1630   9847
```

From the preceding code output, we can make the following observations:

- The loss and accuracy based on test data are 0.385 and 0.829 respectively. These results, based on the test data, also show better model performance compared to the previous model with the test data.
- The confusion matrix shows a similar pattern that we observed for the training data. Negative movie review sentiments are correctly classified at a rate of about 86.9% for the test data.
- Similarly, positive movie review sentiments are correctly classified by the model at a rate of about 78.8% for the test data.
- This behavior is consistent with the model performance that was obtained using the training data.

Although trying the `adam` optimizer improves overall movie review sentiment classification performance, it still retains bias when correctly classifying one category compared to the other. A good model should not only improve the overall performance, but it should also minimize any bias when correctly classifying a category. The following code provides a table showing the number of negative and positive reviews in the `train` and `test` data:

```
# Number of positive and negative reviews in the train data
table(train_y)
train_y
    0     1
12500 12500

# Number of positive and negative review in the test data
table(test_y)
test_y
    0     1
12500 12500
```

It can be seen from the preceding output of code that this movie review data is balanced where both train and test data has 25,000 reviews each. This data is also balanced in terms of the number of positive or negative reviews. Both train and test datasets have 12,500 positive and 12,500 negative movie reviews each. Hence, there is no bias in the amount of negative or positive reviews provided to the model for training. However, the bias seen when correctly classifying negative and positive movie reviews is certainly something that needs improvement.

In the next experiment, let's explore with more LSTM layers and see whether or not we can obtain a better movie review sentiment classification model.

Experimenting with the LSTM network having an additional layer

In this second experiment to improve the performance of the classification model, we will add an extra LSTM layer. Let's have a look at the following code:

```
# Model architecture
model <- keras_model_sequential() %>%
         layer_embedding(input_dim = 500, output_dim = 32) %>%
         layer_lstm(units = 32,
                    return_sequences = TRUE) %>%
         layer_lstm(units = 32) %>%
         layer_dense(units = 1, activation = "sigmoid")

# Compiling model
model %>% compile(optimizer = "adam",
         loss = "binary_crossentropy",
         metrics = c("acc"))

# Fitting model
model_three <- model %>% fit(train_x, train_y,
         epochs = 10,
         batch_size = 128,
         validation_split = 0.2)

# Loss and accuracy plot
plot(model_three)
```

By adding an extra LSTM layer to the network, as shown in the preceding code, the total number of parameters with these two LSTM layers will now increase to 32,673 compared to 24,353 that we had previously with one LSTM layer. This increase in the number of parameters will also lead to higher training time when training the network. We are also retaining the use of the Adam optimizer when compiling the model. We are keeping everything else the same as what we had used in the previous model.

A simple flow chart for the network architecture with two LSTM layers used in this experiment, is shown in the following screenshot:

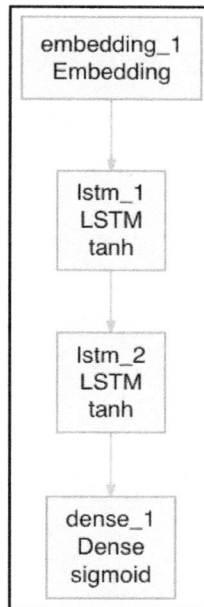

The preceding flow chart shown for the LSTM network highlights the two layers in the architecture and activation functions used. In both LSTM layers, tanh is used as the default activation function. In the dense layer, we continue to use the sigmoid activation function that we used earlier.

After training the model, the accuracy and loss values for each epoch is stored in `model_three`. We use the loss and accuracy values in `model_three` to develop the following plot:

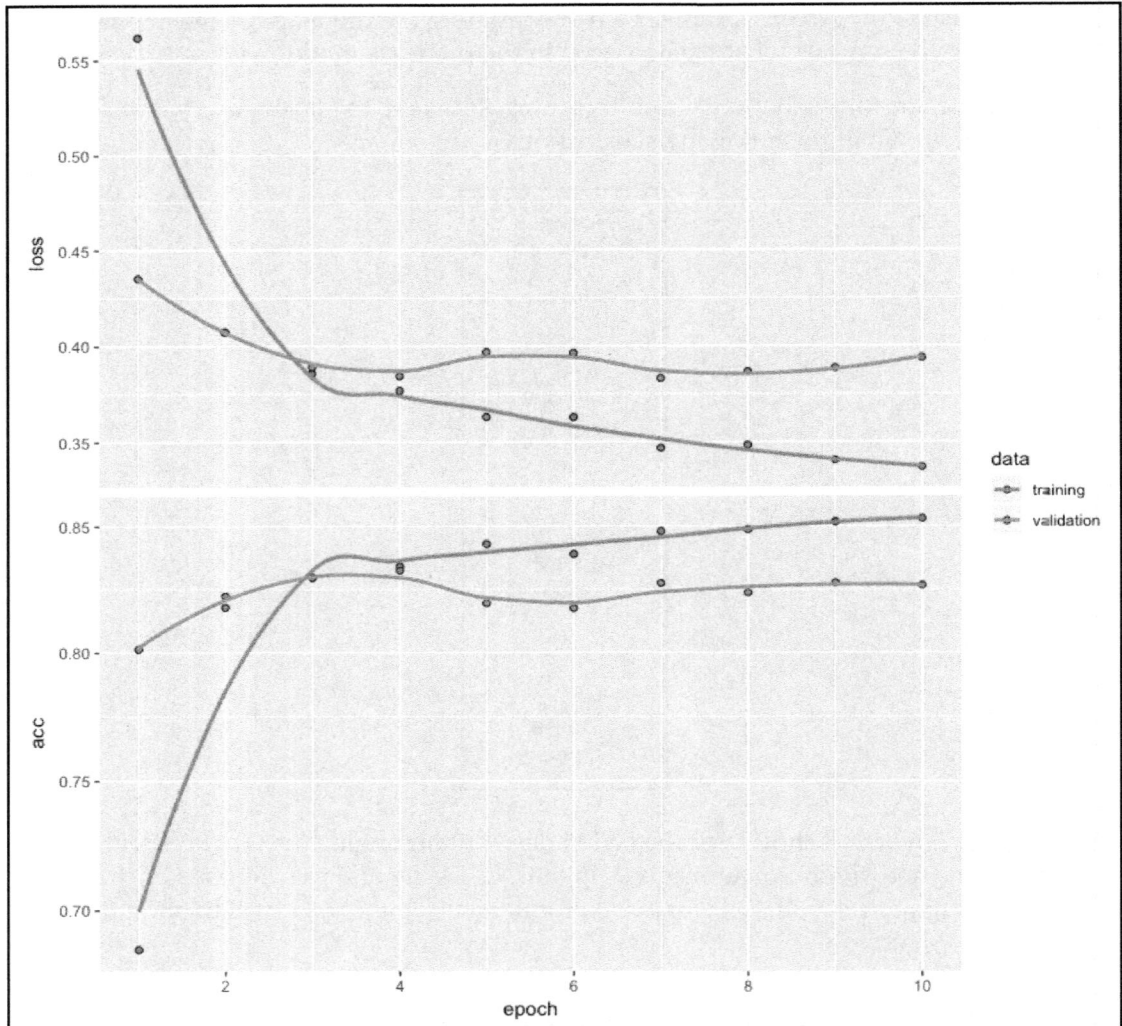

From the loss and accuracy plot shown, we can make the following observations:

- The plot for loss and accuracy values doesn't indicate the presence of an over-fitting problem since the curves for the training and validation data are close to each other.

- As in the earlier model, the loss and accuracy for the validation data seem to remain flat for the last few epochs, indicating ten epochs are sufficient for training the model, and increasing the number of epochs is not likely to improve results.

We can now obtain the loss, accuracy, and confusion matrix for the training data using the following code:

```
# Loss and accuracy
model %>% evaluate(train_x, train_y)
$loss
[1] 0.3396379
$acc
[1] 0.85504

pred <- model %>%   predict_classes(train_x)

# Confusion Matrix
table(Predicted=pred, Actual=imdb$train$y)
         Actual
Predicted    0     1
        0 11245  2369
        1  1255 10131
```

From the preceding code output, we can make the following observations:

- The loss and accuracy values based on training data are obtained as `0.339` and `0.855` respectively. Both loss and accuracy show improvement compared to the earlier two models.
- We can use this model to make predictions for each review in the training data, compare them with actual labels, and then summarize the results in the form of a confusion matrix.
- For the training data, the confusion matrix shows that the model correctly classifies negative movie reviews about 90% of the time and correctly classifies positive reviews about 81% of the time.
- So, although there is an overall improvement in the model performance, we continue to observe bias when correctly classifying one category compared to the other.

After reviewing the performance of the model using training data, we will now repeat the process with the test data. Following is the code for obtaining the loss, accuracy, and confusion matrix:

```
# Loss and accuracy
model %>% evaluate(test_x, test_y)
$loss
[1] 0.3761043
$acc
[1] 0.83664

pred1 <- model %>%   predict_classes(test_x)

# Confusion Matrix
table(Predicted=pred1, Actual=imdb$test$y)
         Actual
Predicted    0     1
        0 10916  2500
        1  1584 10000
```

From the preceding code output, we can make the following observations:

- For the test data, the loss and accuracy values are 0.376 and 0.837 respectively. Both results show a better classification performance compared to the previous two models for the test data.
- The confusion matrix shows that negative movie reviews are correctly classified at a rate of about 87.3%, and positive reviews are correctly classified at a rate of about 80%.
- Hence, these results are consistent with those obtained using the training data and show a similar bias to that we observed for the training data.

To summarize, by adding an extra LSTM layer, we were able to improve the movie review sentiment classification performance of the model. However, we continue to observe bias when correctly classifying one category compared to the other category. Hence, although we obtained moderate success in improving model performance, there is scope to further improve the classification performance of the model.

Experimenting with a bidirectional LSTM layer

A bidirectional LSTM, as the name indicates, not only uses the sequence of integers provided as input but also makes use of its reverse order as additional input. There could be situations where this approach may help to achieve further model classification performance improvements by capturing useful patterns in the data that may not have been captured by the original LSTM network.

For this experiment, we will modify the LSTM layer in the first experiment, as shown in the following code:

```
# Model architecture
model <- keras_model_sequential() %>%
        layer_embedding(input_dim = 500, output_dim = 32) %>%
        bidirectional(layer_lstm(units = 32)) %>%
        layer_dense(units = 1, activation = "sigmoid")
# Model summary
summary(model)
Model
```

Layer (type)	Output Shape	Param #
embedding_8 (Embedding)	(None, None, 32)	16000
bidirectional_5 (Bidirect	(None, 64)	16640
dense_11 (Dense)	(None, 1)	65

```
Total params: 32,705
Trainable params: 32,705
Non-trainable params: 0
```

From the preceding code output, we can make the following observations:

- We converted the LSTM layer into a bidirectional LSTM layer using the bidirectional () function.
- This change doubles the number of parameters related to the LSTM layer to 16,640, as can be seen from the model summary.
- The total number of parameters for this architecture now increases to 32,705. This increase in the number of parameters will further reduce the speed at which the network will be trained.

Here is a simple flow chart for the bidirectional LSTM network architecture:

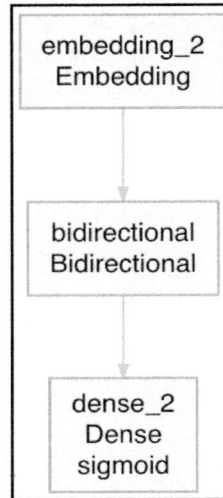

```
┌─────────────────────┐
│   embedding_2       │
│   Embedding         │
└─────────────────────┘
          │
          ▼
┌─────────────────────┐
│   bidirectional     │
│   Bidirectional     │
└─────────────────────┘
          │
          ▼
┌─────────────────────┐
│   dense_2           │
│   Dense             │
│   sigmoid           │
└─────────────────────┘
```

The flow chart for the bidirectional LSTM network shows embedding, bidirectional, and dense layers. In the bidirectional LSTM layer, `tanh` is used as the activation function and the dense layer uses the `sigmoid` activation function. The code for compiling and training the model is as follows:

```
# Compiling model
model %>% compile(optimizer = "adam",
         loss = "binary_crossentropy",
         metrics = c("acc"))

# Fitting model
 model_four <- model %>% fit(train_x, train_y,
         epochs = 10,
         batch_size = 128,
         validation_split = 0.2)

# Loss and accuracy plot
plot(model_four)
```

As seen from the preceding code, we will continue to use the `adam` optimizer and keep the other settings the same as earlier for compiling and then fitting the model.

After we train the model, the accuracy and loss values for each epoch are stored in `model_four`. We use the loss and accuracy values in `model_four` to develop the following plot:

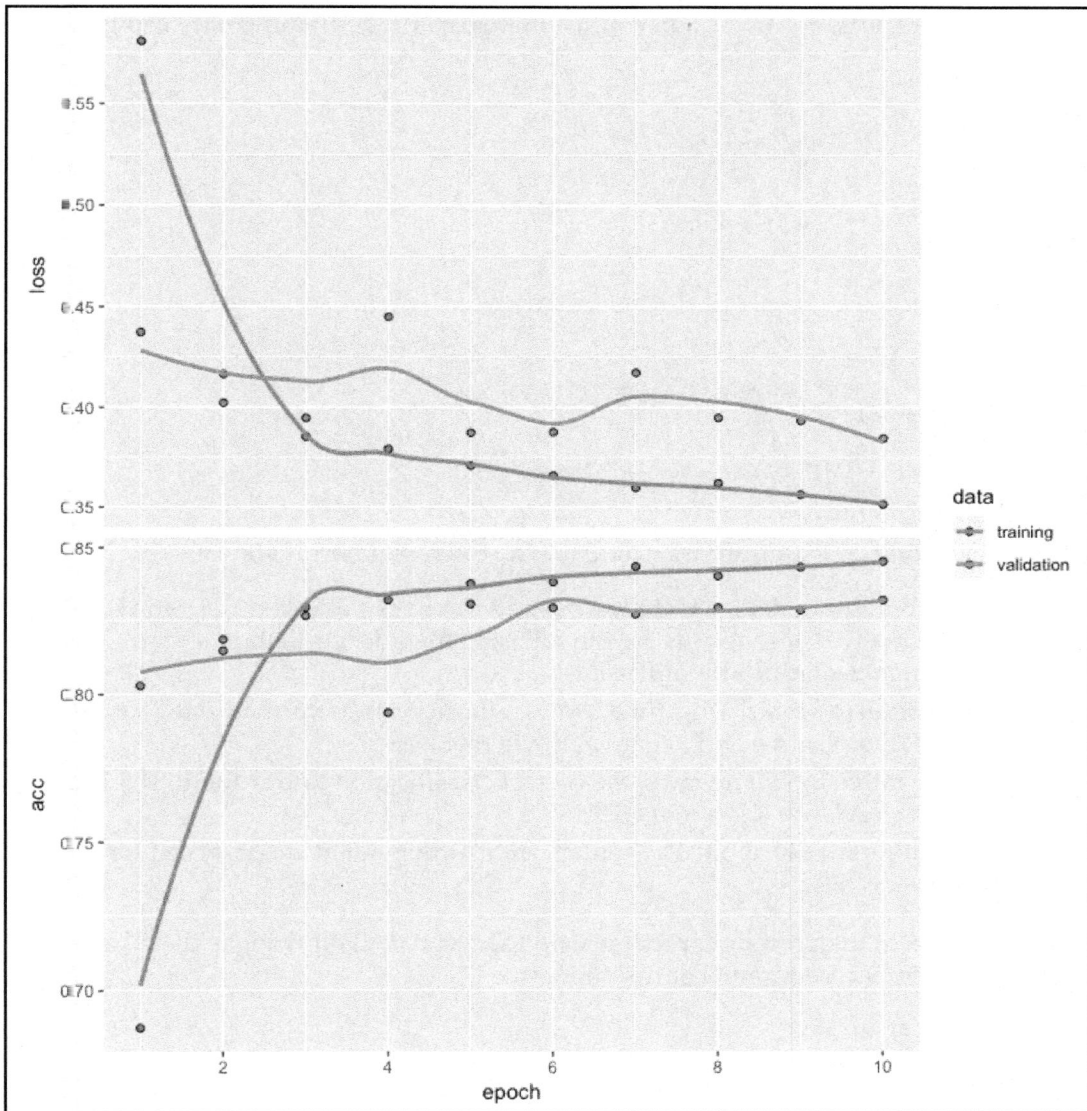

From the preceding plot, we can make the following observations:

- The loss and accuracy plot doesn't show any cause for concern regarding over-fitting as the lines for training and validation are reasonably close to each other.
- The plot also shows that we do not need more than ten epochs to train this model.

We will obtain the loss, accuracy, and confusion matrix for the training data using the following code:

```
# Loss and accuracy
model %>% evaluate(train_x, train_y)
$loss
[1] 0.3410529
$acc
[1] 0.85232

pred <- model %>%   predict_classes(train_x)

# Confusion Matrix
table(Predicted=pred, Actual=imdb$train$y)
        Actual
Predicted     0     1
        0 10597  1789
        1  1903 10711
```

From the preceding code output, we can make the following observations:

- For the training data, we obtain loss and accuracy values of 0.341 and 0.852 respectively. These results are only marginally inferior to the previous results and are not significantly different.
- The confusion matrix this time shows a more even performance for correctly classifying positive and negative movie reviews.
- For negative movie reviews, the correct classification rate is about 84.8% and for positive reviews, it is about 85.7%.
- This difference of about 1% is much smaller than what we observed for the earlier models.

We will now repeat the preceding process with the test data. Following is the code for obtaining the loss, accuracy, and confusion matrix:

```
# Loss and accuracy
model %>% evaluate(test_x, test_y)
$loss
[1] 0.3737377
$acc
[1] 0.83448

pred1 <- model %>%   predict_classes(test_x)

#Confusion Matrix
table(Predicted=pred1, Actual=imdb$test$y)
        Actual
```

```
Predicted     0     1
        0 10344  1982
        1  2156 10518
```

From the preceding code output, we can make the following observations:

- For the test data, the loss and accuracy values are 0.374 and 0.834 respectively.
- The confusion matrix shows that the negative reviews are correctly classified by the model at a rate of about 82.8%.
- This model correctly classifies positive movie reviews at a rate of about 84.1%.
- These results are consistent with those obtained for the training data.

The experiment with bidirectional LSTM helped to obtain somewhat comparable performance in terms of loss and accuracy than that were obtained with two LSTM layers in the previous experiment. However, the main gain that is observed is in achieving results where we can correctly classify a negative or positive movie review with much better consistency.

In this chapter, we used the LSTM network to develop a movie review sentiment classification model. When data involves sequences, LSTM networks help to capture long term dependencies in the sequence of words or integers. We experimented with four different LSTM models by making some changes to the model and the results for the same are summarized in the following table.

This table summarizes the performance of the four LSTM models:

Model	LSTM Layers	Optimizer	Data	Loss	Accuracy	Accuracy for Negative Reviews or Specificity	Accuracy for Positive Reviews or Sensitivity
One	1	rmsprop	Train	0.375	82.8%	74.1%	91.4%
			Test	0.399	81.9%	73.3%	90.7%
Two	1	adam	Train	0.360	84.3%	88.9%	79.7%
			Test	0.385	82.9%	86.9%	78.8%
Three	2	adam	Train	0.339	85.5%	90.0%	81.0%
			Test	0.376	83.7%	87.3%	80.0%
Four	bidirectional	adam	Train	0.341	85.2%	84.8%	85.7%
			Test	0.374	83.4%	82.8%	84.1%

We can make the following observations from the preceding table:

- Out of the four models that were tried, the bidirectional LSTM model provided better performance compared to the other three models. It has the lowest loss value based on test data.
- Although overall accuracy is slightly lower for the fourth model compared to the third model, accuracy for correctly classifying negative and positive reviews is much more consistent, varying from 82.8% to 84.1%, or a spread of only about 1.3%.
- The third model seems biased toward negative reviews that correctly classifies such reviews at a rate of 87.3% for the test data. For the third model, the correct classification of positive reviews in the test data is only at 80%. Hence, the spread between the correct classification of negative and positive reviews for the third model is more than 7%.
- The spread between sensitivity and specificity is even higher for the first two models.

Although the fourth model provides good results, additional improvements can certainly be explored by experimenting further with other variables. Variables that can be used for further experiments may include the number of most frequent words, use of pre versus post for padding and/or truncation, the maximum length used for padding, the number of units in the LSTM layer, and the choice of another optimizer at the time of compiling the model.

Summary

In this chapter, we illustrated the use of LSTM networks for developing a movie review sentiment classification model. One of the problems faced by recurrent neural networks that we used in the previous chapter is that it involves difficulty in capturing long-term dependency that may exist between two words/integers in a sequence of words or integers. **Long Short-Term Memory (LSTM)** networks are designed to artificially retain long-term memories that are important when dealing with long sentences or a long sequence of integers.

In the next chapter, we will continue to work with text data and explore the use of **Convolutional Recurrent Neural Networks (CRNNs)**, which combine the benefits of **Convolutional Neural Networks (CNNs)** and **Recurrent Neural Networks (RNNs)** into a single network. We will illustrate the use of this type of network with the help of an interesting and publicly available text dataset, `reuter_50_50`.

12
Text Classification Using Convolutional Recurrent Neural Networks

Convolutional neural networks (CNNs) have been found to be useful in capturing high-level local features from data. On the other hand, **recurrent neural networks (RNNs)**, such as **long short-term memory (LSTM)**, have been found to be useful in capturing long-term dependencies in data involving sequences such as text. When we use CNNs and RNNs in the same model architecture, it gives rise to what's called **convolutional recurrent neural networks (CRNNs)**.

This chapter illustrates how to apply convolutional recurrent neural networks to text classification problems by combining the advantages of RNNs and CNNs networks. The steps that are involved in this process include text data preparation, defining a convolutional recurrent network model, training the model, and model assessment.

More specifically, in this chapter, we will cover the following topics:

- Working with the reuter_50_50 dataset
- Preparing the data for model building
- Developing the model architecture
- Compiling and fitting the model
- Evaluating the model and predicting classes
- Performance optimization tips and best practices

Working with the reuter_50_50 dataset

In the previous chapters, when dealing with text data, we made use of data that had already been converted into a sequence of integers for developing deep network models. In this chapter, we will use text data that needs to be converted into a sequence of integers. We will start by reading the data that we will use to illustrate how to develop a text classification deep network model. We will also explore the dataset that we'll use so that we have a better understanding of it.

In this chapter, we will make use of the `keras`, `deepviz`, and `readtext` libraries, as shown in the following code:

```
# Libraries used
library(keras)
library(deepviz)
library(readtext)
```

For illustrating the steps involved in developing a convolutional recurrent network model, we will make use of the `reuter_50_50` text dataset, which is available from the UCI Machine Learning Repository: https://archive.ics.uci.edu/ml/datasets/Reuter_50_50#.

This dataset contains text files in two folders, with one folder for the training data and another for the test data:

- The folder containing the training data has 2,500 text files with 50 articles each from 50 authors.
- Similarly, the folder containing the test data also has 2,500 text files with 50 articles each from the same 50 authors.

Reading the training data

We can access the `reuter_50_50` dataset by going to `Data` folder from the link that we provided for the UCI Machine Learning Repository. From here, we can download the `C50.zip` folder. When unzipped, it contains a `C50` folder containing `C50train` and `C50test` folders. First, we will read the text files from the `C50train` folder using the following code:

```
# Reading Reuters train data
setwd("~/Desktop/C50/C50train")
temp = list.files(pattern="*.*")
k <- 1; tr <- list(); trainx <- list(); trainy <- list()
for (i in 1:length(temp)) {for (j in 1:50)
```

```
        { trainy[k] <- temp[i]
          k <- k+1}
author <- temp[i]
files <- paste0("~/Desktop/C50/C50train/", author, "/*")
tr <- readtext(files)
trainx <- rbind(trainx, tr)}
trainx <- trainx$text
```

With the help of the preceding code, we can read data on 2,500 articles from the C50train folder into trainx and also save information about the author's names into trainy. We start by setting the working directory to the C50train folder using the setwd function. The C50train folder contains 50 folders named after 50 authors, and each folder contains 50 articles written by the corresponding author. We assign a value of 1 to k and initiate tr, trainx, and trainy as a list. Then, we create a loop so that the author's name is stored in trainy, which contains the author's names for each article, and so that trainx contains the corresponding articles written by the authors. Note that, after reading data on these 2,500 text files, trainx also contains information about file names. Using the last line of code, we retain data on only 2,500 texts and remove information about the file names that we will not need.

Now, let's look at the content of text file 901 from the train data using the following code:

```
# Text file 901
trainx[901]
[1] "Drug discovery specialist Chiroscience Group plc said on Monday it is
testing two anti-cancer compounds before deciding which will go forward
into human trials before the end of the year.\nBoth are MMP inhibitors, the
same novel class of drug as British Biotech Plc's potential blockbuster
Marimastat, which are believed to stop cancer cells from spreading.\nIn an
interview, chief executive John Padfield said Chiroscience hoped to have
its own competitor to Marimastat in early trials next year and Phase III
trials in 1998."

# Author
trainy[901]
[[1]]
[1] "JonathanBirt"
```

From the preceding code and output, we can make the following observations:

- The test file 901 in trainx contains certain news items about drug trials by the Chiroscience Group
- The author of this short article is Jonathan Birt

Having read the text files and author names for the training data, we can repeat this process for the test data.

Reading the test data

Now, we will read the text files from the C50test folder located within the C50 folder. We will use the following code to do so:

```
# Reuters test data
setwd("~/Desktop/C50/C50test")
temp = list.files(pattern="*.*")
k <- 1; tr <- list(); testx <- list(); testy <- list()
for (i in 1:length(temp)) {for (j in 1:50)
        { testy[k] <- temp[i]
        k <- k+1}
        author <- temp[i]
        files <- paste0("~/Desktop/C50/C50test/", author, "/*")
        tr <- readtext(files)
        testx <- rbind(testx, tr)}
testx <- testx$text
```

Here, we can see that the only change in this code is that we are creating testx and testy based on the test data located within the C50test folder. We read 2,500 articles from the C50test folder into testx and save information about the author's names into testy. Once again, we use the last line of code to retain data on only 2,500 texts from the test data and remove information on file names, which isn't required for our analysis.

Now that we've created the training and test data, we will carry out data preprocessing so that we can develop an author classification model.

Preparing the data for model building

In this section, we will prepare some data so that we can develop an author classification model. We will start by using tokens to convert text data that is available in the form of articles into a sequence of integers. We will also make changes to identify each author by unique integers. Subsequently, we will use padding and truncation to arrive at the same length for the sequence of integers that represent the articles by 50 authors. We will end this section by partitioning the training data into train and validation datasets and then carrying out one-hot encoding on the response variables.

Tokenization and converting text into a sequence of integers

We will start by carrying out tokenization and then converting the articles, which are in text form, into a sequence of integers. To do this, we can use the following code:

```
# Tokenization
token <- text_tokenizer(num_words = 500) %>%
        fit_text_tokenizer(trainx)

# Text to sequence of integers
trainx <- texts_to_sequences(token, trainx)
testx <- texts_to_sequences(token, testx)

# Examples
trainx[[7]]
[1] 98    4   41   5    4   2   4  425   5   20   4   9   4  195   5  157   1   18
[19] 87    3   90   3   59  1 169 346   2   29  52 425   6   72 386 110 331   24
[37] 5     4    3  31    3  22   7  65  33 169 329  10 105   1 239  11   4   31
[55] 11  422    8  60  163 318  10  58 102   2 137 329 277  98  58 287  20   81
[73] 3   142    9   6   87   3  49  20 142   2 142   6   2  60  13   1 470    8
[91] 137 190   60   1   85 152   5   6 211   1   3   1  85  11   2 211 233   51
[109] 233 490    7 155    3 305   6   4  86   3  70   4   3 157  52 142   6  282
[127] 233   4  286  11  485  47  11   9   1 386 497   2  72   7  33   6   3    1
[145] 60    3  234  23   32  72 485   7 203   6  29 390   5   3  19  13  55  184
[163] 53   10    1  41   19 485 119  18   6  59   1 169   1  41  10  17 458   91
[181] 6    23   12   1    3   3  10 491   2  14   1   1 194 469 491   2   1    4
[199] 331 112  485 475   16   1 469   1 331  14   2 485 234   5 171 296   1   85
[217] 11  135  157   2  189   1  31  24   4   5 318 490 338   6 147 194  24  347
[235] 386  23   24  32  117 286 161   6 338  25   4  32   2   9   1  38   8  316
[253] 60  153   27 234  496 457 153  20 316   2 254 219 145 117  25  46  27    7
[271] 228  34  184  75   11 418  52 296   1 194 469 180 469   6   1 268   6  250
[283] 469  29   90   6   15  58 175  32  33 229  37 424  36  51  36   3 169   15
[307] 1    7  175   1  319 207   5   4

trainx[[901]]
[1] 74 356 7   9 199  12  11  61 145 31  22 399 79 145   1 133   3   1  28 203
[21] 29   1 319  3  18 101 470 31  29  2  20   5  33 369 116 134   7   2  25  17
[41] 303  2   5 222 100  28   6   5
```

From the preceding code and output, we can observe the following:

- For tokenization, we specify `num_words` as 500, indicating that we will use the 500 most frequent words from the text in the training data.
- Note that using `fit_text_tokenizer` automatically converts text into lowercase and removes any punctuation that can be observed in the articles containing text data. Converting text into lowercase helps us avoid duplicates of words, where one may contain lowercase alphabetical characters and another may have uppercase alphabetical characters. Punctuation is removed since it doesn't add value when developing the author classification model with text as input.
- We use `texts_to_sequences` to convert the most frequent words in the text into a sequence of integers. The reason for doing this is to convert the unstructured data so that it has a structured format, which is required by deep learning models.
- The output of text file 7 shows a total of 314 integers that are between 1 and 497.
- Looking at the output for text file 901 (the same example in the training data that we reviewed earlier), we can see that it consists of 48 integers between 1 and 470. The original text consists of over 80 words and those words that do not belong to the 500 most frequent words are not represented in this sequence of integers.
- The first five integers, that is, 74, 356, 7, 9, and 199, correspond to the words `group`, `plc`, `said`, `on`, and `monday`, respectively. Other words at the beginning of the text that haven't been converted into integers do not belong to the top 500 most frequent words in the articles.

Now, let's look at the number of integers per article in the training and test data. We can do this with the following code:

```
# Integers per article for train data
z <- NULL
for (i in 1:2500) {z[i] <- print(length(trainx[[i]]))}
summary(z)
   Min. 1st Qu.  Median    Mean 3rd Qu.    Max.
   31.0   271.0   326.0   326.8   380.0   918.0

# Intergers per article for text data
z <- NULL
for (i in 1:2500) {z[i] <- print(length(testx[[i]]))}
summary(z)
   Min. 1st Qu.  Median    Mean 3rd Qu.    Max.
   39.0   271.0   331.0   329.1   384.0  1001.0
```

From the preceding summary, we can make the following observations:

- The number of integers per article in the training data ranges from 31 to 918, with a median of about 326 words.
- Similarly, the integers per article range from 39 to 1001 for the test data, with a median of about 331.
- If the number of most frequent words is increased from 500 to a higher value, the median number of words is also expected to increase. This may lead to suitable changes needing to be made in the model architecture and parameter values. As an example, an increase in the number of words per article may call for more neurons in the deep network.

A histogram of the number of integers per text file for the training data is as follows:

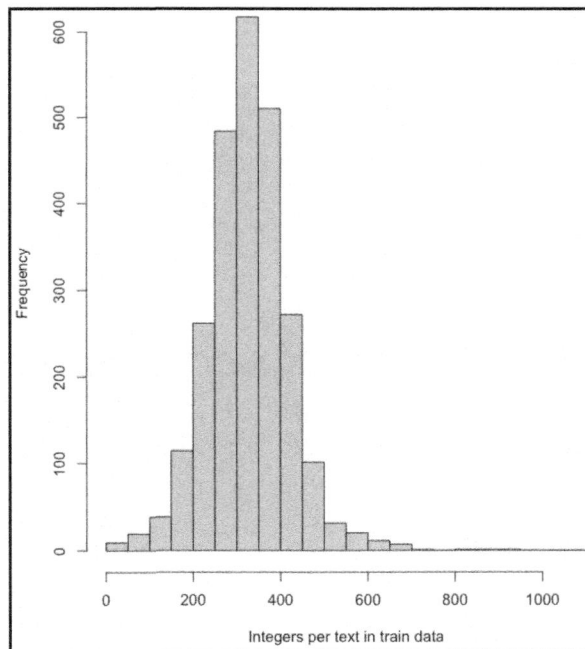

The preceding histogram of integers per text file for the training data shows the overall pattern, with a mean and median of about 326. The tail of this histogram is slightly longer toward the higher value, giving it a moderately right-skewed or positively-skewed pattern.

Now that we've converted the text data into a sequence of integers, we will change the labels for the train and text data into integers as well.

Changing labels into integers

When developing deep learning networks for classification problems, we always use responses or labels in the form of integers. Author names for the train and test text data are stored in `trainy` and `testy`, respectively. Both `trainy` and `testy` are lists of 2,500 items that contain the names of 50 authors. To change the labels into integers, we can use the following code:

```
# Train and test labels to integers
trainy <- as.factor(unlist(trainy))
trainy <- as.integer(trainy) -1
testy <- as.factor(unlist(testy))
testy <- as.integer(testy) -1

# Saving original labels
trainy_org <- trainy
testy_org <- testy
```

As we can see, to convert labels containing author names into integers, we need to unlist them and then use integers from 0 to 49 to represent the 50 authors. We can also use `trainy_org` and `testy_org` to save these original integer labels for later use.

Next, we will carry out padding and truncation to make the data on a sequence of integers have an equal length for each article.

Padding and truncation of sequences

When developing the author classification model, the number of integers for each training and test text data need to be of equal length. We can achieve this by padding and truncating the sequence of integers, as follows:

```
# Padding and truncation
trainx <- pad_sequences(trainx, maxlen = 300)
testx <- pad_sequences(testx, maxlen = 300)
dim(trainx)
[1] 2500  300
```

Here, we are specifying the maximum length of all the sequences, that is, `maxlen`, to be 300. This will truncate any sequences that are longer than 300 integers in an article and add zeroes to sequences that are shorter than 300 integers in an article. Note that for padding and truncation, a default setting of "pre" has been used and is not specifically indicated in the code.

This means that for truncation and padding, the integers at the beginning of the sequence of integers are impacted. For padding and/or truncation toward the end of the sequence of integers, we can make use of `padding = "post"` and/or `truncation = "post"` within the code. We can also see that the dimensions of `trainx` show a 2,500 x 300 matrix.

Let's look at the output from text files 7 and 901 in the train data, as follows:

```
# Example of truncation
trainx[7,]
  [1]    5 157   1  18  87   3  90   3  59   1 169 346   2  29  52 425
 [17]    6  72 386 110 331  24   5   4   3  31   3  22   7  65  33 169
 [33]  329  10 105   1 239  11   4  31  11 422   8  60 163 318  10  58
 [49]  102   2 137 329 277  98  58 287  20  81   3 142   9   6  87   3
 [65]   49  20 142   2 142   6   2  60  13   1 470   8 137 190  60   1
 [81]   85 152   5   6 211   1   3   1  85  11   2 211 233  51 233 490
 [97]    7 155   3 305   6   4  86   3  70   4   3 157  52 142   6 282
[113]  233   4 286  11 485  47  11   9   1 386 497   2  72   7  33   6
[129]    3   1  60   3 234  23  32  72 485   7 203   6  29 390   5   3
[145]   19  13  55 184  53  10   1  41  19 485 119  18   6  59   1 169
[161]    1  41  10  17 458  91   6  23  12   1   3   3  10 491   2  14
[177]    1   1 194 469 491   2   1   4 331 112 485 475  16   1 469   1
[193]  331  14   2 485 234   5 171 296   1  85  11 135 157   2 189   1
[209]   31  24   4   5 318 490 338   6 147 194  24 347 386  23  24  32
[225]  117 286 161   6 338  25   4  32   2   9   1  38   8 316  60 153
[241]   27 234 496 457 153  20 316   2 254 219 145 117  25  46  27   7
[257]  228  34 184  75  11 418  52 296   1 194 469 180 469   6   1 268
[273]    6 250 469  29  90   6  15  58 175  32  33 229  37 424  36  51
[289]   36   3 169  15   1   7 175   1 319 207   5   4

# Example of padding
trainx[901,]
  [1]    0   0   0   0   0   0   0   0   0   0   0   0   0   0   0   0
 [17]    0   0   0   0   0   0   0   0   0   0   0   0   0   0   0   0
 [33]    0   0   0   0   0   0   0   0   0   0   0   0   0   0   0   0
 [49]    0   0   0   0   0   0   0   0   0   0   0   0   0   0   0   0
 [65]    0   0   0   0   0   0   0   0   0   0   0   0   0   0   0   0
 [81]    0   0   0   0   0   0   0   0   0   0   0   0   0   0   0   0
 [97]    0   0   0   0   0   0   0   0   0   0   0   0   0   0   0   0
[113]    0   0   0   0   0   0   0   0   0   0   0   0   0   0   0   0
[129]    0   0   0   0   0   0   0   0   0   0   0   0   0   0   0   0
[145]    0   0   0   0   0   0   0   0   0   0   0   0   0   0   0   0
[161]    0   0   0   0   0   0   0   0   0   0   0   0   0   0   0   0
[177]    0   0   0   0   0   0   0   0   0   0   0   0   0   0   0   0
[193]    0   0   0   0   0   0   0   0   0   0   0   0   0   0   0   0
[209]    0   0   0   0   0   0   0   0   0   0   0   0   0   0   0   0
[225]    0   0   0   0   0   0   0   0   0   0   0   0   0   0   0   0
[241]    0   0   0   0   0   0   0   0   0   0   0   0  74 356   7   9
```

```
[257] 199  12  11  61 145  31  22 399  79 145   1 133   3   1  28 203
[273]  29   1 319   3  18 101 470  31  29   2  20   5  33 369 116 134
[289]   7   2  25  17 303   2   5 222 100  28   6   5
```

From the preceding output, we can make the following observations:

- Text file 7, which had 314 integers, has been reduced to 300 integers. Note that this step removed 14 integers at the beginning of the sequence.
- Text file 901, which had 48 integers, now has 300 integers, which has been achieved by adding zeros at the beginning of the sequence to artificially make the total number of integers 300.

Next, we will partition the training data into train and validation data, which will be required for training and assessing the network at the time of fitting the model.

Data partitioning

At the time of training the model, we use `validation_split`, which uses a specified percentage of training data to assess validation errors. The training data in this example contains data of the first 50 articles from the first author, followed by 50 articles from the second author, and so on. If we specify `validation_split` as 0.2, the model will be trained based on the first 80% (or 2,000) articles from the first 40 authors, and the last 20% (or 500) articles written by the last 10 authors will be used for assessing validation errors. This will cause no input from the last 10 authors to be used in the model training. To overcome this problem, we will randomly partition the training data into train and validation data using the following code:

```
# Data partition
trainx_org <- trainx
testx_org <- testx
set.seed(1234)
ind <- sample(2, nrow(trainx), replace = T, prob=c(.8, .2))
trainx <- trainx_org[ind==1, ]
validx <- trainx_org[ind==2, ]
trainy <- trainy_org[ind==1]
validy <- trainy_org[ind==2]
```

As we can see, to partition the data into train and validation data, we have used an 80:20 split. We also used the `set.seed` function for repeatability purposes.

After partitioning the train data, we will carry out one-hot encoding on the labels, which helps us represent the correct author with a value of one, and all the other authors with a value of zero.

One-hot encoding the labels

To carry out one-hot encoding on the labels, we will use the following code:

```
# OHE
trainy <- to_categorical(trainy, 50)
validy <- to_categorical(validy, 50)
testy <- to_categorical(testy, 50)
```

Here, we have used the `to_categorical` function to one-hot encode the response variable. We used 50 to indicate the presence of 50 classes since the articles have been written by 50 authors that we plan to classify, using articles that have been written by them as input.

Now, the data is ready for developing the convolutional recurrent network model for author classification based on the articles they have written.

Developing the model architecture

In this section, we will make use of convolutional and LSTM layers in the same network. The convolutional recurrent network architecture can be captured in the form of a simple flowchart:

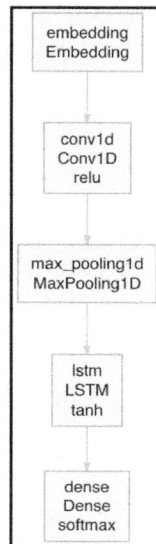

Here, we can see that the flowchart contains embedding, convolutional 1D, maximum pooling, LSTM, and dense layers. Note that the embedding layer is always the first layer in the network and is commonly used for applications involving text data. The main purpose of the embedding layer is to find a mapping of each unique word, which in our example is 500, and turn it into a vector that is smaller in size, which we will specify using `output_dim`. In the convolutional layer, we will use the `relu` activation function. Similarly, the activation functions that will be used for the LSTM and dense layers will be `tanh` and `softmax`, respectively.

We can use the following code to develop the model architecture. This also includes the output of the model summary:

```
# Model architecture
model <- keras_model_sequential() %>%
        layer_embedding(input_dim = 500,
                        output_dim = 32,
                        input_length = 300) %>%
        layer_conv_1d(filters = 32,
                kernel_size = 5,
                padding = "valid",
                activation = "relu",
                strides = 1) %>%
        layer_max_pooling_1d(pool_size = 4) %>%
        layer_lstm(units = 32) %>%
        layer_dense(units = 50, activation = "softmax")

# Model summary
summary(model)
```

Layer (type)	Output Shape	Param #
embedding (Embedding)	(None, 300, 32)	16000
conv1d (Conv1D)	(None, 296, 32)	5152
max_pooling1d (MaxPooling1D)	(None, 74, 32)	0
lstm (LSTM)	(None, 32)	8320
dense (Dense)	(None, 50)	1650

```
Total params: 31,122
Trainable params: 31,122
Non-trainable params: 0
```

From the preceding code, we can make the following observations:

- We have specified `input_dim` as 500, which was used as the number of most frequent words during data preparation.
- For `output_dim`, we are using 32, which represents the size of the embedding vector. However, note that other numbers can also be explored and we will do so later in this chapter, at the time of performance optimization.
- For `input_length`, we have specified 300, which is the number of integers in each sequence.

After the embedding layer, we have added a 1D convolutional layer with 32 filters. In the previous chapters, we used a 2D convolutional layer when working on image classification problems. In this example, we have data involving sequences and, in such situations, a 1D convolutional layer is more appropriate. For this layer, we have specified the following:

- The length of the 1D convolutional window is specified as 5 using `kernel_size`.
- We use `valid` for padding to indicate that no padding is required.
- We have specified the activation function as `relu`.
- The strides of the convolution have been specified at 1.

The convolutional layer is followed by a pooling layer. The following are some of the comments for pooling and the subsequent layer:

- The convolutional layer helps us extract features, while the pooling layer after the convolutional layer helps us carry out downsampling and detect important features.
- In this example, we have specified a pooling size of 4, which means that the size of the output (74) is one-fourth of the input (296). This can also be seen in the model summary.
- The next layer is the LSTM with 32 units.
- The last layer is a dense layer with 50 units for the 50 authors, along with the `softmax` activation function.
- The `softmax` activation function makes all 50 outputs have a total value of one and thus allows them to be used as probabilities for each of the 50 authors.
- As we can see from the summary of the model, the total number of parameters in this network is 31,122.

Next, we will compile the model, followed by training it.

Compiling and fitting the model

In this section, we will compile the model and then train the model using the `fit` function using the training and validation dataset. We will also plot the loss and accuracy values that were obtained while training the model.

Compiling the model

For compiling the model, we will use the following code:

```
# Compile model
model %>% compile(optimizer = "adam",
        loss = "categorical_crossentropy",
        metrics = c("acc"))
```

Here, we've specified the `adam` optimizer. We're using `categorical_crossentropy` as the loss function since the labels are based on 50 authors. For the metrics, we've specified the accuracy of the author's classification.

Now that the model has been compiled, it's ready for training.

Fitting the model

We will train the model using the following code:

```
# Fitting the model
model_one <- model %>% fit(trainx, trainy,
        epochs = 30,
        batch_size = 32,
        validation_data = list(validx, validy))

# Loss and accuracy plot
plot(model_one)
```

Here, we're training the model using `trainx` as input and `trainy` as output. The model's training is carried out for 30 epochs with a batch size of 32. For assessing the validation loss and validation accuracy for each epoch during the training process, we make use of `validx` and `validy`, which we created earlier by taking approximately a 20% random sample from the training data.

The loss and accuracy values based on the train and validation data for each of the 30 epochs are stored in `model_one`. The following is a plot of this data:

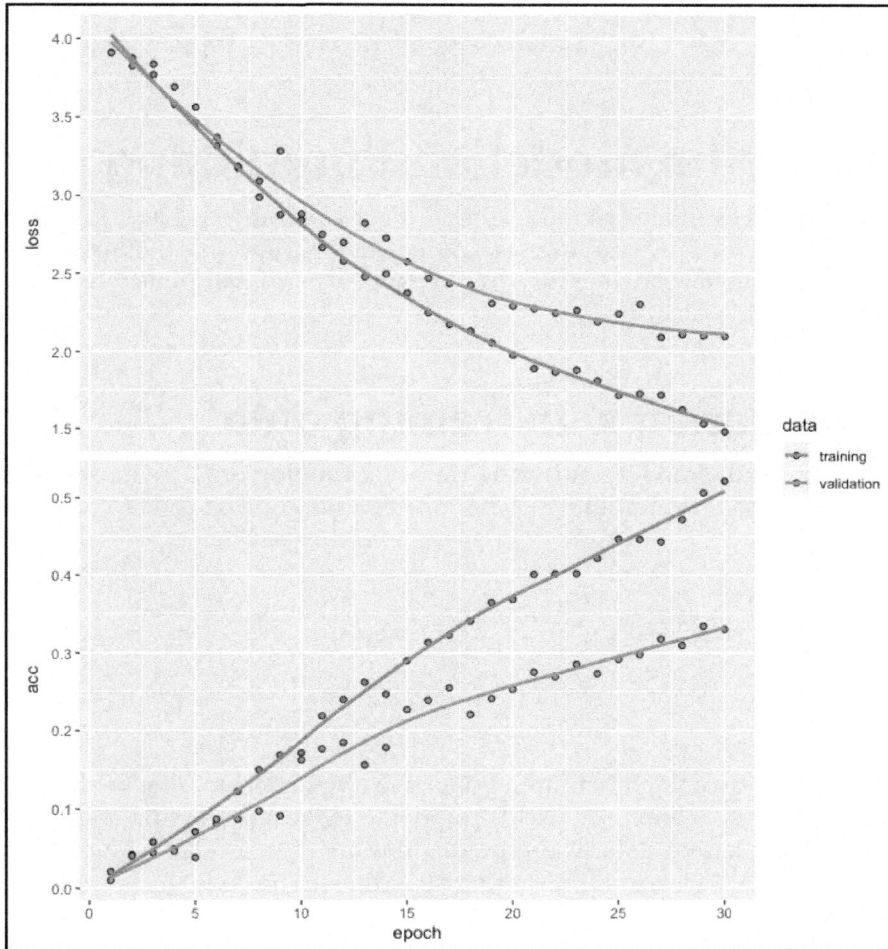

From the preceding plot, we can make the following observations:

- The loss values for the training and validation data reduce as we go from 1 to 30 epochs. However, the loss values for the validation data reduce at a slower pace compared to those for the training data as the training proceeds.
- The accuracy values for the training and validation data show a similar pattern in the opposite direction.

- Increasing the number of epochs during training is likely to improve the loss and accuracy values; however, divergence between the curves is also expected to increase, with this potentially leading to an overfitting situation.

Next, we will evaluate `model_one` and make predictions using training and test data.

Evaluating the model and predicting classes

In this section, we will evaluate the model based on our training and test data. We will obtain accuracy by correctly classifying each author using a confusion matrix for the training and test data to gain further insights. We will also use bar plots to visualize the accuracy of identifying each author.

Model evaluation with training data

First, we will evaluate the model's performance using training data. Then, we will use the model to predict the class representing each of the 50 authors. The code for evaluating the model is as follows:

```
# Loss and accuracy
model %>% evaluate(trainx, trainy)
$loss
[1] 1.45669
$acc
[1] 0.5346288
```

Here, we can see that, by using the training data, we obtain a loss value of about 1.457 and an accuracy of about 0.535. Next, we use the model to make a prediction about the classes for the articles in the training data. These predictions are then used to arrive at an accuracy reading for each of the 50 classes representing 50 authors. The code that's used to achieve this is as follows:

```
# Prediction and confusion matrix
pred <- model %>%   predict_classes(trainx_org)
tab <- table(Predicted=pred, Actual=trainy_org)
(accuracy <- 100*diag(tab)/colSums(tab))
  0  1  2  3  4  5  6  7  8  9 10 11 12 13 14 15 16 17 18 19 20 21 22 23 24
 82 40 30 10 54 46 54 82  8 56 46 36 76 18 52 90 50 56  8 66 80 24 30 46 32
 25 26 27 28 29 30 31 32 33 34 35 36 37 38 39 40 41 42 43 44 45 46 47 48 49
 46 88 62 22 64 76  2 74 88 72 74 76 86 70 60 86 38 32  0 48  6 24 76  8 22
```

In the preceding code, to conserve space, we haven't printed the output of the confusion matrix since it will be a 50 x 50 matrix. However, we have used information in the confusion matrix to arrive at the model's accuracy by correctly predicting each author based on the articles they have written. The output that we've obtained is as follows:

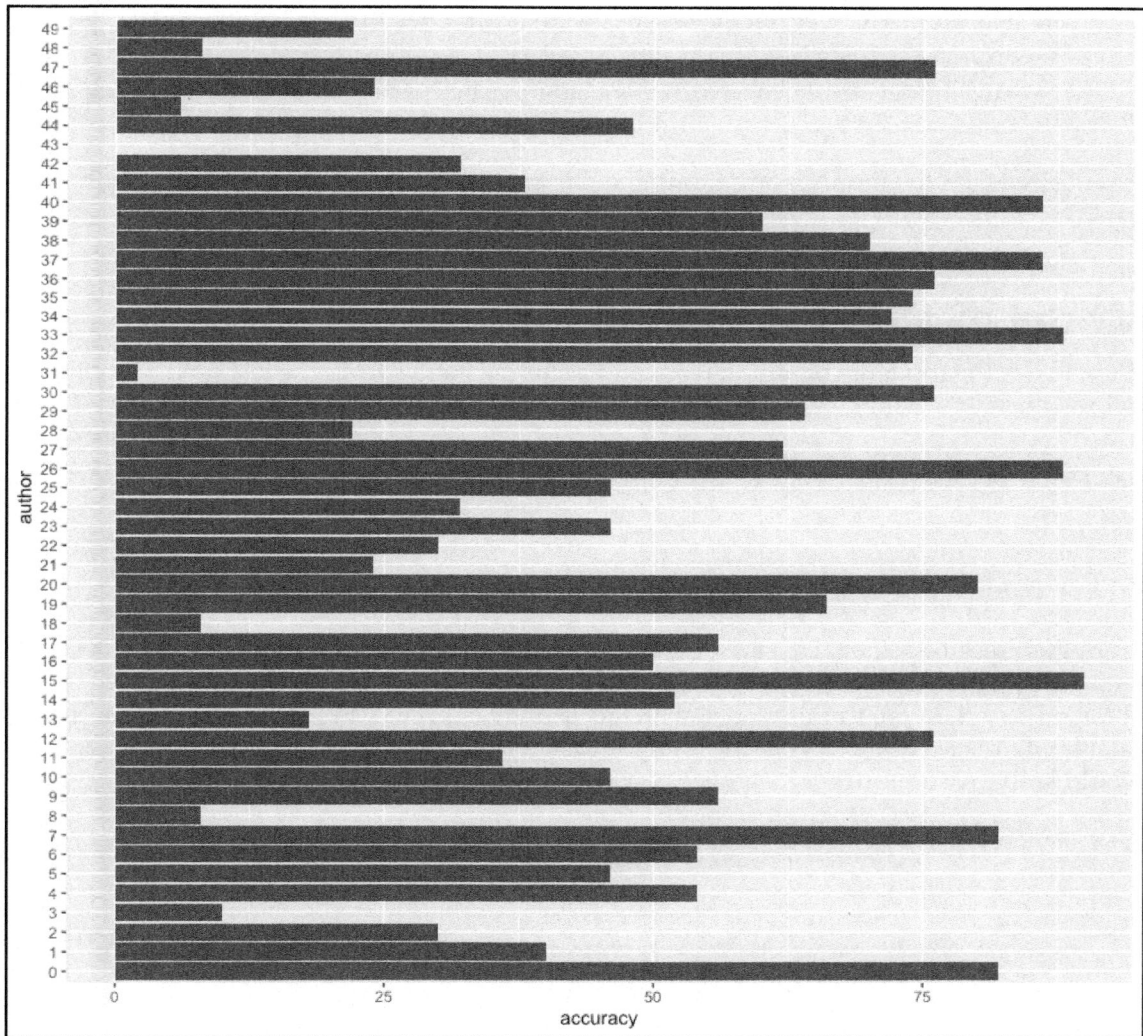

The preceding bar plot provides further insight into the model's performance with respect to each author:

- The accuracy of correctly classifying an author has the highest value of 90% for author 15.
- The accuracy of correctly classifying an author has the lowest value of 0% for author 43.
- This model struggles to correctly classify articles from certain authors, such as those labeled 3, 8, 18, 31, 43, 45, and 48.

Having assessed the model using training data, we will repeat this process with the test data.

Model evaluation with test data

We will use the model to obtain the loss and accuracy values from the test data using the following code:

```
# Loss and accuracy
model %>% evaluate(testx, testy)
$loss
[1] 2.460835
$acc
[1] 0.2508
```

From the preceding code, we can see that the loss and accuracy values based on the test data are 2.461 and 0.251, respectively. Both of these results are inferior to the ones we obtained based on the training data, which is usually expected. Predicting the classes and calculating the accuracy of classification for each author, as shown in the following code, would help provide further insights:

```
# Prediction and confusion matrix
pred1 <- model %>%   predict_classes(testx)
tab1 <- table(Predicted=pred1, Actual=testy_org)
(accuracy <- 100*diag(tab1)/colSums(tab1))
  0  1  2  3  4  5  6  7  8  9 10 11 12 13 14 15 16 17 18 19 20 21 22 23 24
 22 28  2  2 28 14 14 20  6 28 24  8 28  8 46 84 14 36 10 50 40 12  4 22  4
 25 26 27 28 29 30 31 32 33 34 35 36 37 38 39 40 41 42 43 44 45 46 47 48 49
 18 54 38 12 34 46  0 52 26 48 40 26 84 46 18 24 26 10  0 46  0  4 38  0 10
```

The information in the confusion matrix is stored in `tab1`, which is used for arriving at the accuracy of correctly classifying articles from each author. The results are as follows:

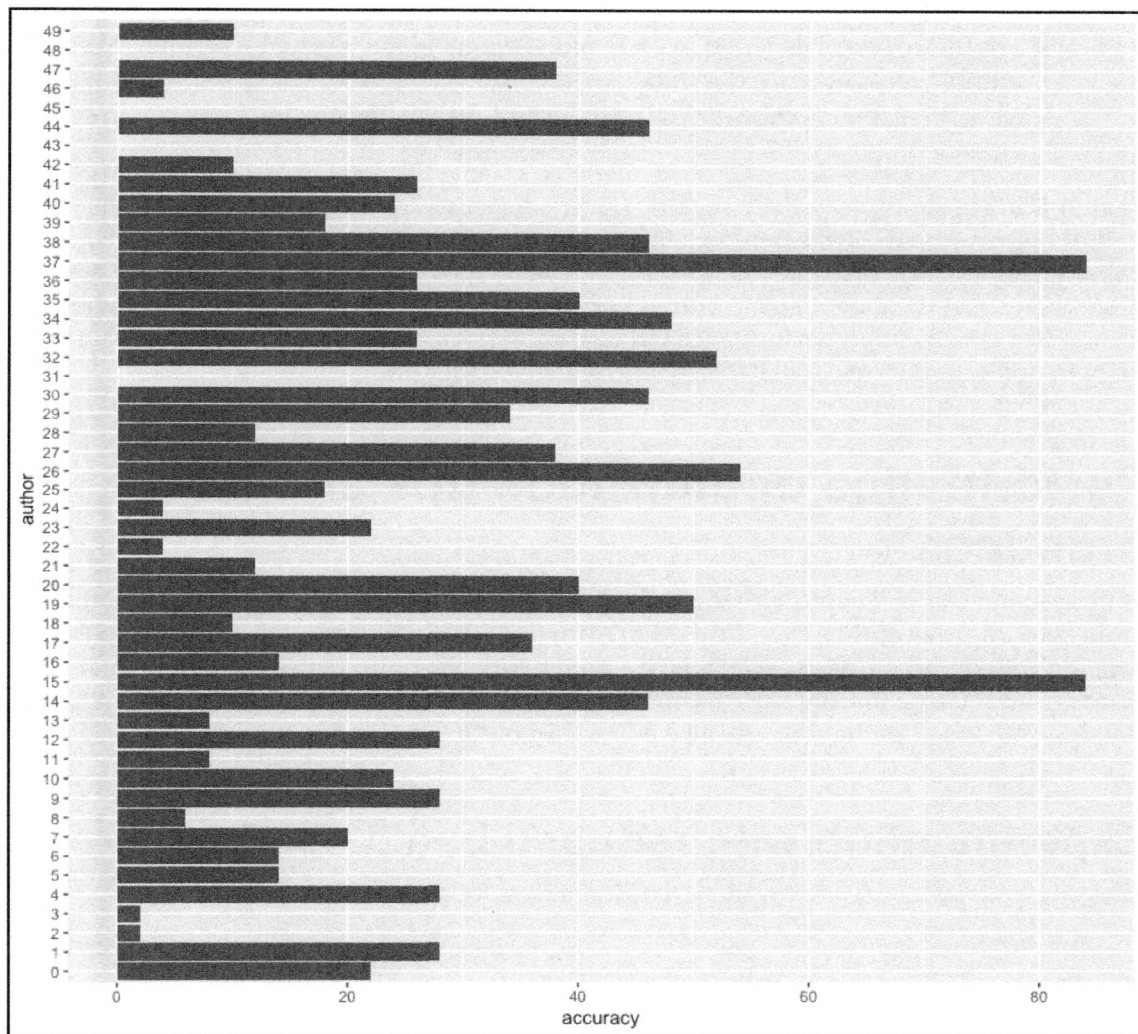

An overall accuracy of about 25% for the test data already suggested significantly inferior performance based on the test data. This can also be seen in the preceding bar chart. Let's take a look at some of the observations we can make from this:

- For the authors labeled 31, 43, 45, and 48, none of the 50 articles written by each author were correctly classified.
- More than 80% of the articles from the authors labeled 15 and 38 were correctly classified.

From this initial example, we can see that our model classification performance needs further improvement. The differences in performance that we have observed between the training and test data also indicate the presence of an overfitting problem. Thus, we need to make changes to the model architecture to obtain a model that not only provides higher accuracy in classification performance but also shows consistent performance between the training and test data. We will explore this in the next section.

Performance optimization tips and best practices

In this section, we will explore changes we can make to the model architecture and other settings to improve author classification performance. We will carry out two experiments, and, for both of these two experiments, we will increase the number of most frequent words from 500 to 1,500 and increase the length of the sequences of integers from 300 to 400. For both experiments, we will also add a dropout layer after the pooling layer.

Experimenting with reduced batch size

The code that we'll be using for this experiment is as follows:

```
# Model architecture
model <- keras_model_sequential() %>%
        layer_embedding(input_dim = 1500,
                        output_dim = 32,
                        input_length = 400) %>%
        layer_conv_1d(filters = 32,
                kernel_size = 5,
                padding = "valid",
                activation = "relu",
                strides = 1) %>%
        layer_max_pooling_1d(pool_size = 4) %>%
```

```
            layer_dropout(0.25) %>%
            layer_lstm(units = 32) %>%
            layer_dense(units = 50, activation = "softmax")

# Compiling the model
model %>% compile(optimizer = "adam",
            loss = "categorical_crossentropy",
            metrics = c("acc"))

# Fitting the model
model_two <- model %>% fit(trainx, trainy,
            epochs = 30,
            batch_size = 16,
            validation_data = list(validx, validy))

# Plot of loss and accuracy
plot(model_two)
```

From the preceding code, we can make the following observations:

- We will update the model architecture by specifying `input_dim` as 1,500 and `input_length` as 400.
- We will reduce the batch size that's used at the time of fitting the model from 32 to 16.
- To address the overfitting problem, we have added a dropout layer with a rate of 25%.
- We have kept all other settings the same as those we had used for the previous model.

The loss and accuracy values based on the training and validation data for each of the 30 epochs is stored in `model_two`. The results can be seen in the following plot:

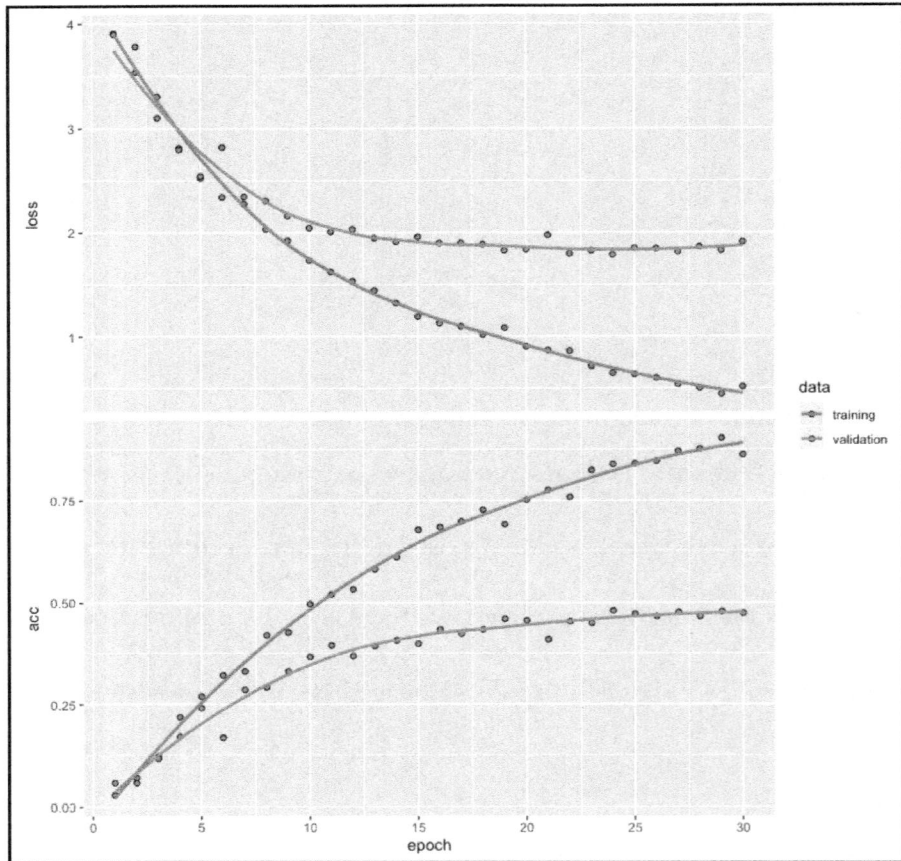

The preceding plot indicates that the loss and accuracy values for the validation data stay flat for the last few epochs. However, they do not deteriorate. Next, we will obtain the loss and accuracy values based on the training and test data using the `evaluate` function, as follows:

```
# Loss and accuracy for train data
model %>% evaluate(trainx, trainy)
$loss
[1] 0.3890106
$acc
[1] 0.9133034
```

```
# Loss and accuracy for test data
model %>% evaluate(testx, testy)
$loss
[1] 2.710119
$acc
[1] 0.308
```

From the preceding code and output, we can observe that the loss and accuracy values for the training data show better results compared to the previous model. However, for the test data, although the accuracy value is better, the loss value is slightly worse.

The accuracy that was obtained by correctly classifying the articles in the testing data from each author can be seen in the following bar plot:

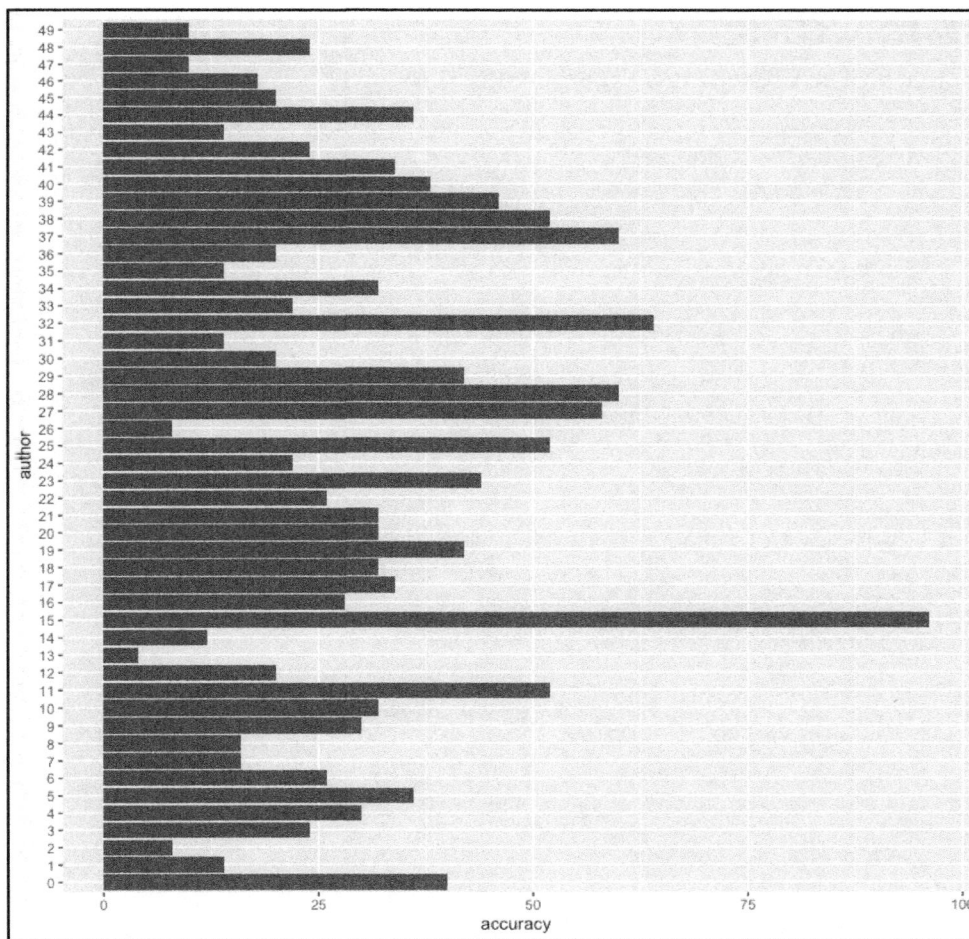

From the preceding bar plot, we can make the following observations:

- The bar plot visually shows improvements compared to the previous model.
- In the previous model, for the test data, we had four authors with no articles classified correctly. However, now, we don't have any authors with no correct classification.

In the next experiment, we will look at more changes we can make in an effort to improve the author's classification performance even further.

Experimenting with batch size, kernel size, and filters in CNNs

The code that will be used for this experiment is as follows:

```
# Model architecture
model <- keras_model_sequential() %>%
        layer_embedding(input_dim = 1500,
                        output_dim = 32,
                        input_length = 400) %>%
        layer_conv_1d(filters = 64,
              kernel_size = 4,
              padding = "valid",
              activation = "relu",
              strides = 1) %>%
        layer_max_pooling_1d(pool_size = 4) %>%
        layer_dropout(0.25) %>%
        layer_lstm(units = 32) %>%
        layer_dense(units = 50, activation = "softmax")

# Compiling the model
 model %>% compile(optimizer = "adam",
        loss = "categorical_crossentropy",
        metrics = c("acc"))

 # Fitting the model
 model_three <- model %>% fit(trainx, trainy,
        epochs = 30,
        batch_size = 8,
        validation_data = list(validx, validy))

# Loss and accuracy plot
plot(model_three)
```

From the preceding code, we can make the following observations:

- We have reduced the kernel size from 5 to 4.
- We have increased the number of filters for the convolutional layer from 32 to 64.
- We have reduced the batch size from 16 to 8 while training the model.
- We have kept all other settings the same as what was used for the previous model.

The loss and accuracy values based on the training and validation data for each of the 30 epochs are stored in `model_three`. A plot of this data is as follows:

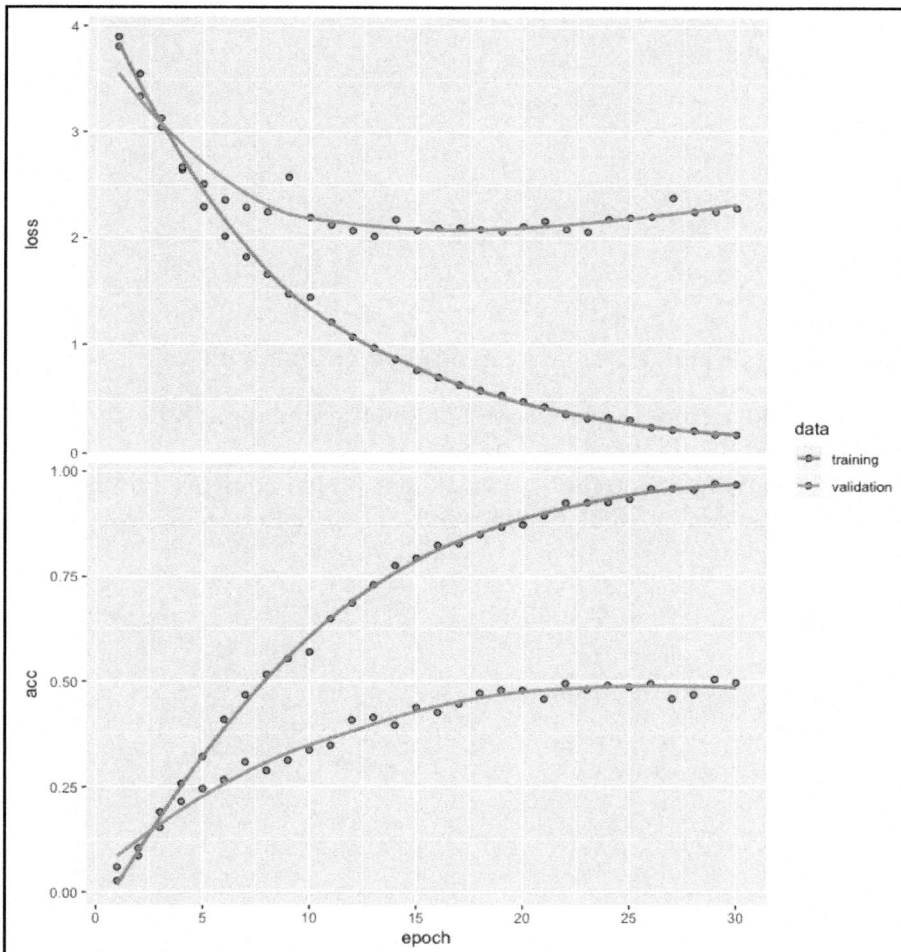

The plot for the loss and accuracy shows the following:

- The accuracy values for the validation data remain flat for the last few epochs, whereas it increases at a relatively slower pace in the last few epochs for the training data.
- The loss values based on the validation data start to increase during the last few epochs and continue to decrease for the training data.

Now, we will obtain the loss and accuracy values based on the train and test data using the `evaluate` function, as follows:

```
# Loss and accuracy for train data
model %>% evaluate(trainx, trainy)
$loss
[1] 0.1093387
$acc
[1] 0.9880419

# Loss and accuracy for test data
model %>% evaluate(testx, testy)
[1] 3.262691
$acc
[1] 0.337
```

From the preceding code and output, we can observe the following:

- The loss and accuracy values based on the training data show an improvement compared to the previous two models.
- For the test data, although the loss value is higher compared to the first two models, an accuracy value of about 34% shows better accuracy in classifying author articles.

The following bar plot shows the accuracy of correctly classifying the authors of articles in the test data:

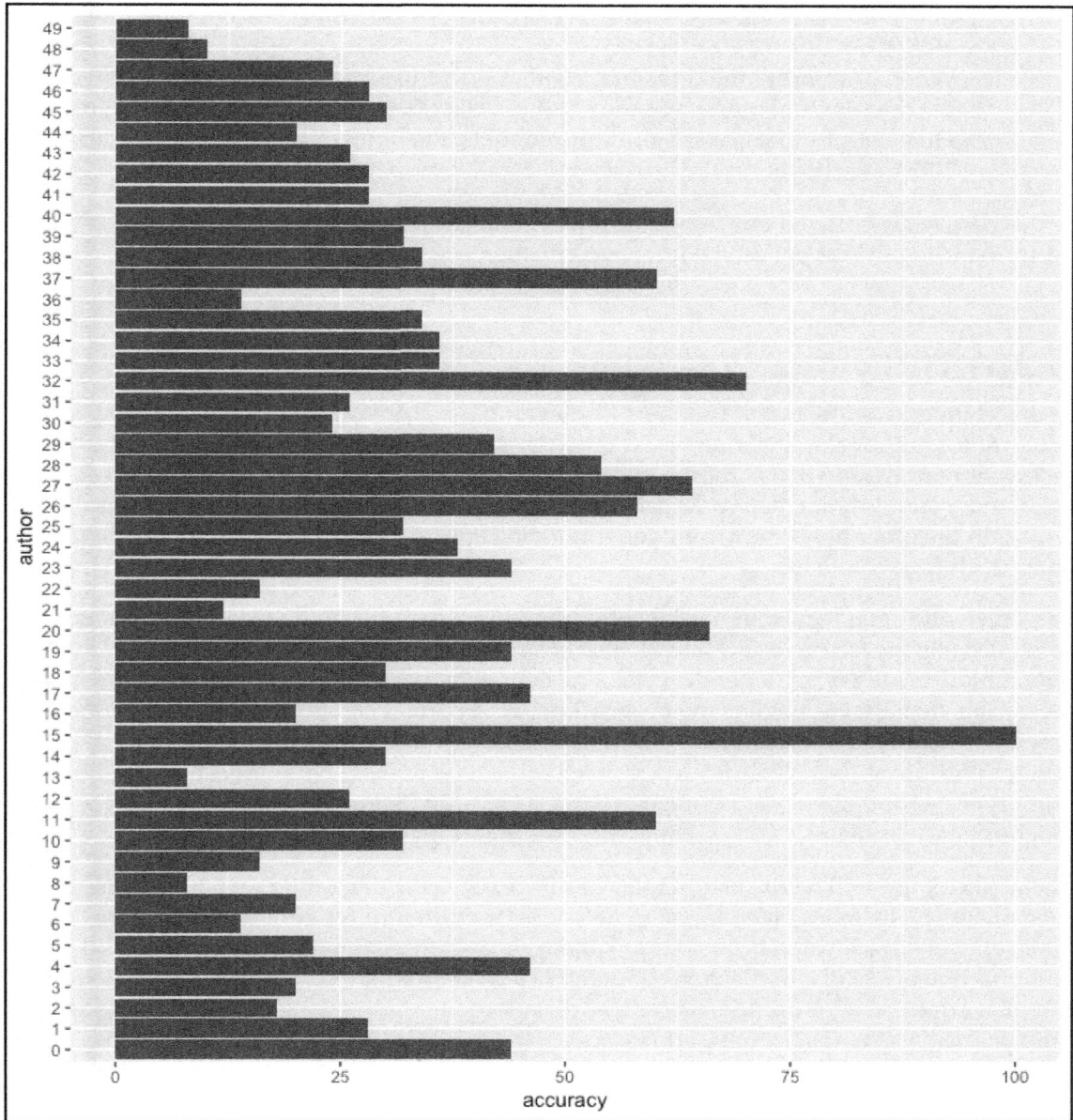

From the preceding bar plot, we can observe the following:

- The accuracy of correctly classifying articles from each author shows better performance compared to the previous two models since we don't have any authors with zero accuracy.
- When comparing the three models that we've used so far using test data, we can see that the first model has four authors classified with 50% or higher accuracy. However, for the second and third models, the number of authors classified with 50% or higher accuracy increases to 8 and 9, respectively.

In this section, we carried out two experiments that showed that the author classification performance of the model can be improved further.

Summary

In this chapter, we illustrated the steps for developing a convolutional recurrent neural network for author classification based on articles that they have written. Convolutional recurrent neural networks combine the advantages of two networks into one network. On one hand, convolutional networks can capture high-level local features from the data, while, on the other hand, recurrent networks can capture long-term dependencies in the data involving sequences.

First, convolutional recurrent neural networks extract features using a one-dimensional convolutional layer. These extracted features are then passed to the LSTM recurrent layer to obtain hidden long-term dependencies, which are then passed to a fully connected dense layer. This dense layer obtains the probability of the correct classification of each author based on the data in the articles. Although we used a convolutional recurrent neural network for the author classification problem, this type of deep network can be applied to other types of data involving sequences, such as natural language processing, speech, and video-related problems.

The next chapter will be the last chapter of this book and will go over tips, tricks, and the road ahead. Developing deep learning networks for different types of data is both art and science. Every application brings new challenges, as well as an opportunity for us to learn and improve our skills. In the next chapter, we will summarize some such experiences that can turn out to be very useful in certain applications and help save a significant amount of time in arriving at models that perform well.

Section 5: The Road Ahead

This section discusses the road ahead for putting deep learning techniques into action and related tips and tricks.

This section contains the following chapter:

- Chapter 13, *Tips, Tricks, and the Road Ahead*

Tips, Tricks, and the Road Ahead 13

In this book, we covered how to apply various deep learning networks to develop prediction and classification models. Several tips and tricks that we covered were unique to certain application areas and helped us arrive at better prediction or classification performance for the models that we developed.

In this chapter, we will go over certain tips and tricks that will be very handy when you continue your journey of applying these methods to new data and different problems. We will cover four topics in total. Note that these approaches haven't been covered in the previous chapters, but we will make use of some of the examples from them to illustrate their use.

In this chapter, we will cover the following topics:

- TensorBoard for training performance visualization
- Visualizing deep network models with LIME
- Visualizing model training with tfruns
- Early stopping of network training

TensorBoard for training performance visualization

For visualizing deep network training performance, TensorBoard is a useful tool that is available as part of the TensorFlow package. We will rerun the deep network model that we used in Chapter 2, *Deep Neural Networks for Multi-Class Classification*, where we used CTG data to develop a multi-class classification model for patients. For the code related to data processing, the model architecture, and compiling the model, you can refer to Chapter 2, *Deep Neural Networks for Multi-Class Classification*.

The following is the code for model_one from Chapter 2, *Deep Neural Networks for Multi-Class Classification*:

```
# Fitting model and TensorBoard
setwd("~/Desktop/")
model_one <- model %>% fit(training,
                           trainLabels,
                           epochs = 200,
                           batch_size = 32,
                           validation_split = 0.2,
                           callbacks = callback_tensorboard('ctg/one'))
tensorboard('ctg/one')
```

From the preceding code, we can observe the following:

- We have set a working directory, which will be the desktop where the results of training the model will be stored for visualization on TensorBoard.
- The model is fit using additional feature callbacks, where we use the callback_tensorboard function to store data in the ctg/one folder on the desktop for visualization later.
- Note that the ctg directory is automatically created at the time of fitting the model.
- Finally, the tensorboard function is used for visualization using data stored in the ctg/one folder.

The following screenshot is of TensorBoard:

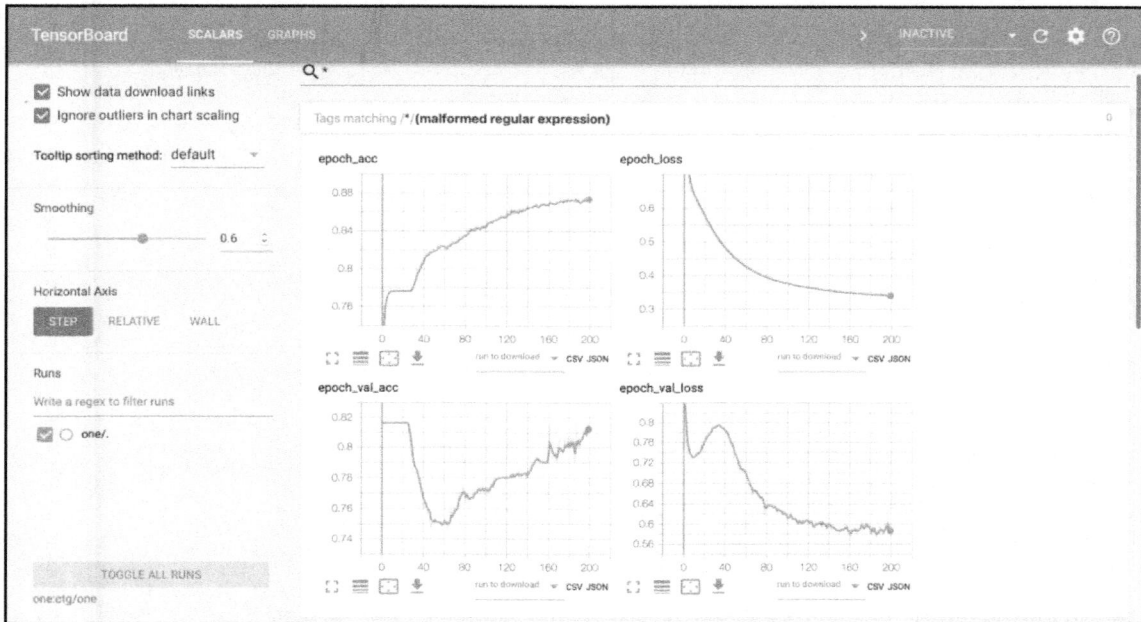

The preceding screenshot shows the loss and accuracy plots for the training and validation data for 200 epochs. This was used for training the model. This visualization on TensorBoard is interactive in nature and provides the user with additional options so that they can explore and understand the model performance's during the training process.

As we have seen in all the chapters in this book that have illustrated the use of various deep learning methods, improving the performance of a classification or prediction model involves extensive experimentation. To help with such experimentation, one of the key benefits of using a TensorBoard is that it allows model performance to be compared very easily using interactive visualization.

We ran three more models from Chapter 2, *Deep Neural Networks for Multi-Class Classification,* and stored model training data within subfolders two, three, and four of the ctg folder. Run the following code for TensorBoard visualization:

```
# TensorBoard visualization for multiple models
tensorboard(c('ctg/one', 'ctg/two', 'ctg/three', 'ctg/four'))
```

The preceding code creates TensorBoard visualizations for all four models. A screenshot of the resulting TensorBoard page is as follows:

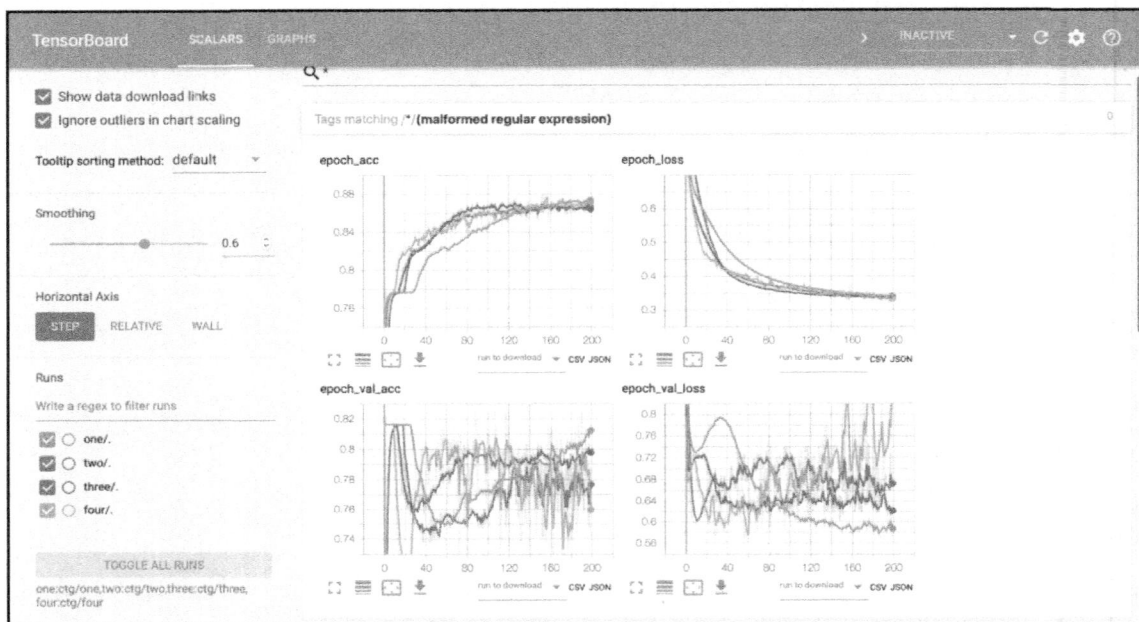

The preceding visualization shows the loss and accuracy values for the training and validation data for all four models. The following are some observations that we can make about this plot:

- The results for the four models that were run are presented in different colors to allow us to quickly identify them and make comparisons.
- The loss and accuracy values based on the validation data show higher variability in the results compared to what can be observed by the training data.
- An option to download any plot or related data is also provided.

The ability to visualize different models with different parameter values can be useful when we're making choices about the type of architecture to use for the deep network, the number of epochs, the batch size, and other model-related attributes that are of interest. It can also provide us with directions for further experimentation if needed and help us compare current and past results.

Visualizing deep network models with LIME

In the application examples that we've provided so far in this book, after we developed a classification or prediction deep network model, we carried out visualizations to view the overall performance of the models. These assessments are done using training and test data. The main idea behind such an assessment is to obtain an overall or global understanding of the model's performance. However, there are situations where we want to obtain a deeper understanding and also interpretations for a specific prediction. For example, we may be interested in understanding the main features or variables that have influenced a specific prediction in the test data. Such "local" interpretations are the focus of a package called **Local Interpretable Model-Agnostic Explanations**, or **LIME**. LIME can help provide deeper insights into each prediction.

The code for carrying out visualization using LIME for the model we developed in Keras is as follows:

```
# LIME package
library(lime)

# Using LIME with keras
model_type.keras.engine.sequential.Sequential <-
function(x, ...) {"classification"}
predict_model.keras.engine.sequential.Sequential <-
   function(x,newdata,type, ...) {p <- predict_proba(object=x,
x=as.matrix(newdata))
         data.frame(p) }

# Create explainer using lime
explainer <- lime(x = data.frame(training),
           model = model,
           bin_continuous = FALSE)

# Create explanation
explanation <- explain(data.frame(test)[1:5,],
               explainer    = explainer,
               n_labels     = 1,
               n_features   = 4,
               kernel_width = 0.5)
testtarget[1:5]
[1] 0 0 0 2 2
```

As shown in the preceding code, we use two functions to be able to use LIME with the Keras model. In the first function, we indicate that we will be working with a classification model. The second function obtains prediction probabilities. In this section, we will use `model_one` from `Chapter 2`, *Deep Neural Networks for Multi-Class Classification*. Then, we'll use the `lime` function with the training data, the model (that is, `model_one`), and specify the binning of continuous variables as `FALSE`. The resulting explainer is used with the `explain` function, where we will specify the number of labels to use as one and specify the number of most important features to use for each case as four. We specify the kernel width as 0.5. We can also see that the first three patients in the test data have the class labeled as 0, indicating that they belong to the normal patient category. Similarly, the 4th and 5th patients in the test data have been labeled as 2, indicating that they belong to the pathological patient category.

We obtained the following plot using `plot_features(explanation)`:

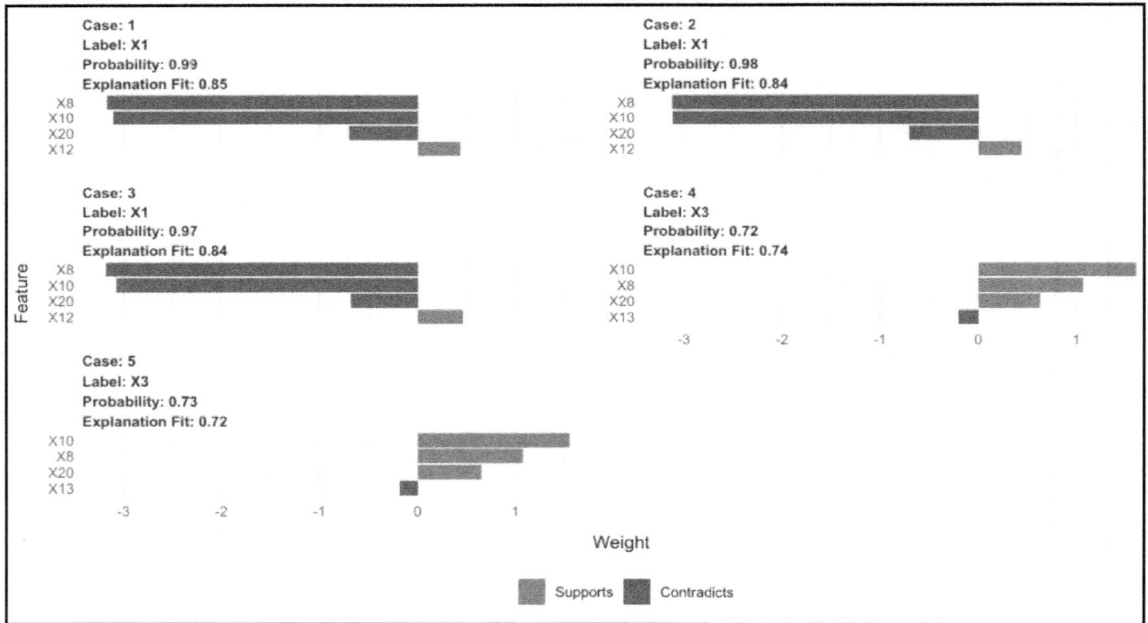

The preceding plot provides individual plots for the first five patients in the test data. Here are some of the observations that can be made from this plot:

- All five patients have been correctly classified.
- The first three patients have been classified as belonging to a class labeled as 0, representing a normal patient.

- The remaining two patients are classified as belonging to a class labeled as 2, representing a pathological patient.
- The prediction probability for the first three cases is 0.97 or above and the prediction probability for the 4th and 5th patients is 0.72 and above.
- This plot depicts the four most important features that have contributed to the specific classification of each patient.
- Features with blue bars support the model's conclusion, whereas features with red bars contradict the model's conclusion for each patient.
- Higher values for the X8, X10, and X20 variables seem to have a higher influence on a patient being classified as pathological.
- Higher values for the X12 variable seems to influence a patient being classified as normal.

The following heatmap can be obtained using `plot_explanations(explanation)`:

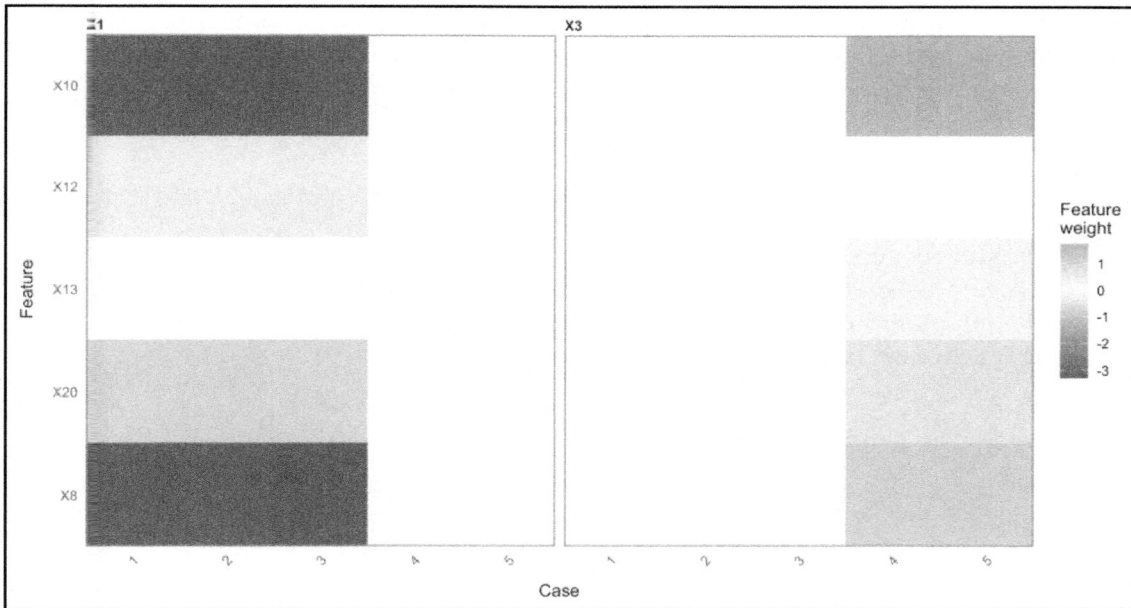

We can make the following observations from the preceding heatmap:

- The heatmap makes comparing the different variables for each patient easier and thus helps with interpretation.
- It summarizes the results of the case, feature, and label combination and doesn't provide as much detail as the previous plot.
- For class-X1, or patients labeled as normal (1, 2, and 3), all four features (X8, X10, X12, and X20) have very similar weights.
- For class-X3, or patients labeled as pathological (4 and 5), once again, all four features (X8, X10, X13, and X20) have an approximately similar weight.

Visualizing model training with tfruns

When we run a deep network model using Keras, we can make use of tfruns to visualize a loss and accuracy plot, as well as other model-related summaries. Although we can also obtain the plot and related summaries when required, the main advantage of using tfruns is that we can obtain them all in one place. We can make use of the following code to achieve this:

```
library(tfruns)
training_run("mlp_ctg.R")
```

In the preceding code, the R file that's being referenced contains the code to run model_one from Chapter 2, *Deep Neural Networks for Multi-Class Classification*. The mlp_ctg.R file may be stored on the computer when we run the code. As soon as we have run the code, the following interactive screen is automatically presented:

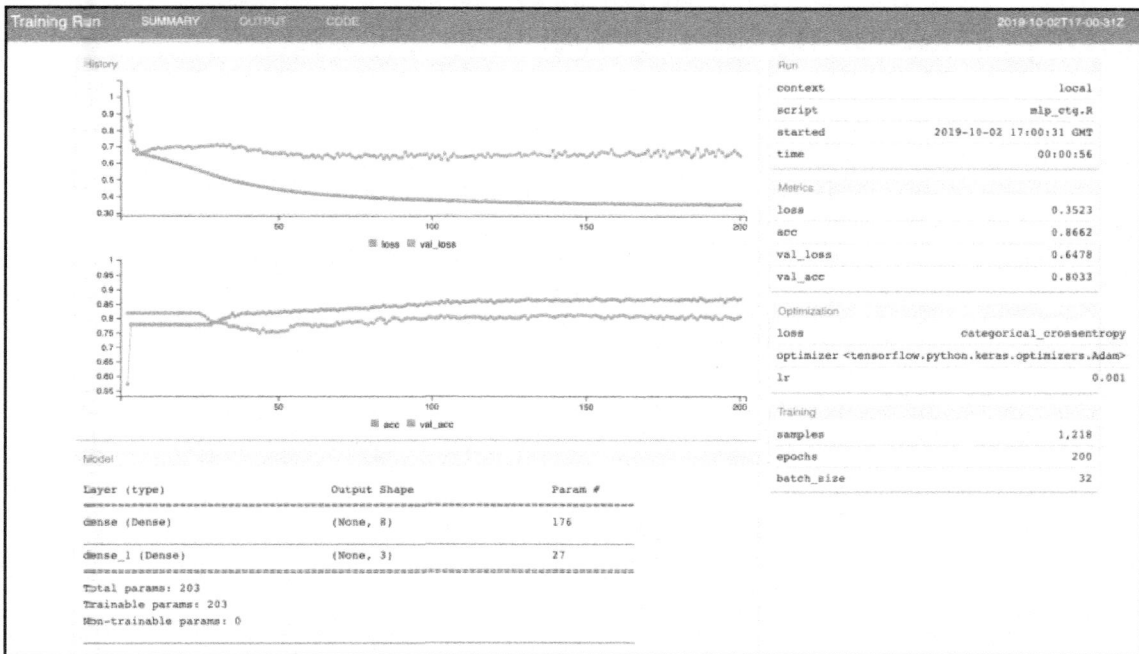

The page shown in the preceding screenshot provides the following:

- An interactive plot of the loss and accuracy values for the training and validation data
- A model summary based on the model's architecture
- Information regarding the run, including the time it took to complete all epochs
- A numeric summary in the form of accuracy and loss, based on the training and validation data
- The samples that were used, the number of epochs, and the batch size that was specified

Early stopping of network training

When training a network, we specify the number of epochs we need in advance, without knowing how many epochs will actually be needed. If we specify the number of epochs to be too few compared to what is actually required, we may have to train the network again by specifying more epochs. On the other hand, if we specify too many more epochs than what are actually needed, then this may lead to an overfitting situation and we may have to retrain the network by reducing the number of epochs. This trial and error approach can be very time-consuming for applications where each epoch takes a long time to complete. In such situations, we can make use of callbacks that can help stop the network training at a suitable time.

To illustrate this problem, let's develop a classification model with the CTG data from Chapter 2, *Deep Neural Networks for Multi-Class Classification*, using the following code:

```
# Training network for classification with CTG data (chapter-2)
model <- keras_model_sequential()
model %>%
  layer_dense(units = 25, activation = 'relu', input_shape = c(21)) %>%
  layer_dense(units = 3, activation = 'softmax')
model %>% compile(loss = 'categorical_crossentropy',
                  optimizer = 'adam',
                  metrics = 'accuracy')
history <- model %>% fit(training,
                         trainLabels,
                         epochs = 50,
                         batch_size = 32,
                         validation_split = 0.2)
plot(history)
```

In the preceding code, we have specified the number of epochs as 50. Once the training process is completed, we can plot the loss and accuracy values for the training and validation data, as follows:

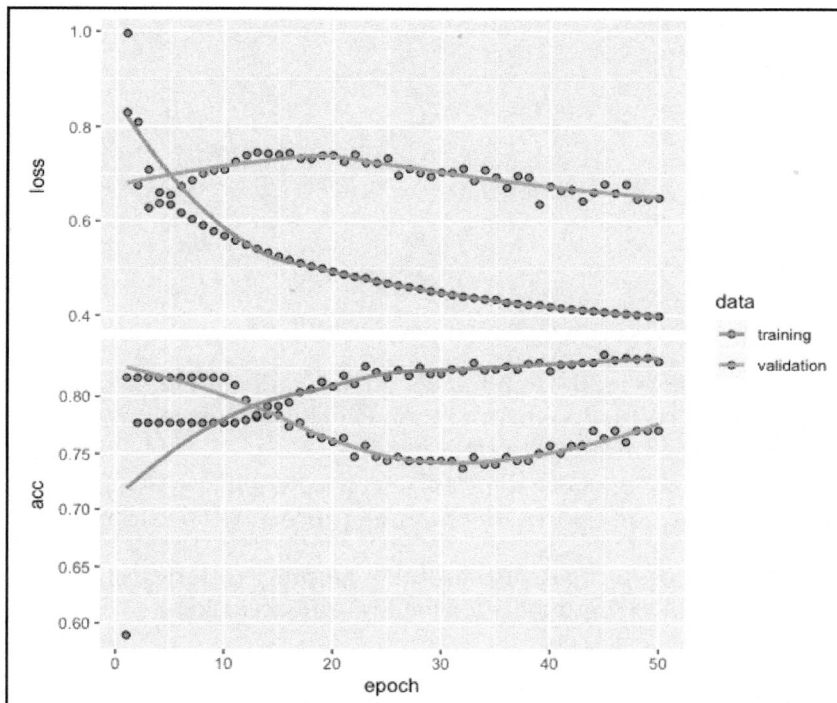

From the preceding plot, we can observe the following:

- We can observe that the loss values for the validation data decrease initially for the first few epochs and then start to increase.
- The plot also shows that, after the first few epochs, the loss values for the training and validation data show divergence and tend to go in the opposite direction.
- If we would like to stop the training process much earlier instead of waiting for all 50 epochs to be completed, then we can make use of the callback feature that's available in Keras.

The following code includes the callback feature within the `fit` function at the time of training the network:

```
# Training network with callback
model <- keras_model_sequential()
model %>%
   layer_dense(units = 25, activation = 'relu', input_shape = c(21)) %>%
   layer_dense(units = 3, activation = 'softmax')
model %>% compile(loss = 'categorical_crossentropy',
                  optimizer = 'adam',
```

```
                            metrics = 'accuracy')
history <- model %>% fit(training,
                         trainLabels,
                         epochs = 50,
                         batch_size = 32,
                         validation_split = 0.2,
                         callbacks = callback_early_stopping(monitor =
"val_loss",
                                                   patience = 10))
       plot(history)
```

In the preceding code, early stopping is included for callbacks:

- The metric that we used for monitoring was validation loss values. Another metric that can be tried in this situation is validation accuracy since we are developing a classification model.
- We have specified patience to be 10, which means that when there are no improvements for 10 epochs, the training process will be stopped automatically.

The plot for the loss and accuracy are also useful in helping us decide on the appropriate values for patience. The following plot is for the loss and accuracy:

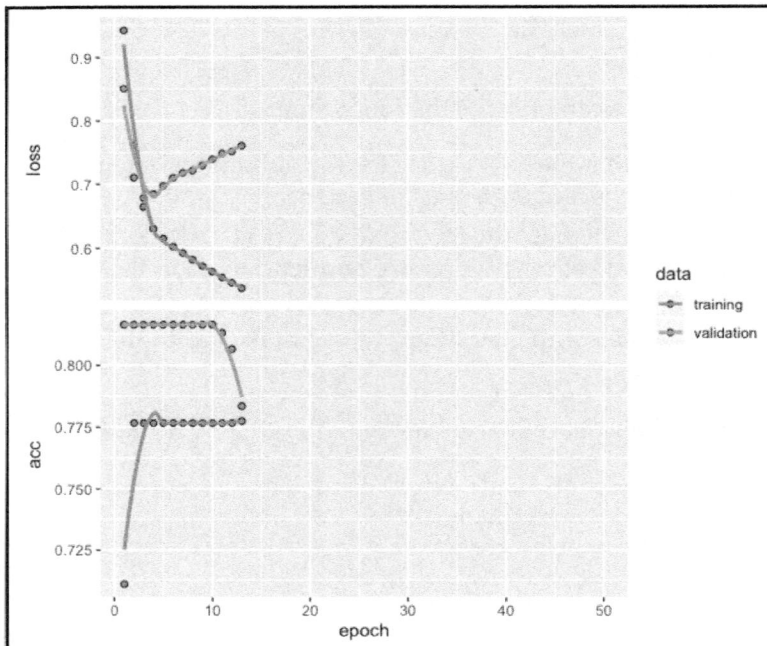

As we can see, this time, the training process didn't run for all 50 epochs and stopped as soon as there were no improvements in the loss values for 10 epochs.

Summary

Developing classification and prediction models using deep learning networks involves extensive experimentation to arrive at models with high-quality performance. To help with this process, there are various methods that are very useful for visualizing and controlling network training. In this chapter, we went over four such useful methods. We saw that TensorBoard provides a tool that we can use to assess and compare model performance after training the network with different architectures and other changes in the model. The advantage of using TensorBoard lies in the fact that it brings all the necessary information together in one place in a user-friendly way. There are also situations where we want to understand how the main features or variables on a specific prediction are influenced when using a classification or prediction model. In such situations, we can visualize the impact that the main features will have using LIME.

Another useful tip that we illustrated in this chapter is visualization with the help of tfruns. When developing a deep network model, we come across various plots and summaries related to a specific model. Using tfruns, we can visualize all the information in one place with the help of an interactive screen. Another tip or trick that will be very useful in the journey ahead is the use of callbacks to automatically stop the training process when a suitable classification or prediction model has been developed. All the methods that were discussed in this chapter can be very useful for the journey ahead, especially when you're working on complex and challenging problems.

Other Books You May Enjoy

If you enjoyed this book, you may be interested in these other books by Packt:

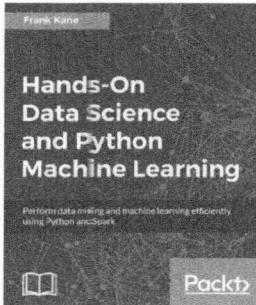

Hands-On Data Science and Python Machine Learning
Frank Kane

ISBN: 978-1-78728-074-8

- Learn how to clean your data and ready it for analysis
- Implement the popular clustering and regression methods in Python
- Train efficient machine learning models using decision trees and random forests
- Visualize the results of your analysis using Python's Matplotlib library
- Use Apache Spark's MLlib package to perform machine learning on large datasets

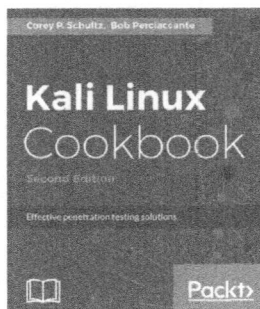

Kali Linux Cookbook - Second Edition
Corey P. Schultz, Bob Perciaccante

ISBN: 978-1-78439-030-3

- Acquire the key skills of ethical hacking to perform penetration testing
- Learn how to perform network reconnaissance
- Discover vulnerabilities in hosts
- Attack vulnerabilities to take control of workstations and servers
- Understand password cracking to bypass security
- Learn how to hack into wireless networks
- Attack web and database servers to exfiltrate data
- Obfuscate your command and control connections to avoid firewall and IFS detection

Leave a review - let other readers know what you think

Please share your thoughts on this book with others by leaving a review on the site that you bought it from. If you purchased the book from Amazon, please leave us an honest review on this book's Amazon page. This is vital so that other potential readers can see and use your unbiased opinion to make purchasing decisions, we can understand what our customers think about our products, and our authors can see your feedback on the title that they have worked with Packt to create. It will only take a few minutes of your time, but is valuable to other potential customers, our authors, and Packt. Thank you!

Index

URL 161
Internet Movie Database (IMDb) 217, 240

K

Keras R packages 11
Keras
  used, for creating deep neural network model for regression 66, 67
  used, for fitting deep neural network model for regression 67

L

Local Interpretable Model-Agnostic Explanations (LIME)
  about 29
  deep network models, visualizing 319, 320, 322
long short-term memory (LSTM) 28
LSTM model
  accuracy plot 266, 267
  best practices 270
  experimenting, with Adam optimizer 270, 271, 272, 273, 274
  fitting 265
  loss plot 266, 267
  performance optimization 270
LSTM network architecture 264, 265
LSTM network model
  compiling 265
  creating 263
  model evaluation, with test data 269
  model evaluation, with train data 267, 268
  performance, evaluating 267
LSTM network, with additional layer
  experimenting with 274, 275, 277, 278
LSTM networks
  need for 262

M

MNIST image data
  processing 195, 197
model training
  visualizing, with tfruns 322, 323
movie review
  maximum sequence length 233, 234
multi-class classification 23

N

National Research Council (NRC) 222
network training
  about 202, 203
  early stopping 324, 325
  initial setup, for saving fake images and loss values 201
normalization 13

O

one-hot encoding 37

P

padding
  about 222
  text sequences 242
prediction model, developing with Boston Housing dataset
  best practices 76
  data normalization 65
  data, partitioning 64, 65
  data, preparing 63
  deeper network architecture 72, 73
  log transformation, of output variable 76, 77, 78
  model evaluation 69, 70
  model improvement 72
  model prediction 69, 70, 71, 72
  neural network, visualizing 63, 64
  performance 79, 80
  performance optimization tips 76
  results 74, 75, 76
pretrained image classification model
  about 160
  best practices 182
  evaluation 179
  evaluation, with test data 181, 182
  evaluation, with training data 179, 180
  experimenting with VGG16, as pretrained network 188, 190, 191
  experimenting, with Adam optimizer 182, 184, 185
  hyperparameter tuning 185, 186, 188
  image, reading 161, 162, 163
  input, preprocessing 163, 164

performance optimization tips 182
predicion 179

R

rectified linear units (relus) 135
recurrent neural network model
  accuracy values 246
  activation functions, using 252, 253, 254
  best practices 249
  calculation of parameters 244
  compiling 245, 246
  data, testing 249
  data, training 248
  developing 243, 244
  fitting 246
  loss values 246
  maximum length, for padding sequences 256, 257, 258, 259
  model evaluation 248
  model prediction 248
  number of units, in simple RNN layer 250, 251, 252
  performance optimization tips 249
  recurrent layers, adding 254, 255, 256
recurrent neural networks (RNNs) 28
regression problems 24
reuter_50_50 dataset
  test data, reading 288
  training data, reading 286, 287
  working with 286
root mean square propagation (RMSProp) 39

T

TensorBoard
  about 29
  performance visualization, training 316, 317,
318
test data
  prediction probabilities 98
text classification, with RNNs
  data, preparing for model building 240, 241, 242
text data
  preparing, for model building 262, 263
text datasets 216
text datasets, Keras 217, 218
text sequences
  padding 242
text
  converting, into sequences of integers 220
tfruns
  about 29
  model training, visualizing 322, 323
tokenization 219
transfer learning 26
true negative 21
true positive 21
truncation 221
tweet sentiment classification model
  best practices 233
  developing 222, 223, 224
  evaluating, with test data 232, 233
  evaluating, with training data 231, 232
  evaluation 231
  performance optimization tips 233
  prediction 231
  tokenization 220

U

UCI machine learning repository 216, 217

V

VGG16 188

Printed in Great Britain
by Amazon

27318902R00196